modern bodies

modern

bodies

Dance and

American Modernism

from Martha Graham

to Alvin Ailey

Julia L. Foulkes

The University of North Carolina Press

Chapel Hill & London

© 2002
The University of North Carolina Press
All rights reserved
Designed by Richard Hendel
Set in Monotype Garamond
by Tseng Information Systems, Inc.
Manufactured in the United States of America

The paper in this book meets the guidelines for
permanence and durability of the Committee on
Production Guidelines for Book Longevity of
the Council on Library Resources.

Library of Congress
Cataloging-in-Publication Data
Foulkes, Julia L.
Modern bodies : dance and American modernism
from Martha Graham to Alvin Ailey /
by Julia L. Foulkes.
p. cm. — (Cultural studies of the United States)
Includes bibliographical references and index.
ISBN 0-8078-2698-7 (cloth : alk. paper) —
ISBN 0-8078-5367-4 (pbk. : alk. paper)
1. Modern dance—United States—History.
I. Title.   II. Series.
GV1623 .F68   2002
792.8—dc21   2001059758

cloth 06 05 04 03 02   5 4 3 2 1
paper 06 05 04 03 02   5 4 3 2 1

FRONTISPIECE.
*Helen Tamiris in "Joshua Fit for
Battle" from* Negro Spirituals.
*Photograph by Thomas Bouchard,
© Diane Bouchard. (Jerome Robbins
Dance Division, The New York
Public Library for the Performing
Arts, Astor, Lenox and Tilden
Foundations)*

Portions of this work appeared
previously, in somewhat different
form, as "Dance Is for American
Men: Ted Shawn and the Intersection of Gender, Sexuality, and
Nationalism in the 1930s," in
*Dancing Desires: Choreographing
Sexualities On and Off the Stage,* ed.
Jane C. Desmond, © 2001,
reprinted by permission of the
University of Wisconsin Press,
and "'Angels Rewolt!': Jewish
Women in Modern Dance in the
1930s," *American Jewish History*
88 (June 2000): 233–52.

To my folks,
with gratitude and love,
from your dancing
daughter

contents

illustrations

acknowledgments

After ferrying me back and forth to dance classes for years, my father began to ask me whether I had learned any new steps. With all the precociousness of a teenager wrapped up in an obsession, I would reply with some exasperation that I was beyond the point where I learned new steps; I now only put steps together in new ways and perfected them.

One of the greatest joys in moving between dance classes and academic classrooms has been the realization that there are always new steps to learn. And I have been lucky to have had exceptional teachers all along the way. In giving me exacting attention and measured guidance, Kathy Peiss has put forth a model of scholarship to which I will continue to strive. Special thanks to Lewis Erenberg for asking the question "Do you dance?" when I first mentioned researching dance, and then advising me throughout the project. Yvonne Daniel, Tim Gilfoyle, David Glassberg, Susan Hirsch, William Johnston, Kimerer LaMothe, John McManamon, Carl Nightingale, Charles Rearick, and Sterling Stuckey have given me crucial insight and encouragement. I am indebted to Maggie Lowe, who has been a compassionate and insightful commentator from the beginning of the project to its end. I thank the anonymous readers, Alan Trachtenberg, Sian Hunter, and many at the University of North Carolina Press who significantly bettered the book.

For financial support, my thanks to the American Historical Association, American Jewish Archives, Harvard Theatre Collection of Houghton Library, Rockefeller Archive Center, Rockefeller Foundation, Society for the Preservation of American Modernism, and University of Massachusetts at Amherst. The Dance Collection in the Performing Arts Library of the New York Public Library has been a second home to me for years now, and I would like to express my appreciation for the consistent help of the pages and librarians there, especially Phil Karg, Monica Mosely, and Charles Perrier. I owe special thanks to Ed Bailey, Robert Wilson, and Staci Levin of Fish & Neave for prompt and compassionate counsel.

In 1997–98, I was the Rockefeller Foundation Postdoctoral Fellow at the Center for Black Music Research, Columbia College Chicago, and my time there remains one of the most pleasurable experiences of my professional life. The Center, founded and directed by Samuel Floyd Jr., provides a respectful, warm, and communal environment that allows people to flourish in their work. Johann Buis, Suzanne Flandreau, Samuel Floyd Jr., Trenace Ford, Marsha Heizer, Helen Walker Hill, Morris Phibbs, and Marcos Sueiro have my deepest gratitude. I have also found that curious, encouraging spirit at New School University, where I have been inspired by conversations with colleagues, especially Philip Bennett, Linda Dunne, Wendy Kohli, Jenny Lynn McNutt, Tim Quigley, Joe Salvatore, Jonathan Veitch, and Gina Luria Walker.

Friends—including Mike Barsanti, Abby Burbank, Catherine Candy, Frank Forts, Carole Harris, Daniel Harris, Rebecca Houston, Laurie Krauz, Kasia Malinowska, Caroline and Tony Murray, Jena Osman, Karen Plafker, Sharon Preiss, and the working dreamers at the fishbowl—have sustained me through the long years of work on this project, and I am deeply grateful. Above all, I have been propped up by the laughter, consolation, and wisdom of Sam Elworthy, Rebecca Foster, Donna and Malik Geraci, Leslie Schwerin, and Maire Vieth. And for joyful distraction and comfort during the final push, I thank Brian Kane.

My family has followed my many steps, from dance classes to performances and now a book on the history of dance. Anne and Tom Foulkes, Sky, Sue, Tucker, and Tyler Foulkes, Christy, Brian, Casey, Max, and Jake McCullough have regularly been in the audience. And they have never stopped reminding me that I always have a place in their homes and hearts, as dancer and scholar, but also as daughter, sister, and aunt. This book exists because of the constancy of their support and love.

modern bodies

You do not realize how the headlines that make
daily history affect the muscles of the human body.
—Martha Graham

introduction

From 5 to 12 January 1930, four modern dance companies performed on alternating nights at Maxine Elliott's theater on 39th Street in New York City. Calling themselves the Dance Repertory Theatre, Martha Graham, Doris Humphrey, Helen Tamiris, and Charles Weidman joined together to share the almost insurmountable costs of theatrical productions. The content of the week's performances conveyed the range of ideas that engaged modern dancers: from Graham's *Heretic* (1929), a battle between an individual and society, to Tamiris's pull of the body against forces of gravity and oppression in *Three Negro Spirituals* (1928); from the clever pantomime of Weidman's *Marionette Theatre* (1929) to Humphrey's *The Life of the Bee* (1929), a dramatization of Maurice Maeterlinck's 1901 study on the hierarchical authority of the queen bee and the pitiless duties of worker bees. Poised at the perilous moment after the stock market crash of October 1929 and the start of a new decade, modern dancers steeped themselves in the social, political, and aesthetic issues of the day.

Reviewers hailed the week, seeing a new solidity and momentum in the group effort that moved this art form beyond scattered, individual accomplishments to a growing force in the arts that deserved wider recognition. John Martin, the first dance critic at the *New York Times,* appointed in 1927, declared of the week, "The American dance has come of age."[1] The *New Yorker* had a more coy view, proclaiming that the new art form was "an entity capable of standing on its own legs—and what legs some of them are!"[2] Margaret Gage, a critic writing in *Theatre Arts Monthly,* offered the most trenchant commentary. She asked, "What is 'modernism' in the American art of the dance?" Looking for associations with the scientist Albert Einstein and philosopher Alfred North Whitehead, intellectuals she thought responsible for revealing "the impersonal grandeur of . . . new vistas," Gage heralded modern dancers' abstract design and choreographic adventure. But the true connection with the intellectuals' innovations was the dancers' "unswerving and unsentimental directness of idea presented in a style dictated wholly by that idea, with everything ruthlessly whittled away that is nonessential to the main structural lines." What dancers added to this new mode of thinking was "the communal presentation of [an] idea," and this Gage identified as the "vital kernel of 'modernism' in the American art of the dance."[3] A few weeks before the Dance Repertory Theatre performance, Doris Humphrey had ruminated on just this conundrum of how forceful group movement comes out of the drives and thoughts of individual dancers: "[W]ith one hand I try to encourage them to be individuals—to move and think regardless of me or anyone else. And in rehearsals also it is necessary to contradict all that and make them acutely aware of each other, so that they may move in a common rhythm."[4] This tension between individual identity and communal harmony lay at the core of the new modern dance.

The trickling effects of World War I, rapid changes prompted by the technology of the machine age, and the boom and then swoop of the economy created a ferment that could not be ignored, and artists seized the opportunity to define a new role for the arts in the United States. *Revolt in the Arts,* a compendium of manifestos by representatives of theater, film, dance, music, literature, and painting put together by Oliver Sayler and published in 1930, advanced the idea that a refiguring was taking place across the arts. In creation, distribution, and appreciation of the arts, Sayler saw "unrest, confusion, chaos"—a revolt so complete that it entailed "a vast, overwhelming readjustment of values, involving not alone the arts as such but our whole understanding and conception of life."[5] This tumult stirred up political debates, and modern dancers tackled questions about the utility of art that had been pushed into the public arena by the growing appeal of Communism and socialism: Whom did art serve, and what was its function in society? In answer, modern dancers exalted individual expression and primal body movements. Proclaiming the worth of every body, modern dancers believed in the power of conjoining that variety in group movement. In its conception and its practice, modern dance illustrated the social tension between the heralding of the individual and the possibilities of mass appeal and participation. Whether Humphrey's *The Life of the Bee,* which criticized a hierarchical social structure, or Graham's paean to individual fortitude, *Heretic,* modern dance embodied the conflict and potential of creating a democratic whole out of distinct individuals.

This tension had a different resonance in dance than in other art forms because of the medium of dance: bodies. The *New Yorker* comment on "the legs" of this new movement exposed the unavoidability of judging this art form without consideration of the bodies that moved on stage. Jane Dudley, an active participant in different modern dance groups in the 1930s, called the new spectacle on stages "modern bodies: the kind of bodies you'd see in a Picasso, or in a Matisse."[6] The reference to the work of Pablo Picasso and Henri Matisse is telling, not only because these painters gave dance heightened meaning in several of their works, including Picasso's *Three Dancers* (1925) and Matisse's ongoing series *The Dance* (1905), but also because they placed the large, overwhelming presence of bodies at the center of their paintings, capturing meaning in bodily forms rather than in landscapes. Modernist painters also rejected lifelike renderings of people and places. They broke with tradition by fragmenting images, emphasizing the relation of one thing to another, juxtaposing inner and outer realities, and finding new ways to integrate opposites and contradictions. Moving from Europe to America via such events as the 1913 New York Armory show of cubism and postimpressionist painting, modernism gathered momentum in the United States as writers, musicians, sculptors, and painters experimented with the formal elements that made up their art forms.[7]

Like Picasso, Matisse, and other modernist painters, modern dancers created new ways for people to see themselves, from disjointed, angular composites of body parts to colorful, rounded, fluid outlines. New images came out of new roles. Modern dance was distinct from other artistic genres in the groups of people it attracted: white women (many of whom were Jewish), gay men, and some African American men and women. Women held leading roles on stage and off, replacing the common stage image of the sexual ingenue with that of the pioneering individual who moved her own body with disquieting, abrupt force. Gay men, too, recast the effeminate image of the sissy into a hardened, heroic, dancing American athlete. African American dancers, however, did not find an easy place within this new American art form, even though the theme of African Americans' rise

FIGURE I.I. *Helen Tamiris in "Joshua Fit for Battle" from* Negro Spirituals. *Photograph by Thomas Bouchard, © Diane Bouchard. (Jerome Robbins Dance Division, The New York Public Library for the Performing Arts, Astor, Lenox and Tilden Foundations)*

from oppression dominated many of the stories of white modern dancers' choreography, such as Tamiris's *Negro Spirituals*. In their slighted role, African American dancers and choreographers defined the limits of modern dancers' communal visions, and in their own productions they explored other conceptions of dance, of modern times, and of the United States by thrusting Africa and the Caribbean onto American stages.[8]

This vital new force in the arts inevitably evoked questions about how America could be portrayed in dance, what was American in the arts, and what it meant to be an American. In many ways, modern dance productions portrayed the United States as a society composed of heroic individuals, a theme also found in post office murals and Federal Theatre productions created out of the government-sponsored Works Progress Administration (WPA). One of the most celebrated plays of the era was Thornton Wilder's *Our Town* (1938), which eulogized Americans' ability to group together quirky individuals in both life and death. But modern dancers enacted a more radical concept. Marginalized groups of gay men, Jewish women, and African American men and women flocked to a fledgling art form that was based on physical expression. Defined by external physical characteristics or so-called deviant sexual practices, the social identities of these dancers shaped the means by which they contributed to defining America. And their physical differences and exploration of body movement showed the limits of pluralism and assimilation in the 1930s and, particularly, the depth and endurance of racial fracture.

Modern dance began and remains a place where people on the edges of society congregate and express themselves. In the 1930s modern dancers shaped their art form within the democratic, pluralist Popular Front thrust of the times and attempted to appeal to a large audience, from workers in labor unions to townspeople in rural areas of the Midwest. The changing political climate of the 1940s was one reason that in the wake of World War II modern dancers shed their efforts to appeal to a mainstream audience and gravitated to a less constraining setting in colleges and universities and among the avant-garde. Because of their commitment to flouting both aesthetic and social conventions, modern dancers shifted their goals in the postwar years; most modern dancers chose iconoclasm, conforming their art to intellectual ideals. Ballet and musical theater took up the nationalist call more resoundingly in this era, with Russian émigré George Balanchine and his newly formalized American ballet leading the way. The evolution of modern dance into an esoteric art form illuminates the course of modernism in the United States where social roles reinforced a marginal path. White women, African American men and women, and gay men created in modern dance a malleable art form within which they might re-imagine conventional social roles. But that very malleability and radical re-visioning have kept modern dance on the fringe of the arts and the rim of society.

Modern dance's liminal place, though, lends it importance in offering an original perspective on how the arts reflect and contribute to the struggles and composition of our world. The instructiveness of dance begins with its elusiveness—the active embodiment of an idea, practice, or historical era *and* its fleetingness. The inability to fix or stop the moment of dance allows for continual transformation of our finite bodies. James Baldwin elegantly described the power of performance as "the unmistakable silence in which [the performer] and the audience re-create each other."[9] Dance resides within that hope of re-creation. It offers the possibility that our bodies are not always a prison of flesh and that we can change our physical presentation to the world and alter the way we see ourselves and others.

The ephemerality of dance, however, eclipses its potential. Each move erases the previous one; Doris Humphrey called dance "the arc between two deaths."[10] The transience of one moment of dance speaks to the fragility of the art form as a whole. The lack of permanence of the artworks, the difficulty in recording and preserving dance or reproducing it in any commodified form, compounds the loss inherent to the art form. Studying dance of the past sharpens our attention to the historical record of bodies' movements, of people, of practices, that is inevitably lost. Filmed documentation of dance was not begun in earnest until the 1960s, so I have pieced together events such as the Dance Repertory Theatre performances by looking at photographs, reviews, choreographic notes, remembrances, and small snippets of film that have survived, or later filmed versions of a work. The ineluctable loss of the performances themselves makes clear that our understanding of the past demands imagination. Beyond the political speeches, magazine advertisements, letters, and music that traditionally compose our view of the past are exuberantly physical beings. This is a project of reclamation of that part of the past—of utterances and meaning expressed through bodies in motion. If Martha Graham is right, and bodies daily accumulate social tensions, triumphs, and woes, dance, then, is a fluid act of revelation whereby newspaper headlines move and get rearranged. In conjuring up these dancers, I most want to carry forward their insistence on placing the movement, suffering, and joy of lived bodies at the center of passionate inquiry and the quest for understanding.

1 : *manifestos*

On 25 April 1922, the American dancer Ruth St. Denis presented a silver "loving cup" to the Russian ballerina Anna Pavlova at a performance of *Giselle* at the Metropolitan Opera house in New York City. The painter Robert Henri, arts patron Otto Kahn, dance writer Troy Kinney, Russian émigré and ballet dancer Adolph Bolm, and St. Denis's dance partner and husband, Ted Shawn, joined St. Denis to pay tribute to Pavlova, whose solo *The Dying Swan* had spawned ballet devotees throughout the world.[1] The passing of the cup to Anna Pavlova by Ruth St. Denis, though, signified a change in the American dance scene. St. Denis built on the movement innovations of Isadora Duncan and Loïe Fuller earlier in the century, dancing in bare feet, stylizing gestures, looking outside ballet for movement ideas, and insisting upon a spiritual reverence for the body and its movements. Creating a new theatrical event that mixed small, detailed motions with exotic costumes, sets, and dramatic lighting, mostly portraying Asian themes and subjects, St. Denis moved fluidly between vaudeville, the homes of wealthy patrons, and concert stages. In 1922 her successes, rather than Pavlova's, portended the things to come, because she inspired and trained many who would indelibly alter concert dance in the 1930s.

The nascent American dance scene owed much to the Russian ballet stars Anna Pavlova and Michel Fokine and to Serge Diaghilev's Ballets Russes, whose tours in the 1910s inflamed audiences and provided a glimpse of the European balletic tradition that was being infused with new energy and talent corralled by Diaghilev. The shock of Vaslav Nijinsky's angular, emphatic movement and Igor Stravinsky's relentless, pounding score in *Sacre du Printemps* (1913), the hallmark of European modernism, still rippled. In the United States ballet had neither evoked such shock nor carried such import. Largely a vehicle for titillation or decoration, American ballet teetered between an act in vaudeville, such as a satiric scenario of Fokine's *Cléopâtre* staged by Gertrude Hoffman at Brooklyn's Majestic Theater in 1912, and a backdrop in opera, such as Bolm's *Le Coq d'Or* (1918) for the Metropolitan Opera. Pavlova's performance with Mikhail Mordkin in 1910, followed by the 1916–17 tour of Ballets Russes, changed American perceptions of ballet, moving it more solidly into the realm of art and beauty in its own right. By the 1920s small ballet schools and performances sprouted in cities and towns around the nation, the most evident being those led by Catherine Littlefield in Philadelphia and Ruth Page in Chicago. Heavily influenced by European, and especially Russian, techniques and choreography, ballet began to attract a smattering of practitioners and followers in this country.[2]

Other dance innovations blossomed from the United States at the turn of the century. Isadora Duncan and Loïe Fuller began dancing in ways distinct from ballet and the dance done in vaudeville shows, freeing movement from the constraining technique of ballet and the flashiness of vaudeville and using it to convey philosophical, religious, or artistic ideas and beliefs. Isadora Duncan drew on Hellenic ideals of government, art, architecture, and philosophy to liberate the body in reverence to the freedom of the individual spirit. Freeing her body from the corset, she reinvented walking, skipping, and leaping and elevated dance from a popular entertainment to the hallowed halls of art and nature, sometimes performing barefoot in flowing white tunics on forested lawns to classical music. Loïe Fuller experimented with early motion picture techniques to explore the dimensions of light by creating shadows and refractions through a diaphanous, flowing costume, transforming scientific inventions into new theatrical visions.[3]

Duncan and Fuller received their greatest fame in Europe, largely because of new approaches to movement spreading throughout Europe, but their innovations laid the foundation for the success of Ruth St. Denis in the United States. Born in 1879 in Somerville, New Jersey, Ruth Dennis grew up amid the turn-of-the-century attention to physical culture that was nurtured in her own home by her mother. Determined to raise a healthy girl, Dennis's mother took her to classes in the Delsarte system of movement. In this theory of the body and its meaning, developed by a nineteenth-century French philosopher, François Delsarte, certain zones of the body—head, heart, and lower limbs—corresponded to different philosophical states—

mind, soul, and life, respectively. To this attention to physicality, Dennis's mother added a Christian devotion, a strong will, and attendance at the spectacles that came into town at the Palisades Amusement Park, including P. T. Barnum's circus and *Egypt through the Centuries* (1892). The combination inspired Dennis to put movement to theatrical use. Working in dime museums, vaudeville, and variety shows, Dennis navigated through the theatrical world of the turn of the century, picking up costume and stage tips, making distinctions in audiences and venues, and learning a variety of dance steps, from clog dances and Irish jigs and reels to skirt dancing and gymnastic trickeries. In 1900 she ended up in the company of David Belasco, a vaudeville impresario, and it was here that she began to develop a vision of herself as a solo dancer where she could combine her deep religiosity with theatrical flair. Seeing a poster advertising Egyptian Deity cigarettes, she began researching other cultures and in 1905 left Belasco for a new career in staging dancing pictures of foreign lands under a new name, Ruth St. Denis.[4]

St. Denis's Hindu-inspired *Radha* (1906) served as her entrée into a solo career in theaters and private performances in the homes of society women. In the early twentieth century the arts were a respected avocation for white middle- and upper-class girls and women, but a rare vocation. Training in the arts was to produce cultured girls and women as another sign of education and manners, not professional artists. Wealthy white women began to host dance soloists in their homes as a way in which to display their cultured worldview; in so doing, they also supported those women who were struggling to form careers as artists and loosen dance from its vaudeville and burlesque ties. In 1898, for example, Isadora Duncan danced at the Newport, Rhode Island, summer residence of Ellen Mason, a Bostonian. The patrons of the dance concert were all women and included Mrs. William Astor of New York City. Ruth St. Denis also performed in homes, often as a part of a benefit or charitable cause, including a 1914 birthday party for Anna Howard Shaw, one of the leaders of the women's suffrage movement. This patronage by elite members of society gave dance a new cultural legitimacy.[5]

The patronage of women also solidified the association of dance as an artistic medium for women. Ruth St. Denis, Loïe Fuller, and Isadora Duncan all embodied the much talked about New Woman emerging at the turn of the century. Throwing off layers of petticoats, emboldened women fought for more public roles and the right to vote. These new ideas included an embrace of "free love," looser sexual mores, and unfettered movement in dance halls and on stage that reflected a less restrained attitude toward bodies. Dancers such as Duncan and St. Denis disrobed: they took off corsets and put on bloomers, allowing more freedom of the legs and torso. The birth of more expressive dance on the West Coast aided this liberation from binding clothes. Duncan grew up in San Francisco, and the New Jersey–born St. Denis ended up founding a school, Denishawn, with her husband and partner, Ted Shawn, in Los Angeles in 1915. The school's explorations in movement suited the southern Californian scene with its new, quickly dominant movie industry. Denishawn students appeared in films, filling out dramatic scenes such as the Babylonian episode in D. W. Griffith's *Intolerance,* and actresses, such as Lillian and Dorothy Gish, came to Denishawn for dance lessons. The sun and warmth of the climate mixed with the more sexually open attitude of Hollywood to create a welcome dance beginning for young women. Doris Humphrey's mother recognized the sexual implications of this liberation when she wrote Humphrey soon after she went to Denishawn in 1917. Reacting to comments from others, she asked Doris if licentiousness permeated the choreography or school.[6] Humphrey did not respond directly to this query, but it seems likely that modern dance freed young women psychically from the remnants of their strict upbringing as well as physically from the residue of Victorian notions of women's bodily weaknesses.[7]

This liberation extended beyond concert stages and movies to a less flagrant but more pervasive growth in dance that was occurring in the dance halls, settlement homes, and public parks of major cities in United States, especially New York, in the first decades of the twentieth century. "Dance madness" consumed working- and middle-class men and women in the 1910s and 1920s, and dance halls became a public arena in which men and women mingled and bartered for sexual favors. Dance halls and cabarets allowed for exploration of body movement, from the stylized one-step of Vernon and Irene Castle to the turkey trot, with its flapping arms and legs that resembled those of its namesake. The avid interest in dance and experimentation by young men and women sparked the concern of Progressive Era reformers, who denounced this kind of dancing as sexually promiscuous. Indeed, dancing of all kinds exposed how relationships between men

FIGURE 1.1. *Ruth St. Denis and Ted Shawn seated on a rock, surrounded by students. Martha Graham is second from right, looking downward. (Jerome Robbins Dance Division, The New York Public Library for the Performing Arts, Astor, Lenox and Tilden Foundations)*

and women, and the prescribed gender roles for men and women, were embroiled in other issues of the era, with its increasing immigration, particularly from southern and eastern Europe, rapid industrialization, overflowing cities, and political battles over women's suffrage, labor relations, and the role of the United States in world affairs.[8]

The attempt to shape and control this new interest in physical expression was perhaps most obvious in settlement homes, where middle-class white women used dance to instruct young working-class girls in acceptable ways to move, act, and be proper Americans. Dance historian Linda Tomko has uncovered these activities, primarily centered in New York but also present in Chicago and Boston, which fostered a wave of physical expression among girls and women and placed dance in a realm dominated by middle-class white women. Led by Jane Addams, the founder of Hull-House in Chicago, these women had carved out roles for themselves in the creation of settlement houses that provided needed services in immigrant neighborhoods. Believing that the environment in which people live shapes their actions, settlement house workers lived in poor neighborhoods, offering a model of domestication and behavior based on white middle-class ideals such as restraint, cleanliness, and well-defined roles for girls and boys. Despite these restrictive models aimed at molding the vast variety of immigrants into acceptable citizens, the mostly female settlement house workers also put forth an active, involved, communal role for women.[9]

Dance existed within this setting as an expressive outlet for young immigrant girls. Influenced by the ideas of British artists and thinkers John Ruskin and William Morris, settlement house workers used art to serve a social end by grouping people together in friendly ways, providing activity to enrich minds, and restoring the creativity and beauty that was thought to be siphoned off in industrial society. Sisters Alice and Irene Lewisohn ran the artistic activities at the Henry Street Settlement House, founded by Lillian Wald in 1893 on the Lower East Side of New York City, and Irene took particular interest in dance. American-born daughters of a German Jewish immigrant father, they directed their attention to the new influx of eastern European Jews.[10] Eastern Europeans quickly dominated the Jewish population in New York City, and German Jews who had long resided in America hoped to instruct the new arrivals on how to fit into society. German Jews worried about certain traits that eastern European Jews brought with them—particularly Orthodox religious beliefs and political activism—and wanted to quell any anti-Semitism that the eastern European Jews might provoke and by which German Jews might be harmed. To that end, the Lewisohn sisters promoted cultural rather than political activities, hoping to bridge the different cultures by putting on street pageants, beginning in 1906, resplendent with the stories and costumes of homelands. They soon became more ambitious and in 1915 built a theater called the Neighborhood Playhouse located just a few blocks from the Henry Street Settlement House. Their first production, *Jephthah's Daughter,* based on the story in the Book of Judges, drew mixed responses. "The radically inclined were disappointed that the Old Testament was used as a source, rather than Andreyev or Gorky, and the conventionally minded were shocked at the bare feet of the dancers," Alice Lewisohn Crowley remembered.[11] In this maelstrom of varying values and beliefs, dance had a place as a form of expression and communication that did not require spoken language.

Helen Tamiris, the organizer of the Dance Repertory Theatre, was born into this environment in 1902. The only daughter of Russian Jewish immigrants, Helen Becker grew up amidst poverty, squalid living conditions, and the endless work of garment sweatshops on the Lower East Side of Manhattan. The early death of her mother, when Helen was three, added to the family's difficulties. Along with two of her four brothers, Becker found solace in creativity. One brother was an artist, another a sculptor, while Helen began her dance career with classes at the Henry Street Settlement House.[12] Taking classes from Irene Lewisohn and Blanche Talmud, Becker picked up a variety of movements, from pantomimic gestures to folk dances. She went from her dance classes at Henry Street to a job at the Metropolitan Opera, first utilizing her folk dance lessons, then turning to ballet. She was inspired by Pavlova and began to re-train her body, forgetting what she had learned at the settlement house about "allowing the movement to flow out from the chest through the arms and legs . . . to start each movement from the center—the seat of the heart and lungs—and soul." Instead, ballet required concentrating on legs and feet, stiffly holding her neck, and keeping the spine immovable, "as though a rod had been tied to the vertebrae."[13] She conquered ballet well enough to continue at the

Metropolitan for a couple of years and then, in the early 1920s, went on tour to South America with the Bracale Opera Company.[14] The trip inspired her to seek out new forms of art and literature, and a romantic liaison with a South American writer brought about a christening with a new name from a poem about an ancient Persian queen: "Thou art Tamiris, the ruthless queen who banishes all obstacles."[15]

When she returned to the United States the obstacle Tamiris set about banishing was ballet. The artificiality of ballet began to annoy her, and pointe work prompted the scornful remark, "Toe dancing . . . Why not dance on the palms of the hands?"[16] She developed a reputation as "wild Becker" because she would not stay in the lines of the corps and her exuberance overtook others on the stage. By the mid-1920s other dancers with backgrounds similar to Tamiris's, many of whom also began their dance training at the Henry Street Settlement House, turned to modern dance rather than ballet. The bare feet of modern dance attracted poor dancers who could not afford pointe shoes, recalled Faith Rehyer Jackson. Poverty influenced political ideology among early modern dancers because they wanted to move with "that proletariat feeling of moving in a group and they could afford one leotard," as Jackson put it. Brought up in the teeming political atmosphere of the Lower East Side, these women turned to body movement to express their social and political ideals.[17]

These dancers merged art and politics, finding ways to respond to social conditions and make political statements through dance. Giving new meaning and relevance to movement, nascent modern dancers in the 1920s vilified ballet, theatrical dance, and even the mentor of many of them, Ruth St. Denis. In their eyes, ballet was a fantastical picture of femininity in alabaster imported from Europe, too elitist and foreign to speak to the American masses. Revue dancing was formulaic, designed to surprise and please the audience with acrobatic stunts and, as Tamiris described it, "some high kicking hitting the head from the back over and over again 32 times—64 times with the music furiously getting louder and louder until the audience would break out in applause."[18] Even St. Denis prompted scorn because she performed a potpourri of dance styles that featured more authentic costumes than authentic movement in the mix of steps from ballet, Isadora Duncan, and Asian sources.[19] This break of the modernists in dance was less formal and more revolutionary than the passing of a silver loving cup at a gala performance. The aesthetic issues involved large, serious questions and ideals about American society.

Tamiris articulated much of what was at stake in a "Manifest[o]" she included in the program of her second solo concert on 29 January 1928. It was a smattering of claims ranging from specific scolding ("To give primary importance to facial expression is just as bad as to give primary importance to the feet") to broad philosophical precepts ("There are no general rules"). Throughout Tamiris stressed that dance was its own art, neither a supplement to music, a simplistic mode of narration, nor a bodily prop for costumes. Even more important, dance must spring from "the age we live in" and be "a product of nationality." "The dance of today must have a dynamic tempo and be valid, precise, spontaneous, free, normal, natural and human," she concluded.[20]

For modern dancers sustenance came from abstract thoughts, freedom of will, purposeful work—and finding others with the same commitment. They followed the mission of Oliver Sayler, outlined in his 1930 book *Revolt in the Arts,* in which he claimed that "art has become our necessity" and that all the arts were "intricately interrelated."[21] Modern dancers involved themselves in this larger movement of change in the arts, reading Nietzsche for inspiration, seeking out the music of contemporary American composers such as Wallingford Riegger for accompaniment to their dances, and mining the poetry of Hart Crane and William Carlos Williams for provocative titles for their works. Otto Luening, a composer and conductor who had worked in Europe, commented that the modern dancers he knew were not at all interested in the European dancers he had seen: "They were interested mostly that I knew James Joyce."[22] Joyce's distinctive literary style of writing sentences that mimicked the elliptical, roaming way people think correlated to modern dancers' mission to use the body to convey philosophical and emotional principles. Doris Humphrey's attraction to the music of Henry Cowell, who played the piano with various parts of his body, exemplified modern dancers' affinity with other artists flailing traditions and finding new ways to deliberate ideas.[23]

For modernist artists what most mattered was individual expression and having the artistic product relay that intellectual or emotional process. For modern dancers life was effortful and weighty; their grounded movements and intense faces embodied this idea. More specifically, the Nietzschean duality of restraint and liberation, Apollo and Dionysus, formed the basis of their movement styles. Martha Graham devised the principle of contraction and release based on the example of breathing. Centered in the torso, a contraction hollowed out the stomach and rounded the back; the release freed the body again, straightening the spine. Doris Humphrey's fall and recovery worked on the same principle of duality. Following gravity, Humphrey let the body fall toward earth in various ways, only to reflect off and lift again. Humphrey believed "the arc between two deaths" to be the life between two moments of stasis, the extreme ends of an oppositional dualism.[24] The unending repetition of these cycles through body movement—dancing—represented the coexistence and occasional unity of these contrary elements.

Modern dancers displayed this battle of opposites on both psychological and social levels. In her first solo concert, Tamiris performed *Subconscious* (1927), which "juxtapose[d] movement suggesting inhibited activity as against free activity" and ended in a bold emergence from "grey swirling mist . . . free and unfettered."[25] Graham had a less sanguine view when she placed the struggle of opposites in society in *Heretic* (1929). To simple percussive rhythms by Louis Horst, stolid group actions of women dressed in black opposed the dramatic, forceful moves of the individual danced by Graham, costumed in white (see figure 1.2). The group formed an immobile semicircle around the individual, in effect confining her. The piece repeated the individual's fight with the circle of masses three times and ended with the individual—after a prototypical, agonizing fall backward—lying on the floor face down, conquered and condemned. Graham thus relayed both the importance and the impotency of the individual. The music reinforced this idea with its lyrical theme, to which only Graham danced, and a forceful pounding motif, to which the group moved. While confirming the clash between the individual and society and predicting a pessimistic end, *Heretic* underscored the inevitability of that struggle.

If dualism was modern dancers' philosophical paradigm, minimalism was their style. Following Gertrude Stein's aphorism "So little is more," they rebelled against the theatrical spectacles of Denishawn with their numerous props, settings, and lush costumes and danced instead on bare stages in plain dresses with stark lighting.[26] "Like the modern painters and architects, we have stripped our medium of decorative unessentials. Just as fancy trim-

FIGURE I.2. *Martha Graham and Group in* Heretic. *Photograph by Soichi Sunami. (Jerome Robbins Dance Division, The New York Public Library for the Performing Arts, Astor, Lenox and Tilden Foundations)*

mings are no longer seen on buildings, so dancing is no longer padded," Graham declared.[27] Her 1930 solo, *Lamentation,* was a landmark example (see figure I.3). A solitary dancer sat on a bench enshrouded in a tubular costume that restricted the arms and legs and covered the head so that only the feet and face were visible. Movements emanated from the torso and reverberated through the fetus-like shape. This dance distilled one emotion—grief—into the strained, yearning movements of a confined body.

This ability to convey emotion through structured form was what *New York Times* dance critic John Martin stressed as modern dance's importance. Martin devoted years to explaining and advocating modern dance in newspaper articles, lectures at the New School for Social Research, and books.

FIGURE 1.3. *Martha Graham in* Lamentation. *Photograph by Soichi Sunami. (Jerome Robbins Dance Division, The New York Public Library for the Performing Arts, Astor, Lenox and Tilden Foundations)*

He believed that a set vocabulary of movement dominated classic dance (which he thought of as ballet) and resulted in an artificial, machine-like beauty. A modern dancer, on the other hand, was "never willing to make his body a machine for manufacturing designed in space, but insists that it always be recognized as a body . . . devoted wholly to the transfer of a heightened emotional perception of reality from his own experience to the understanding of the spectator." Abstracted from personal experience, emotion was an elemental and universal quality.[28]

With scorn for Denishawn and ballet, Graham wrote in 1930 that "we have had a dance of 'appearance' rather than a dance of 'being'—instead of an art which was the fruit of a people's soul, we had entertainment."[29] "Being" translated into a concern with such elemental philosophical principles as duality, a minimalist style with little decoration in costumes or settings, the use of movement to convey emotion, and an interest in "primitive" cultures. The search for foundational elements of thought and aesthetic style had inspired many European modernist artists to explore African art and culture.[30] Following this impulse, Graham sought that same primitive inspiration within the United States as a way to help modern dancers define their dance as an American art form. She identified "two forms of indigenous dance" in America that would be useful, that of the African American and that of the Native American, and expressed their appeal in dualistic terms: "The Negro dance is a dance toward freedom, a dance to forgetfulness, often Dionysiac in its abandon and the raw splendour of its rhythm—it is a rhythm of disintegration. The Indian dance, however, is not for freedom, or forgetfulness, or escape, but for awareness of life, complete relationship with that world in which he finds himself; it is a dance for power, a rhythm of integration."[31] Graham began exploring these ideas in choreography and in 1931 created one of her masterworks, *Primitive Mysteries,* which examined contemporary Native American religiosity, a mixture of missionaries' Catholicism with tribal beliefs. Like the earlier *Heretic,* the structure of the piece contrasted an individual woman costumed in white (abstractly, the Virgin Mary) with a large group of women surrounding her in darker costumes. Unlike *Heretic,* harmonious interaction, both physically and psychically, existed between the individual and the group. The dance affirmed the oneness of the group and the significance of the ritual itself. Turning from the pessimism she saw around her and displayed in *Heretic,* Graham found the harmony she wished for in an idealization of Native American culture.[32]

Modern dancers utilized the spiritual traditions of Native Americans in developing a "rhythm of integration" and culled from African and African American dance traditions the freeing of the whole body for a "rhythm of disintegration." African dance and spiritual traditions featured full-body shaking and loose-jointed motions that highlighted the impulse and origin of the movement rather than its stylized continuation. Modern dancers propounded the importance of the torso and pelvis as the center and instigation of movement that differed greatly from ballet's tightly held, rigid spine, its stationary hips, and active legs moving in circular and vertical extensions. White modern dancers did not endorse the circular motions of the hips that African American modern dancers utilized, but their embrace of the fluidity of the body, where one motion spawned a reactive motion, echoed the kinetic principles underlying the rhythmic impulses of African-related dance.[33]

Talk of rhythm in general reflected the more widespread blending of African American, Native American, and white traditions and the porousness of these categories, particularly in the realm of American culture. The literary critic Mary Austin identified "American rhythm" as stemming from Native American songs and dances popularized to the point that rhythm was "perhaps the very mode of consciousness itself."[34] In the work of sexologists such as Havelock Ellis and the poetry of modernists such as Hart Crane and Theodore Roethke, rhythm often connoted sex and was linked to animalistic passions and urges that primitive people supposedly exemplified. Crane's "Star kissing star through wave on wave onto / Your body rocking!" in his poem "Voyages" (1926) and Roethke's "I measure time by how a body sways" in his later poem "I Knew a Woman" (1958) gave a physical pace to their poetry.[35] Modern dancers joined these thinkers in maintaining that sex and dance were manifestations of a spiritual rhythmic force that formed the very foundation of life. "Rhythm so permeates every aspect of human beings, and indeed, of the known world, that it might be compared to the ambience of existence," Humphrey wrote, and she urged dancers to return to this inherent foundation.[36] In their use of angular, often disjunctive movements, modern dancers hoped to signify the pattern and connectedness that rhythm implied.

Harmony, in fact, was the first abstract idea Humphrey attempted to choreograph. In 1927, still officially working with Denishawn, Humphrey claimed to be "so tired of the dinky little dances and decorative or character or cute ballets, that I've gone to the extreme of abstractness."[37] To new music by Clifford Vaughn, which he produced as she choreographed, Humphrey focused on color. She researched the subject extensively, thinking about how color related to emotional expression, musical theory, and light. In a passionate description in her notebook, Humphrey related the interaction between groups of primary colors that merged into new colors, creating vibration rather than form. Using costumes and lighting, for example, dancers grouped as red and yellow mixed so that an orange scarf emerged from their motion. At the end, "all the flaming colors are laid down in rhythmic patterns—in a pyramidal form—up high steps to a climax, where a silver streak molds itself into a stream of light that goes up to infinity."[38] *Color Harmony* (1927) was an auspicious break with the dance of the past, revealing the abstract and theoretically rich ideas modern dancers brought to choreography.

St. Denis probably prompted Humphrey's initial thoughts on color and harmony with a 1924 article, "The Color Dancer," in Denishawn's magazine. This same article also inspired another St. Denis devotee, Edna Guy, to think about color's "psychology and symbolism."[39] Guy's thoughts about color had expanded by the end of the decade, when she explained to St. Denis that "someday I should like to do a mass movement thing with instead of colors in costumes symbolizing—have colors in bodies symbolize. Girls and boys from white to the very black."[40] Guy's idea never came to fruition, however, and, as a young African American woman, she found that her hopes for a career in concert dancing were often stymied. In all of St. Denis's and Humphrey's research about color, the hues of skin color did not appear on their theoretical palette. The easy ignorance among white Americans of racial discrimination was common in the 1920s, even though the mix of many different kinds of people was also increasingly common, particularly in New York City. Many white New Yorkers traveled uptown, imbibing the thrill and adventure of going to Harlem and commingling with "colored" people. Whether or not they grappled with questions of color like Edna Guy did, white modern dancers were a part of the stream uptown, where blues and jazz music trumpeted both the lingering sadness and the carefree attitude of life after the Great War.[41]

The nightclubs of Harlem such as the Cotton Club remain an enduring image of the 1920s with its uncomfortably sharp picture of white voyeurs of showy spectacles made up of black dancers and musicians, but the cultural activities of African Americans, and often the whiteness of the audience, went beyond nightclubs. During the 1920s, African Americans published books at presses that previously had denied publication to black authors; Broadway theaters hosted more and more African American revues; some shows, such as *Showboat* (1927) and Eugene O'Neill's play *All God's Chillun* (1924) had interracial casts; and even African American painters (Aaron Douglas, Palmer Heyden), a classical composer (William Grant Still), and opera singers (Roland Hayes and, later, Marian Anderson) began to enter the elite institutions that supported those arts.[42] James Weldon Johnson, in his 1930 book *Black Manhattan,* celebrated the recent success of African American artists and attributed it to the rising black population in crowded urban locales in the North, the result of African Americans' fleeing the fields of the South, lured by factory jobs first accessible to them during World War I. The artistic activity reflected a resurgence, not a new phenomenon, Johnson reminded readers, because "for many generations the Negro has been a creative artist and a contributor to the nation's common cultural store."[43] What was new were the labels "New Negro" and "Harlem Renaissance," a more positive response from whites, and a concerted effort by some African Americans to inspire and guide artistic output.

Dance was a part of this flowering. In Paris, Josephine Baker thrilled audiences at the Théâtre de Champs-Elysées in 1925 and the Folies Bergères in 1926; in New York, Bill "Bojangles" Robinson dominated the tap scene in Broadway shows and then in movies of the 1930s, and Florence Mills made a splash with her dancing and singing ability in the 1924 all-black revue *Dixie to Broadway,* which differed from previous shows that usually centered around male comedians. In 1927 a new dance craze hit the dance floors of New York: the lindy hop celebrated Charles Lindbergh's solo jump across the Atlantic in an airplane and dazzled spectators at Harlem's Savoy Ballroom with its airborne lifts, fast footwork, and solo breakaways full of improvisation.

Edna Guy awoke to dance in this atmosphere, sparked by African American concert singers Roland Hayes and Paul Robeson and a 1922 performance of Ruth St. Denis. Guy sent a note to St. Denis after the performance, a poetic reverie, signed "Edna Guy, Colored Girl." For the next few years Guy sought out St. Denis in correspondence and dance classes, hoping to join Denishawn. St. Denis encouraged Guy's lofty dreams but only intermittently helped with the many obstacles she faced. Guy struggled to find teachers and classes that would accept her and then to find jobs. Although she recognized that chorus dancing held no "beauty" (and St. Denis concurred), Guy sought such jobs because this kind of dance was seen as African Americans' forte and because concert dance groups would not employ her. Even in show dancing, however, she encountered discrimination. She soon came to the realization that she could only hope for a specialty part, because "the chorus girls are all to [sic] light for me to be in with them."[44]

Guy was caught by prejudices that pushed her to chorus jobs and then thwarted her success even in that realm. By the late 1920s she gravitated to the inchoate modern dance movement, theoretically open to *every* body. Working with Hemsley Winfield, who had achieved some success in the little theater movement, Guy participated in the first modern dance performance of African Americans on 6 March 1931, when Winfield's new company, Bronze Ballet Plastique, performed at the Saunders Trade School in Yonkers in a benefit for the Colored Citizens Unemployment and Relief Committee. Six weeks later, Guy co-directed and danced with Winfield's Negro Art Theatre Dance Group when it performed the "First Negro Dance Recital in America" in a small theater on the fiftieth floor of the Chanin Building at Lexington Avenue and 42nd Street in midtown Manhattan. Edna Guy and her New Negro Art Dancers followed with their premiere later the same year. The dancing "New Negro" had arrived.[45]

Winfield's Negro Art Theatre Dance Group and Guy's New Negro Art Dancers carried out many of the ideals expressed in the Harlem Renaissance. Hoping to counter stereotypes of being capable only of loose dancing full of hip swings and flailing limbs, Winfield and Guy performed the abstract, highly controlled motions of modern dance that gave each movement a serious, studied intention. Guy had envisioned her importance early on in her training: "I shall be the first colored girl to make the world see that a little negro girl, an American can do beautiful and with much feeling—the creative dances of her soul, and I shall give to other colored boys and girls my thoughts and dreams of beauty in the Dance and in every beautiful thing—they need it so, they just wait for someone to take the first step, to set the example, and I think they will follow. I shall be the one to lead them."[46] Creating new images of African Americans in dance, Guy and Winfield found in modern dance an evolving art form that could be shaped to showcase both the broadened dance capabilities of African Americans and, in theme and choreography, the abilities and the humanity of African Americans in general. Here was an opportunity to enter sanctified realms of art that at this time conveyed values of education, creativity, and sophistication to a degree many thought African Americans incapable of achieving. In her hopeful mission statement, Guy recognized just how unique she would be as "a little negro girl, an American" leading others to see the contributions and rightful place of African Americans in the American arts.

By the end of the 1920s the mission to create an American form of concert dance had begun in earnest, and the important role that social and political ideas would play in realizing this goal was set. Manifestos by Guy, Tamiris, Graham, Humphrey, and others—either written or danced—trumpeted a new force in the American arts. Artistic change meant social change as well. In 1927, just before her tragic death, Isadora Duncan reiterated her belief in the spiritual significance of dance and divided the field into two types of dance, sacred and profane. The duality—and even much of its meaning—remained in place a few years later when, in 1930, Graham shifted it to social categories, Native American and African American. The renaming indicated how this revolutionary dance of being implanted itself in the social composition of America. But it also demonstrated modern dancers' reinforcement of certain prejudices stemming from different kinds of bodies. In their search for a path between what they saw as unsuitable alternatives—the inconsequential fluff of ballet, the exoticism of Denishawn, and the vulgarity of ethnic and African American traditions of show dancing—modern dancers maintained a demarcation between high and low in modernism that denigrated working-class, ethnic, and African

American peoples and cultural expressions even as it utilized and drew from them. "Ballet is as out of style as bustles and leg o'mutton sleeves," and splashy entertainment was devoid of meaning, Humphrey declared.[47]

In *Revolt in the Arts,* Oliver Sayler claimed that "esthetic revolt is the concomitant of social revolt," a principle that modern dancers would prove.[48] Their social revolt may have been less complete than their aesthetic one, but their urgency and passion were compelling. In various talks and articles, Humphrey spelled out her mission as an American modern dancer. "I believe that the dancer must belong to his time and place and that he can only express that which passes through or close to his experience. This new dance of action comes inevitably from the people who had to subdue a continent, to make a thousand paths through forest and plain, to conquer the mountains and eventually raise up towers of steel and glass. The American dance is born of this new world, new life, and new vigor."[49] Manifestos set, modern dancers moved on to establish new roles for themselves in the arts and in society.

2 : *pioneer women*

An illustration in the December 1934 *Vanity Fair* contrasted the modern dancer Martha Graham with Sally Rand, the fan dancer fresh from a scandal over obscenity at the 1933 Chicago World's Fair (see figure 2.1). Describing a fictional "Impossible Interview," the accompanying text to the illustration accentuated the differences between the two dancers. Rand attempted to establish their commonality, saying, "We're in the same racket, ain't we? Just a couple of little girls trying to wriggle along," but Graham rebuked her "haughtily." The conversation ended with a mutual recognition that the two women appealed to different audiences; Rand would "be frowned on in the ladies' clubs," and Graham would "be a flop in a cooch concession," referring to the kind of belly dancing done in burlesque shows. Rand suggested dividing the audiences: "From now on, we'd better split 50–50. You take the ladies, and I'll take the men."[1]

This illustration and the fictional text provocatively captured the complications women faced in dance in the first half of the twentieth century. Dance of all kinds, from vaudeville and burlesque to the concert stages, generally featured women as the main spectacle, a convention that assumed that female bodies were the desired sexual objects of heterosexual male audience members. Modern dancers challenged this convention by displaying different visions of women on stage with the purpose not of titillation but of defiance and demand. Modern dance changed what was on stage, who was in the audience, and the expectations of the audience. Despite this challenge, and the important distinctions separating Graham and Rand, the division between them was not as wide as it appeared in the caricature. In a 1932 Artists Ball in Chicago, Rand appeared as "Madam Godiva" on the same program in which the African American modern dancer Katherine

FIGURE 2.1. *"Impossible Interview," caricature of Martha Graham and Sally Rand. (*Vanity Fair *43, no. 4 [December 1934]: 40. Courtesy of and copyright © by Estate of Miguel Covarrubias)*

Dunham performed *Fantasie Negre*. Rand and Doris Humphrey had appeared on the same program when Humphrey was still in the Denishawn company in the mid-1920s, and Rand later sought and received choreographic suggestions from Humphrey. Both dancers expressed admiration for the other.[2] Female modern dancers worked within and around conventions of femininity, but on stage and off, their status as women always figured into perceptions and judgments of their accomplishments.[3]

The lives and careers of Martha Graham and Doris Humphrey, the leaders of modern dance in the 1930s, demonstrate both the experiences of heterosexual white women in dance and the images and perceptions that followed them in modernism. Recognizing modern dance as a new kind of adventure, Humphrey identified her own role in it as that of a pioneer woman.[4] Modern dance solidified in the decade following the passage of women's suffrage in 1920 and manifested the influence of both the separatist, discriminatory strategy of the women's suffrage movement and the individualist ethos of the failed fight for an equal rights amendment that followed. While female modern dancers did not ardently embrace specific goals about changing the status of women, their roles as choreographers, performers, teachers, and directors of companies placed them in the middle of ongoing debates about what women were capable of, the differences and similarities between men and women, and the role of women as creators of and commentators on American culture.[5]

Graham has been recognized as the foremost modern dancer and choreographer of the twentieth century, perhaps partly due to the fact that she lived through most of the century, being born in 1894 and dying in 1991. She very nearly performed throughout the century as well, beginning in the late 1910s and reluctantly giving her last performance in 1970 at the age of seventy-six. Doris Humphrey is now less well known, having died in 1958 at the relatively early age of sixty-three. But in the 1930s both Graham and Humphrey were the acknowledged leaders of modern dance. Graham drew accolades for her powerful presence on stage; Humphrey received high respect for her choreographic skill. If Graham was the mystical artiste of modern dance, Humphrey was its unremitting theorist and engineer.

Born in Allegheny, Pennsylvania, Martha Graham was the oldest of three daughters (a baby boy died in infancy). Her father, Dr. George Graham, dominated the household and maintained a puritan atmosphere where rules governed both religious and intellectual pursuits. Her mother, purportedly a descendant of Miles Standish and fifteen years younger than her husband, was a quiet though substantive presence. In 1908 the Grahams moved to Santa Barbara, California, to relieve the asthmatic difficulties of Martha's younger sister Mary. California's atmosphere of freedom of expression and liberal thought contrasted sharply with the puritanism of Pennsylvania. For Martha, the differences between the East and West Coasts would become polarized between suppression and paganism, restraint and liberation. This opposition also incorporated the tension between her father's intellectual curiosity and interest in the burgeoning field of psychology and a more sensory understanding of the world, from the almost exclusively female household, that gave credence to intuitiveness and emotions. Lizzie, the Irish Catholic maid, introduced Martha to the sumptuousness of Catholic rituals and ceremonies, but it was Graham's father who added the importance of body movement. As the famous story goes, Dr. Graham scolded five-year-old Martha for lying, telling her that it was immediately obvious in her body because "movement never lies." Graham learned that the body's actions revealed the mind and could tell truths not communicable in other ways. This dancing lesson formed the basis of Graham's legend.[6]

A performance by Ruth St. Denis in Los Angeles in 1911 that featured *Egypta* and *Radha* sparked Graham's interest in pursuing dance. After graduating from Santa Barbara High School in 1913, she attended the Cumnock School of Expression, a junior college in Los Angeles, where she took classes in dance and drama as well as academic subjects. Despite the death of her father in 1914 and the ensuing financial difficulties for her family, Graham graduated from the Cumnock School in 1916. That summer she attended the year-old Denishawn school in Los Angeles and came under the tutelage of Ruth St. Denis and Ted Shawn. Reveling in classes in Delsarte, decorative movements of the body, ballet, and piano, Graham imbibed the freedom and exoticism St. Denis and Shawn promoted. Caressing St. Denis's peacock Piadormor, listening to poetry and passages by Mary Baker Eddy, and learning a dance about the Japanese art of flower arranging, she eventually began teaching and performing herself, starring in *Xochitl* (1920), a ballet by Ted Shawn about an Aztec princess.[7]

Just a year after Graham began at Denishawn, Doris Humphrey appeared at the school for the summer session. It was a bigger pilgrimage to Los Angeles for Humphrey than for Graham. Born in 1895 in Oak Park, Illinois, Humphrey spent her childhood in the Midwest, the adored only child of a newspaperman father who became the manager of the Palace Hotel in Chicago and a mother who was a graduate of Mount Holyoke College and the Boston Conservatory of Music. Humphrey's upbringing was similar to Graham's in that they were both accorded attention and opportunity as daughters that might not have occurred if there had been living sons in the family. In Humphrey's case, her mother took charge of the household and began Doris's training in the arts with dance lessons at the Parker School when she was eight, primarily with Mary Wood Hinman, who also taught at Hull-House and drew from a variety of dance styles from ballroom to folk. Hinman encouraged Humphrey, giving her teaching opportunities beginning when she was sixteen. Humphrey's teaching activities increased dramatically when her father lost his job after the sale of the hotel, and she and her mother became the family breadwinners. Crunched by teaching demands and few performance opportunities, Humphrey sought out renewal in the summer session of Denishawn in 1917 and returned in the summer of 1918, this time to stay.[8]

The different talents and temperaments of Graham and Humphrey determined their different roles at Denishawn. Graham was a short woman with a long torso, a narrow, drawn face, and deep-set eyes; she was ever-watchful, intense, and determined. St. Denis favored the outgoing, vivacious Humphrey. Lithe and tall with striking cheekbones, Humphrey resembled St. Denis physically and by personality far more than Graham. It was Shawn who shepherded Graham, giving her roles in his ballets and eventually helping her to leave Denishawn by recommending her to a friend for a role in the New York vaudeville show, *The Greenwich Village Follies,* in 1923. Graham left that show for a teaching job in Rochester, New York, but returned to New York City in 1926 with a trio of students to perform a complete show of her own choreography.

Humphrey stayed with St. Denis and Shawn longer, traveling to Asia in the mid-1920s on a two-year tour and then helping to run their new school in New York City. She benefited from St. Denis's attention, crafting "music visualizations," a Denishawn invention that portrayed music in both movement and choreographic form. While Humphrey would soon scoff at this literalness, these music visualizations began her lifelong devotion to form and abstraction, elements that became hallmarks of her choreography. In 1928 Humphrey, Charles Weidman, and Pauline Lawrence battled with St. Denis and Shawn over the re-formation of Denishawn. The school had lost popularity, and St. Denis and Shawn hoped to remove the taint of vaudeville that remained from their past, when they had felt compelled to take such jobs for the money. Other elements factored into the reorganization that chaffed the younger dancers even more, however. Shawn felt that company members needed to adhere to a higher moral standard, perhaps a veiled attempt to censure his own adulterous wanderings with men while still married to St. Denis. Perhaps more surprisingly, St. Denis declared that she intended to limit Jewish students in the school "to ten percent of the whole," a general reference to the immigration quotas enacted in 1924 that legislated similar restrictions.. In a letter to her parents recounting the event, Humphrey suggested that this was an attempt to maintain an American origin to the art and an American appearance to the company, particularly when performing abroad. After St. Denis made such declarations about Anglo-Saxon art, she went on to invite Jewish company members to perform in an upcoming performance at Lewisohn Stadium, a hypocrisy that did not go unnoticed by Humphrey.[9] These strains of moral righteousness and anti-Semitism combined with a growing rift in artistic sensibility; Humphrey, Weidman, and Lawrence promptly left Denishawn to start their own troupe, the Humphrey-Weidman Group.

The training and support that Graham and Humphrey received at Denishawn cemented their devotion to dance — as a passion and as a career. Both were teachers at the Denishawn school and often performed in Denishawn concerts, and they formed crucial relationships with other Denishawn company members, although not with each other, that would shape their careers and their lives. Louis Horst, the accompanist for Denishawn, left there to prod Graham's independent efforts. Two Denishawn company members bolstered Humphrey: Charles Weidman became her performing and choreographic partner, and Pauline Lawrence their accompanist, company manager, and indefatigable champion. Graham's and Humphrey's first concerts in the late 1920s reflected the influence of Denishawn, with Graham's *Three Poems of the East* (1926) and *Flute of Krishna* (1926) emulating St. Denis's preoccupation with Asian cultures, and Humphrey's *Piano Concerto in A*

Minor (1928) to Grieg continuing the attempts to translate musical composition into body action. But the seeds of revolt were planted in them at Denishawn as well. Coming to Denishawn when they were twenty-two, Graham and Humphrey both had a sure idea of self and womanhood that was nurtured at the school but could not be contained by it. Championing the call of individual expression and recognizing shifting artistic and social patterns, Graham and Humphrey ventured into new realms of movement and creativity, forging a new artistic path for women.

Although women had gained prominence in other artistic fields by the 1930s—Georgia O'Keeffe in painting, Gertrude Stein in writing, for example—they did not dominate any art form as they did modern dance. The leadership of women in modern dance corresponded with a broadening of opportunities for most women. By the 1920s white American women voted, attended college in record numbers, enjoyed urban nightlife, and worked as a larger percentage of the workforce than before. Many women felt that the battle for equal rights had been won, even though African American women had largely been left out of the suffrage victory due to Jim Crow laws. But the cohesion among some groups of white women that helped pass suffrage began to disintegrate in the wake of that accomplishment. Vociferous debates arose between the National Women's Party, headed by Alice Paul, which worked for an equal rights amendment, and the League of Women Voters, which supported protective legislation for women. Among young women a strong individualist ethos emerged. Writing in *Harper's* in 1927, Dorothy Dunbar Bromley defined the "Feminist—New Style" as a woman who knows that "it is her America, her twentieth-century birthright to emerge from a creature of instinct into a full-fledged individual who is capable molding her own life. And in this respect she holds that she is becoming man's equal."[10] Humphrey opined on what modern dancers should dance about, and her answer reflected the spirit infusing many arenas in which women were involved in the late 1920s and into the 1930s: "There is only one thing to dance about: the meaning of one's personal experience and this experience must be taken in its literal sense as action, and not as intellectual conception."[11] Action and individualism fomented a wave of self-expression that celebrated and explored new definitions of womanhood.

The artistic movement of modernism paralleled this emphasis on individualism but focused on the alienation and isolation of the artist from the larger society that Graham proudly exposed in her 1929 *Heretic,* which dramatized the stoic individual fighting the confining masses. Moving from the nineteenth-century idea of the individual as rational public citizen, the defining unit in a democratic political system, early-twentieth-century individualism included more interiority and expressiveness. Newly professionalized psychologists insisted on the complicated workings of the individual mind, vastly expanding the terrain for understanding individual and societal behavior. Action and thought had an undercurrent of hidden meaning now, not just an overt one, and understanding people required taking account of irrational and rational, known and unknown, possibilities. Sex figured into these new definitions of individualism as sexologists, bohemians, and feminists asserted the strong sexual desire of human beings, emphasizing, to public clamor, women's inclusion in that category. These assertions called for new attention to feelings, connecting, as the philosopher John Dewey put it, "overt . . . activity [with] thought and feeling," joining mind and matter.[12] The newer emphasis on the expressive and internal forms of self allowed for more female participation in the arts, partly because women had been identified with sentiment and feeling over intellect, and also because the process of internalization that these beliefs inspired required little public forum. Modernist artists looked inward first, theoretically without the sanction or prejudice of being a man or woman.[13]

Modern dancers of the 1930s did not make distinctions between men and women in the process of artistic creation, but they did emphasize a different kind of subjectivity. While Picasso made visual the contours of his psyche on a canvas, modern dancers grounded individuality and expressiveness in bodies. "In general, no man can dance convincingly like any other man whose experience lies outside his own, and this is because the body, mirror of every thought and feeling, cannot disassociate itself readily from its movement habits. Here the dance is unique in the aesthetic world," Humphrey explained.[14] With the influence of anthropology and psychology, Katherine Dunham stated it this way: "The constant interplay of conscious and unconscious finds a perfect instrument in the physical form, the human body which embraces all at once."[15] Women modern dancers combined the active spirit inflecting new definitions of womanhood with the modernist internal perspective in expressive movement of their own bodies.

In fact, many modern dancers believed that their art rose above other genres because its source material—bodies—existed prior to words and was thus closer to the raw and basic elements of being that modernist artists sought to expose. Graham lived out her father's dictum that "movement never lies," insisting that bodies needed "only to stand revealed" to manifest this inherent significance.[16] In a theater history published in 1936 the author Sheldon Cheney articulated the common belief of the time that dance was the "mother of all the arts," as did Humphrey, the British sexologist Havelock Ellis, and Isadora Duncan earlier in the century.[17] The gendering of dance cannot be ignored: if dance was the mother of the arts, it was because dance stemmed from bodies. From Judeo-Christian thought through Western philosophy, the perceived sexual temptation of Eve precipitated women's identification with the body side of a mind-body dualism. Women's bodies had innate significance through childbirth; women's affinity for expression through bodies, through dance, was a logical corollary. Women modern dancers did not declare that being a woman led them to a closer connection to their bodies, but in espousing beliefs that body movement revealed natural instincts and feelings, they reinforced the reduction of women to their bodies while at the same time celebrating the uniqueness and profundity of bodily expression.

Although deemed the more natural artistic realm of women, dance still presented problems to women pursuing it as a career. In oral histories and letters, women involved in some capacity in modern dance have indicated the difficulty they experienced in remaining professional concert dancers, often because the low pay prompted them to leave the field for better-paying jobs. Some women's departures coincided with marriage and a long hiatus from, or ending of, any career outside the home.[18] Maintaining a career in the dance field required perhaps an exceptional bounty of fortitude, and many women who had sustained careers married other artists. Sophie Maslow, Jane Dudley, and Anna Sokolow, all important dancers and choreographers, were either married to or involved in long relationships with avant-garde filmmakers and musicians; Sylvia Manning was married to Gene Martel while both were dancing in the Humphrey-Weidman

Group. The complicated personal lives of leading women dancers demonstrated the ingenuity and untraditional gender roles needed to maintain a career in modern dance. German émigré Hanya Holm lived with her adolescent son; Martha Graham lived alone; Helen Tamiris lived unmarried with a man; Katherine Dunham married early, then divorced and married again, this time to a man who designed and made costumes for her productions. Humphrey pieced together an unconventional family with a long-distance marriage to a seaman; Charles Weidman, Pauline Lawrence, and José Limón were her living companions for much of the 1930s. Humphrey's husband persuaded her to marry him partly because he would be paid more and thus be able to contribute financial support for her dance career; downplaying the event, Humphrey relayed her marriage to her parents in a postscript to a letter.[19] Of this group, only Humphrey bore a child during her career, at the relatively late age of thirty-seven. Her attempt to combine motherhood and career prompted harassment by people in her company for the restrictions it placed on their careers (in her resisting long tours, for instance), and also by people outside the dance field, most notably a doctor who called her a "maladjusted woman" for "hanging onto this dance studio in contrast to doing something fundamentally necessary and vital in the world, such as rearing a good son."[20]

Personal complications about gender roles carried over into these women's artistry despite their adherence to a universal vision of the artist that transcended gender. Soon after the Dance Repertory Theatre week in January 1930, Humphrey read Virginia Woolf's *A Room of One's Own* and felt renewed energy from this paean to women's need for independence.[21] After she met her husband-to-be, however, Humphrey embraced another British writer, John Cowper Powys, reading his book of popular philosophy, *In Defence of Sensuality*. In a letter to her husband in 1933, Humphrey agreed with Powys's main thesis: "[T]he male possesses the female; and throughout all eternity this 'act of possession' . . . produces in both of them a long drawn-out ecstasy of magical content." Humphrey qualified her support of this idea, though, warning that women surrendered too easily and lost their "inner self" more often than men. "Submission must stop short of annihilation of the self," she proclaimed.[22] Humphrey also recognized that developing individuality in women required persistence; she wrote to her parents that most girls loved to be dominated.[23] This kind of tenuous hold on their independence could also be seen in modern dancers' invocation of the trope of the pioneer to describe their efforts in forging a new art form from American sources: they interchangeably referred to themselves as pioneers and pioneer *women*.[24] Although they ascribed to idealization as an artist or a pioneer, they were also conscious of themselves as women and of the conditions that placed on their lives. They fluctuated from expressing strong inner selves to revealing struggling egos fighting submission to men, from arguing for a room of their own to joining together in group performances.

. The complications these modern dancers faced as women artists played a fundamental role in the development of the art form by incorporating into it the conflict between the creative individualist and the nurturing partner. Personal expression remained the inspiration and motivating force behind modern dance, but choreographers also sought to move beyond an individualist, internal perspective. Humphrey felt most strongly that her greatest contribution would be her group choreography because "it is only the group composed of individuals which can say anything significant or stirring about contemporary life."[25] Graham gravitated to choreography more reluctantly: "I just began to make up dances, so I would have something to dance," she recalled, and she choreographed more solos for herself than Humphrey did.[26] Both women devoted time and energy to developing dancers and choreographing groups, however, perhaps as a way to impart and solidify an already impermanent art form. Moving beyond themselves meant asserting authority about their artistic visions and extending their impact, both in the power of group movement in performance and in inspiring devotees. Unlike painting or writing, the creative possibilities and challenges burgeoned when Humphrey and Graham choreographed for groups. By their very definition, groups laid bare the problems of forming a collective artistic vision from an individual expression grounded in one's own body. As Humphrey explained, the conundrum was to "encourage them to be individuals" *and* "to move in a common rhythm"—submission that stopped short of annihilation of the self.[27] Women modern dancers succeeded in doing this by remaining true to their vision as choreographers of the group and requiring the members of the company to perform according to their direction. The name and structure of the leading companies manifested their way of combining the individual artist and the followers: Martha Graham and Group, Humphrey-Weidman Group, Hanya Holm and

Group, Tamiris and Group. The individual dancer-choreographer remained the prominent, distinctive, and defining feature of an otherwise anonymous group. Similarly, the dances themselves often featured a soloist (usually the dancer-choreographer for whom the company was named) amid a corps of dancers.

Humphrey created a triumvirate of works, New Dance Trilogy, in the mid-1930s, all revealing aspects of the relationship of individuals to one another. The trilogy began with *New Dance* (1935), which presented the world as it should be. In a pointed response to the idea of only depicting "mass movement," Humphrey "wished to insist that there is also an individual life within that group life."[28] *New Dance* featured three sections—the first for women, the second for men, and the third for men and women together— and celebrated the possible harmony of relationships.[29] The final section best relayed the interplay between solo and group. Beginning with four lines, like the spokes of a wheel, dancers moved around a small center in a large circle that filled the stage (see figure 2.2). Large boxes, placed apart and utilized as pedestals throughout the piece, were piled up in a mountain in the middle of the stage at the end of the piece. The crescendo rose with a speedier tempo as, one by one, individual dancers broke away from the group and danced a solo (which each company member choreographed individually) while the rest of the group shuffled in small steps, clustered on the side or back of the stage. Finished with the solo, the dancer gestured with long, beckoning arms to the group, pulling out another solo dancer, and then climbed back up on the pile of boxes. Dancers whirled from side to side, facing staunchly front and direct to the audience as the curtain dropped. With each dancer turning on an individual axis, the combined force of the whole company spinning ended *New Dance* on a note of vital and dynamic action.

Grant Hyde Code, the public relations director of the Brooklyn Museum and an avid supporter of modern dance, noted the difference between modern dance and ballet's "perpetual flirting" of men and women, declaring that, even if the modern dance group contained both men and women, "one gets . . . the feeling of very strongly organized groups of people. They seem to be social groups, not choruses of men and women. The soloist usually has a very definite feeling of being related to the group if not a part of it. The soloist does not just come out and do a solo while the rest of

FIGURE 2.2. *The Humphrey-Weidman Group in* New Dance. *(Jerome Robbins Dance Division, The New York Public Library for the Performing Arts, Astor, Lenox and Tilden Foundations)*

the dancers remain in the background. The solo seems to be aimed at the group even more than at the spectators."[30] The dominance of the group in modern dance choreography went beyond relations between men and women and formed the foundation from which an individual, or a soloist, could emerge. In the 1930s this common theme of the individual in the group also surfaced in novels, like those of John Steinbeck, and paintings, by Thomas Hart Benton and the regionalist school, for example, but its fullest formal exposition was in live performances of jazz and modern dance. Led by bandleaders like Benny Goodman and Duke Ellington, jazz orchestras in performance pushed at the limits of this theme, with the improvisations of soloists melded into the swinging harmonies and sounds of the full group. Even though modern dance did not involve much improvisation at this time, in the transitory performance of music or dance, the theme of the fundamental reciprocity between individual and group became a lived reality.[31]

Modern dance and jazz were art forms predominantly created by white women and African American men. Both groups had complicated and ambivalent relations to modernist notions of the categories of artist and individual, so dependent on ideas of alienation and isolation. Women were constantly in danger of losing their sense of self, according to Humphrey; W. E. B. Du Bois characterized African Americans' sense of themselves as one of "double consciousness," being at the same time aware both of themselves and of themselves being interpreted by others.[32] The constant presence of the threat of submission or the eyes of others thwarted the peerless insularity of the individual. Instead, white women and African American men constructed art forms that sprang from personal impulses for expression and ended up as patterns of people moving together, or playing instruments together, in a kind of harmony. Humphrey's insistence on the symbiotic relation of the individual to the whole in *New Dance* expressed her belief that solos in dance—and individuals in society—"flow out of the group and back into it again without break and the most important part is always the group."[33] Women's social roles, their qualified understanding of themselves as self and other, produced an interactive art, floating between individual assertion and unified community.

When Humphrey identified modern dance as a pioneering art she recognized not only that there were paths to forge "through forest and plain," but also that the battle included warring with enemies.[34] Many enemies were overt, and, if not exactly vengeful, they were often confused and ambivalent about this new art form. Martha Graham recalled that the New York theater critic Stark Young once protested going to a concert of hers, saying, "Oh must I go? I'm so afraid she's going to give birth to a cube on stage."[35] Although Young proved to be a supporter of modern dance, and the comment reinforced the connection of modern dancers to the stylistic principles of modernist painting, and cubism in particular, it also revealed the troubles women artists confronted in the movement of modernism. Giving birth to children was the biological domain of women, but giving birth to an artistic creation did not necessarily fall within women's purview. And, according to Young, the new life, the cube, was hard, with fierce edges, frozen in shape—in fact, a lifeless form. Young's comment placed the artistic contributions of women, which he described as lifeless, in sharp contrast with their biological function as childbearers and life-givers. Modern dancers' art was not one that lay on a page or canvas, so it was never separate from conceptions about viewing female bodies in motion.[36]

A caricature of Graham printed in *Theatre Arts Monthly* in 1930 reinforced Young's comment and the place of modern dance within modernism (see figure 2.3). Certain cues linked Graham to Picasso in this illustration, particularly the flatness of the image and the strong geometric angles of the right arm perpendicular to the hand and the left arm shooting out in a straight line from the shoulder and forcefully hooked back to the center of the body. While Picasso's *Three Dancers* (1925) suggested the irrationality and alienation of the mind and the individual through the broken images of bodies and disconnected forms on a flat canvas, modern dancers embodied this anguish in physical motions of angular arms and contractions that hollowed out the torso and strenuously bent the body, all performed with force and unease. Manifesting a conflict within the individual, modern dancers intentionally created not a spectacle for the audience's pleasure but a confrontation between audience and performers and within audience members themselves.

The Graham caricature conveyed the sense of confrontation that modernist artists sought, but it also gave Graham far larger and more pointed breasts than she possessed. In contrast, the caricature of Graham and Sally Rand published in *Vanity Fair* in 1934 flattened out Graham's bust. Graham's female attributes were enhanced in a depiction of modernism but lessened in a comparison with another female dancer, relaying the relevance of context in how modern dancers were seen and the inescapability of notions about women that influenced perceptions in all contexts. The *Vanity Fair* illustrator connected Graham to modernist painting with references to Edvard Munch's famous painting *The Scream* (1895) in Graham's hollowed eyes and ghoulish green face, the straight linearity of the body from the outstretched arm to the opposing leg, and the flattened legs jutting sideways with sharply pointed knees. Rand, in contrast, was all circles. From the slightly curved arm overhead through the rounded shoulder, back, and derriere, all the way down to the arched curve of the foot and the painted red toenails, Rand stood swathed in pink swirls. The accompanying text had Graham saying, "You should learn to bare your soul," to which Rand replied, "Say, I got to keep *something* covered." The illustration and exchange

FIGURE 2.3. *Caricature of Martha Graham by Aline Fruhauf.* (Theatre Arts Monthly *14, no. 5* *[May 1930]: 365)*

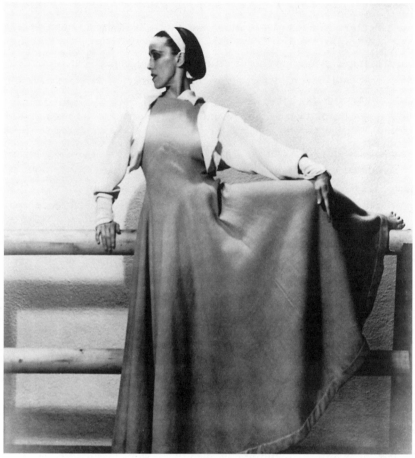

FIGURE 2.4. *Martha Graham in* Frontier. *(Jerome Robbins Dance Division, The New York Public Library for the Performing Arts, Astor, Lenox and Tilden Foundations)*

presented the baring of women's souls as a far less attractive option than the baring of their bodies.

Graham's 1935 solo *Frontier* captured in movement the contrast modern dancers presented. It opened with Graham propping one leg up on a fence, her face in profile staring offstage (see figure 2.4). From the initial movement, the pioneer conquered: first laying claim to the fence, then delineating a space in front of the fence, and finally gazing proprietarily at the surroundings before taking a confident, assured seat on the fence again. The movements echoed the glorification of an individual's strength and resolution with outstretched arms and forceful high kicks, reinforced by Louis Horst's simple, pounding chords, strident and determined. Two ropes went off upward and diagonally forward to the top corners of the stage from the center of a two-tiered fence; Isamu Noguchi's simple design created the illusion of space and open sky, all grounded in an individual's labor and pioneering courage. In staking claim to the land, the American pioneer gained access to the sky and seemingly limitless possibilities.

But did *Frontier* present a pioneer or a pioneer woman? At one point in the dance Graham cradled her arms and rocked her body as if holding and nurturing a child. But very few modern dancers choreographed dances specifically on the theme of women in the 1930s. Miriam Blecher, a leading figure in the workers' dance movement, choreographed *The Woman* (1934), which portrayed "the sort of woman that a worker comes home to," as a reviewer put it.[37] Humphrey gave the most considered view of women in *Dances of Women* (1931), the only remains of which are a few photographs and some movement description. Humphrey's investigation of women may have been provoked by the simple fact that the Humphrey-Weidman Group included both women and men, the only prominent modern dance company until the late 1930s to do so. A work in three sections, *Dances of Women* began with "The Fruitful," an "abstraction of birth." An original dancer in the production described the movement as "like the stem and branches of a tree form, we moved in spasmodic rhythms, with individuals breaking out to the sides, like leaves." The second section, "The Decadent," depicted "pink ladies," as Humphrey called them, women as objects. In "tiny mincing steps," dancers performed "up on their toes, little fingers arched, moving in a boxlike space to tinkling music." In "The Militant," women rebelled. The group shot "one arm up in the air as if striking, while against our repetitious cogmill procession, Doris made a valiant solo attempt at freedom."[38] The full body movements of bent backs and kneeling fetus-like shapes of the first section contrasted sharply with the delicate small motions of fingers and feet of the second section. The straight arms of the third section cried out with strength and might in opposition to the balletic curved arm that framed the face. Humphrey climbed on a box of her own accord, in contrast to a ballerina being lifted by a man (see figure 2.5). *Dances*

FIGURE 2.5. Dances of Women *by Doris Humphrey. Photograph by Soichi Sunami. (Jerome Robbins Dance Division, The New York Public Library for the Performing Arts, Astor, Lenox and Tilden Foundations)*

of Women included a range of views about women, from laborers in birthing to fanciful ladies, but ended on a militant note with women as defiant fighters.

Costumes of both *Dances of Women* and *Frontier* enhanced the themes of strength and expansion and downplayed women's physical attributes of curvier breasts and hips. Modern dance costumes were long dresses covering the body in one piece down to bare feet. The costume fit the torso and either stayed close to the body in a kind of tube or opened a bit wider at the hips to allow for more leg extension. The dress highlighted the actions of the chest and back, and the reverberations of movement through the skirt attracted more attention than motions of the legs themselves. Ballet tutus, in contrast, fit like a corset with a netted skirt fanning out from the waist and ending near the thigh or knee to accentuate the intricate steps of feet encased in pointe shoes. Burlesque costumes mimicked the balletic design with a top like a bustier. The divided sections of ballet and show dancing costumes thus highlighted the movement of particular body parts, while the modern dance one-piece dress suited full body motions. In modern dance costumes, linearity flattened out body shapes and directed audience gazes to the movements of the whole body emanating from the torso.

In *Frontier* and *Dances of Women* Graham and Humphrey eschewed the heterosexual framework of desire between female performer and male audience member that defined ballet and show dancing. They challenged conventional perceptions of femininity on stage by exposing the serious expressive possibilities of bodies. Participants, critics, and some dance historians proclaimed this kind of dance as "sexless," but, more accurately, it was women taking on what many believed were masculine attributes, thereby complicating the perceived categories of male and female physical gestures and appearances.[39] This quality of sexlessness had effects beyond the confusion of conventional gendered movement and appearance: critics and writers endorsed it as a sign of artistic seriousness and worth. While a journalist picked out the Federal Dance Project dancer Sue Remos as "easily the most beautiful of the lot" in a group of auditioning dancers, a dance devotee who attended the audition declared that looks did not matter: "[A] dancer is a dancer, and it doesn't make any difference what she looks like."[40] Variations existed within these pronouncements, however. Many critics considered Graham and the German dancer Mary Wigman the most ugly and manly — "a Humphrey type was prettier" — and the dance critic Walter Terry found in Hanya Holm a "distinct delicacy and an expressive lyricism." Terry even admitted that for impact in a modern dance performance, "a blond has a much harder time than a brunette." "While the feminine contingent of other modern dance companies usually resembled a gang of sexless automatons, Miss Holm's girls inevitably danced with feminine grace and charm," he observed.[41] The exception of Holm only reinforced the more common disavowal of feminine characteristics and embrace of masculine (or at least unfeminine) ones. And the continued comments on sexlessness indicated that women modern dancers were still judged within a framework of sexual attractiveness.

Although cries of manliness dogged modern dancers, suggestions of lesbianism generally did not. In the 1930s women in sport aroused the suspicion of lesbianism when they entered a manly and physically active field.[42] But a participant described the homosocial world of the 1930s Bennington College Summer School of the Dance sessions as having a "convent" quality, which reinforced the sexless image rather than suggesting lesbianism.[43] In fact, within the dance world there may have been lesbian couples. Some dancers believed that Humphrey and her accompanist and company manager Pauline Lawrence were lovers before Humphrey married in 1932; Martha Hill and Mary Jo Shelly, the Bennington College Summer School of the Dance administrators, may also have been lovers.[44] Men in dance, however, overwhelmingly received insinuations and attention to their sexual orientation.

In general, sexual experimentation and relationships were common, probably more so among the New York modern dancers. A student remembered that Graham began a class talking of "free love," and Humphrey, Tamiris, and Graham had eager men following them and had affairs with some of them.[45] They also espoused as their prophet the sexologist Havelock Ellis; in Pauline Lawrence's words, "[H]e sanctions me."[46] Ellis's sensual evocation of *The Dance of Life* linked sex, dancing, and love, imbuing all these acts with religious and artistic significance. Louis Horst, Graham's influential accompanist, composer, and lover in the 1920s to mid-1930s, defined another dimension of the sexual element in modern dance as heterosexual interplay. For him music was masculine and dance was feminine, and their joining as equal art forms in modern dance was the most fruitful union among the arts.[47] With music, set design, and theatrical management all generally dominated by men, Horst's romantic characterization had some basis in reality. The image and the reality also appeared to confirm the naturalness of women in positions of bodily display accompanied and completed by men framing and directing the show.

Ultimately, commonly accepted perceptions of the heterosexual framework of performance, social dancing, and ballet carried over into perceptions of modern dancers. Even in the angular and hard motions of modern dance and the accusations of manliness and sexlessness, modern dancers stayed within a perceived heterosexual mold as female objects of male desire. Graham and Humphrey's confrontation with these perceptions led them to believe that serious artistic intent necessitated a lack of sexual provocation. Sexual movements signified lower art, and modern dancers' attempt at sexlessness revealed the gender, class, and racial prejudices that codified a cultural hierarchy of high and low within modernism. Graham defended this choice by arguing that "ugliness may be beautiful if it cries out with the voice of power."[48]

Comments like these were fodder for the enemies of modern dance. Lincoln Kirstein, the influential patron of American ballet and an avid supporter of modernist painting and architecture, was a prominent one.[49] In a 1934 article acknowledging his bias for ballet and against modern dance, Kirstein highlighted a problem that he felt limited modern dance: the tie to an individual dancer. The magnetism of Martha Graham moved him, but Kirstein felt that the school or system of movement would not survive the original mentor. The problem was that the subject matter of modern dance was the dancer "herself" or "also perhaps vaguely, herself as a particular sort of woman."[50] The use of the female pronoun is notable for its rarity in discussing the motives of artists (even among women modern dancers)— and not coincidental to Kirstein's argument, which linked the ephemerality of the expressive modern dance movement to its inextricability from female bodies. According to Kirstein, ballet and its creative impulses could be transferred from the male choreographer to female dancers and students; the self-expression that rooted modern dance in the body and mind of the female dancer and choreographer could not transcend that base. While the leading women modern dancers unified the mental creative work of the artist as choreographer with the expressiveness of the performer, Kirstein's attitude about this unique circumstance perpetuated notions of the inferiority of women's creativity. Even when using their bodies, to which they were often reduced, to make art, Kirstein argued, women modern dancers could not go beyond their transient physicality in making an enduring artistic contribution.

Kirstein's denunciation points to the ways in which women's place in society determined their place in the arts. Even as Humphrey and Graham perpetuated notions of the artist as a unique seer into the human condition, they also recognized that their art was a part of the "social scene," in Humphrey's words. As a pioneer, Humphrey believed she was inventing not a "new ideology so much as a new form of saying."[51] This stance encompassed her status as a woman and the new ways in which women were expressing themselves, even if she did not specifically identify "pioneer" and modern dance's "new form of saying" this way. Building on historical and ideological associations of women with their bodies and dance as a heterosexual pairing with women on display for men, women modern dancers exposed and altered the potency of moving female bodies on stages from forms of sexual enticement or ethereality to ones of seriousness and profundity. As objects in a performance, women were inevitably seen as female, sexual bodies, but as subjects and inventors in a creative process made up almost exclusively of women, they worked against these assumptions, struggling to embody abstract ideas of individualism, heritage, and collectivity. In this, the new art form of modern dance and the choreography of the 1930s conveyed the contradictions of postsuffrage feminism. Groupings were still generally separated by sex and segregated by race, and all-female modern dance groups did not battle specifically for women's rights. But white women modern dancers continued women's fight for recognition and change under the rubric of individualism, and this opening up of opportunities for women went beyond the leaders of modern dance. Connie Stein Sarason, who took ballet classes as a child in Toledo, Ohio, and modern dance at Ohio State University in the early 1930s, spent one year in New York and the summer at Bennington in 1935; she enthusiastically recalled that this was the best year of her life. Another modern dance student explained about her modern dance teacher that "[it] was my first experience with a woman who was doing something with her life."[52]

Alone on stage in *Frontier,* Graham laid claim to universal concepts as a female artist; her power was unchallenged and not fixed as that of a man or a woman. Her task as a woman and a pioneer artist within American modernism was to turn manly vigor into American strength. In 1930, when Graham promoted a dance of being, she declared America capable of this kind of dance because "its urge is masculine and creative rather than imitative," thus linking feminine urges with mere mimicry; masculine, creative urges transferred into female bodies became "virile gestures."[53] While pushing against perceptions of femininity by taking on masculine gestures, however, white modern dancers and critics perpetuated the notion of essential differences between male and female traits. They emboldened their status as American artists by downplaying female sexuality and challenging the significance of beauty in art. The place of women in American society determined their place in the arts — in dance — but modern dancers subverted sexual appeal into intellectual and emotional weight, furnishing a rare forum for women to collaborate and communicate with others on the pressing issues of the day.

3 : primitive moderns

In the fall of 1932 the noted African American musician and choir director Hall Johnson solicited choreographic help from Doris Humphrey for *Run, Li'l Chillun!*, a folk drama that utilized the work of the anthropologist and writer Zora Neale Hurston. Humphrey wanted to maintain the "primitive and almost . . . untouched" movement of the Bahamian dancers and saw her job as editing the rituals "to fit this dance into the play."[1] Carl Van Vechten, a white author, photographer, and supporter of the Harlem Renaissance, also found ritualistic aspects in the lindy hop, a social dance he attributed to African Americans. Writing in 1930 in terms that modernist artists would appreciate, Van Vechten called the lindy hop "Dionysian," exciting and pleasurable, nearly approaching "the sensation of religious ecstasy. It could be danced, quite reasonably, and without alteration of the tempo, to many passages in the *Sacre du Printemps* of Stravinsky"; the pagan rites in music and dance were transferable from Nijinsky to African American dancers in the Savoy Ballroom in Harlem.[2] This heralding of what Van Vechten and Humphrey saw as the savage, "primitive" nature of dance among black peoples was typical of white modernist artists and set a particular place for African and African American aesthetics within modernism. The elemental force and physical exuberance of black peoples' dancing fit into a vision of the fundamentals of being that white artists sought to expose. In this circumscribed view of the nature of black peoples, the place of African American artists themselves in modernism was quite restricted. If white women found in modern dance a means by which to work within modernism and refute conventional images of femininity, African American men and women had less success in working around modernism's fundamental rift between high and low culture, which mirrored and reinforced social experiences of racial discrimination.[3]

Hemsley Winfield, Edna Guy, Asadata Dafora, and Katherine Dunham trained and performed in the center of these issues, forming racial, cultural, and national identities but contending first and always with racial discrimination that often barred them from the discussions. While segregation persisted in dividing dance studios and theaters into black and white, just as it split cities, collaborations across the color line did occur—in muted ways, like the one between Edna Guy and Ruth St. Denis, or in politically progressive settings, such as Communist Party pageants. More commonly, white modern dancers tackled the theme of African Americans' oppression in their choreography, most early on with Helen Tamiris's *Negro Spirituals* (1928), but they did not employ African American dancers with regularity. Black dancers and choreographers formed their own companies and fused the principles of modern dance with the dance and ritual of the Caribbean and Africa. They established a distinct African American aesthetic in concert dance that drew from, but existed between, the primitive movement that Humphrey noted and the lindy hop and social dance that Van Vechten applauded. Following Guy's entreaty to make "the creative dances of her soul," African American concert dancers molded modern dance to incorporate the push for civil rights as well as the recovery of a transatlantic heritage from Africa through the Caribbean to the stages of the United States.[4]

When Hemsley Winfield plunged into the little theater movement via the Krigwa Players in 1926, he entered a vociferous debate about whether artworks by African Americans were in fact art, fitting into a generally white tradition, or propaganda, whose main purpose was to showcase the talents of a besieged population. These questions peaked in Harlem in the 1920s and reverberated in other cities, especially Chicago, in the 1930s.[5] W. E. B. Du Bois's Krigwa Players, a short-lived national little theater network, was a product of this fervor. Du Bois, one of the leading African American civil rights activists, who helped found the National Association for the Advancement of Colored People and its influential magazine *Crisis,* fastened attention on theater because he thought African Americans were "an essentially dramatic race . . . accustomed to expressing themselves with greater physical and spiritual abandon than most folks." Advocating for a new movement in theater that focused on black rather than white audiences, he called for an African American theater that would be "about us, by us, for us, and near us."[6] This call for art arising from and within African American communities also shaped *The New Negro,* a 1925 anthology of essays, poems, drawings, and short stories, that brought together many of these questions and the people intent upon answering them. Dance had little coverage, except as the subject of poems by Claude McKay and Langston Hughes, and was dismissed by Alain Locke, the editor of the collection, who advocated for the revival of the ancestral arts of Africa, particularly painting and sculpture. Even within a general plea for artistic assertion, dance held an ambivalent place, consigned as a talent of spontaneous expression rather than an art of discipline and respectability.[7]

The already impassioned debate about the role of the arts amongst African Americans intensified in 1926 after the publication of two books by white authors focusing on poor, uneducated black people: Carl Van Vechten's *Nigger Heaven* (1926) and DuBose Heyward's *Porgy* (1925), both of which Doris Humphrey read.[8] In response, *Crisis* published a questionnaire on the purpose and status of the African American arts; the conclusion of the respondents was that a more varied portrayal of African Americans was needed, one that went beyond depictions of desperation and fecklessness.[9] The questionnaire exposed the class outlook that pervaded black Americans' concern with their artistic image. The urging to make artistic renderings of educated, middle-class African Americans followed the dictum set by Du Bois to allow the "thinking element of Negro Americans" to lead and inspire the others.[10] At the same time, black intellectuals George Schuyler and Langston Hughes extended the discussion in two noteworthy articles in the *Nation,* with Hughes praising the "low-down folks, the so-called common element," and the spirituals and jazz with which they were often identified. In opposition, Schuyler pushed Du Bois's loftiness further, insisting that successful African American artists were "just plain American" and, even more tendentious, heavily invested in European traditions of art.[11]

Dance had an uneasy place in this debate. As a social activity, dance exemplified the gaiety and sensuality that most African American critics and intellectuals wanted to offset; as an art form, it had a bodily basis that seemed to overwhelm the possibility of intellectual motivation and purpose. Even in the serious, rigorous realm of the new modern dance, the predominance of women may also have precluded its inclusion in the conceptions of African American arts promoted by educated, mostly male, middle- and upper-class black Americans such as Du Bois, Locke, Schuyler, and Hughes. Hughes was a rare exception in his promotion of jazz, which, like dance, often prompted dismissals by African Americans as an expression of natural talent that they feared would be judged as unsophisticated and too exuberant. Like jazz, modern dance offered a vision of a new, more pluralistic American culture that incorporated democratic principles and racial equality made possible by the unsettling economics and leftist politics of the Great Depression.[12] The limitations of that hope, however, proved more visible in modern dance. Looking at a painting, reading a book, or even listening to jazz on the radio, one could ignore the physical presence of African American artists themselves—an impossibility in dance. Thrusting their bodies on stage, African American concert dancers aggravated and pushed against the racial preconceptions that divided American society and that indelibly shaped the course of their artistry.

Obstacles were apparent from the beginning when African Americans sought dance training. A director barred Edna Guy from applying to the Portia-Mansfield dance camp in Colorado because, she claimed, "some of the girls were southerns [sic] and they just could not be made to understand." A New York ballet mistress also alleged that white students would be dissatisfied and that she would lose money if she allowed Guy into the class.[13] When dance teachers and schools did welcome black students, buildings often banned entry to them and forced out those tenants who allowed them in. In those rare places where African American dancers could take classes, more often than not the studios were a long distance from their home, and the travel by public transportation and the cost of the class became prohibitively expensive.[14] Black students who made it to a dance school beyond their neighborhood were limited in the activities they could do outside of the school. A white Jewish modern dancer of the early 1930s remembered continually asking a black student out for coffee after class and always being refused. She wondered years later if the reason the black woman declined was that there may not have been restaurants in which the woman felt comfortable in the Union Square area of Manhattan where dance studios were located.[15]

For those few who could afford it, private lessons were an alternative to all-white dance classes. Guy settled on this option, but she soon wanted "companionship." She also had continual problems paying for classes. Her parents contributed, as did a patroness from her neighborhood, and St. Denis allowed her to pay in installments. Guy performed duties in exchange for classes and took an occasional job as a model for artists. She even asked St. Denis for loans, and at times St. Denis obliged.[16]

Lighter-skinned African Americans had less trouble because passing as white or foreign was another way to enter white dance studios. Florence Warwick, a black dancer with lighter skin, attended the Bennington Summer School of the Dance in 1938.[17] Katherine Dunham, who began her training in Chicago, had a mixed heritage of French Canadian, Native American, and African American ancestry that may have helped her gain entry into white dance classes. In Philadelphia, Marion Cuyjet passed for white and studied ballet with Catherine Littlefield. Guy also trumpeted her mixed background, claiming, "My grandmother is not a negro—she is Arabian and American Indian. Many people ask her and mother if they are colored. My grandfather was French and colored." The director of the dance camp to which she wanted to apply recommended that Guy send a photograph and perhaps pass as East Indian. Guy easily recognized the hypocrisy: "They will let every other foreign nationality come in their classes expect [*sic*] an American colored girl. Oh! Why are they like that."[18]

Most commonly, African American dancers schooled themselves. Hemsley Winfield established a dance school in Harlem at 35 West 134th Street in 1932, where "in a well-equipped gymnasium, classes are given in the School of the Negro Dance for those interested in Negro Art."[19] The Harlem branch of the YWCA at 137th Street offered dancing classes for adults and children; the school of Grace Giles at Lafayette Hall on 131st Street taught ballet and pointe.[20] Dance schools on the South Side of Chicago, populated largely by African Americans, offered toe, tap, and ballet. Generally training girls for careers as chorus dancers, these schools were featured in the *Chicago Defender* when the Chicago girls moved on to success on the New York stages. It was a parallel world, in many ways, in classes and theaters. In 1933 the white fan dancer Sally Rand went from her success at the Chicago

World's Fair to New York's Paramount Theatre in midtown; the "Sepia Sally Rand," Noma, went from a similar success at the World's Fair to Harlem's Lafayette Theatre.[21]

Occasional crossings of the segregated divide occurred. Katherine Dunham took ballet and modern dance classes in the white dancing schools in Chicago, often as the lone African American student, and in 1930 she attempted to start a black ballet company with the white poet and dancer Mark Turbyfill. They encountered firm resistance.[22] Turbyfill and Dunham enlisted the help of Edith Sampson, a prominent African American philanthropist and lawyer in Chicago, to raise money for the project, but their efforts were unsuccessful. Dunham and Turbyfill also had to move from a studio in the Loop because the manager of the building did not want African Americans coming in and out. After moving south to 57th Street in Hyde Park, they had very few students, and Dunham's classes devoted to "basic rhythms as they related to the Negro" waned. In August 1930 they accepted white students in the classes to help pay rent.[23]

Resistance came in ways beyond geographical segregation, too. When Turbyfill met with New York dancer and choreographer Agnes de Mille, de Mille told him that a black ballet was "all wrong." "She reminds me that it has never been done, that it isn't physiologically in the picture. I tell her that I'm not thinking of a physiological picture, but rather an abstract one," he wrote in his diary.[24] Dunham fought prejudices among African Americans as well. She thought students dropped out too early because they assumed they were "natural born" performers and dancers. Dunham stressed the need for discipline and training in dance and criticized white viewers for praising African American dancers "too quickly." She also recognized a mistake she made in naming one of her first dance companies the Negro Dance Group, saying, "[T]he Negro mothers immediately disapproved! They refused to send their children to me for fear they *might* be taught Negro dancing!" In contrast, her ballet classes were always crowded.[25] The definitions of "Negro dancing" as tap and social dancing pervaded black communities as well as white ones and challenged Dunham's attempts to teach and choreograph modern dance and ballet.

Dunham's collaboration with Turbyfill ended in December 1930, but she kept dancing. In the Artists' Ball of 1932, a program intended to provide money for artists hard-hit by the Depression, she performed *Fantasie Negre,* choreographed by her Russian ballet teacher, Ludmilla Speranzeva, to music by African American composer Florence Price. In 1933 Dunham set up a dance studio called the Negro Dance Art Studio, this time deeply within the segregated black community of Chicago's South Side at 3638 South Parkway. Margaret Bonds and Florence Price were listed as pianists and composers for the school. Dunham and modern dance were a part of a larger African American artistic community—apparently as a subset of women within that.[26]

Dunham's inclusion in Chicago's Artists' Balls represented a kind of integration within the dance world. Although none of the major modern dance groups employed black dancers in the late 1920s and early 1930s, some African American dancers appeared occasionally. For Communist Party pageants, Edith Segal, a Brooklynite born of Jewish immigrants from eastern Europe, depicted a proletarian revolution against racial and labor discrimination led by the combined force of white and black workers in *Black and White, Unite and Fight*.[27] Segal often appeared in the dance with Allison Burroughs, whose father was a Party leader and active in Du Bois's Krigwa Players.[28] Randolph Sawyer appeared with lesser known choreographers Senia Gluck-Sandor and Felicia Sorel in productions in New York as early as 1926. Most often, Sawyer danced roles suitable to his skin color, such as the Blackamoor in *Petrouchka* (1931). Similarly, Ruth Page, a prominent white ballet dancer and choreographer in Chicago, cast Dunham in a small but important role in *La Guiablesse* in 1933. With music by the noted African American composer William Grant Still, *La Guiablesse* depicted a folkloric tale of love from Martinique. Page solicited Dunham to gather a large group of African American youth for background roles. Page herself first performed the leading role of a "she-devil" who forces a tragic ending between lovers, played by Dunham and her first husband, Jordis McCoo. When the production moved from the Chicago World's Fair to the Chicago Grand Opera the next year, Dunham danced the lead. In most integrated productions in the early 1930s, African Americans dancers added authenticity with specifically identified black roles, but they were not used beyond those roles.

Even if white modern dance companies had employed African American dancers, they certainly would have encountered problems in touring. Edna Guy accompanied Ruth St. Denis on a tour, but not as a dancer; she was a personal assistant attending to details such as costume repairs. On tour in 1930 a rift occurred when St. Denis refused to fight Jim Crow segregation policies that persisted in hotels, restaurants, and transportation in the South, and Guy's relations with St. Denis and other company members began to fray. St. Denis eventually fired Guy for the tension she was causing amongst other students, but Guy understood the conflict differently: "You say I'm ungrateful to all you've done for me. And not honest. What do you know about anything outside of your Hotel. . . . All that I have ever been or hoped to be is lost in these weeks—because of the south and its high standards. Mary [a white friend] always said not to put so much belief in you and you were like all other white people. But because you had beauty I stayed and wanted to stay near you."[29] Guy and St. Denis continued to be in touch, and St. Denis appeared at a talk organized by Guy on "Dance as an Art" at the Harlem YMCA on 138th Street in May 1931. But racial tensions underlay their relationship and severely restricted Guy's career with Denishawn. She was never an official member of the company, although she did appear in some student recitals. The problem that arose on tour exposed the menial roles that Guy actually fulfilled in St. Denis's life: those of seamstress and maid.[30]

The small, even daily, achievements of Edna Guy and Hemsley Winfield in New York City and Katherine Dunham in Chicago were pathbreaking successes in showing that African Americans could master different dance styles and treat many subjects, ranging from abstract studies such as *Plastique* and *Song without Words* to evocations of spirituals and *African Themes*. In early 1934 Winfield died prematurely of pneumonia at the age of twenty-seven, and Guy plodded along, frustrated by persistent racism and performing only rarely before giving up dance by the end of the 1930s. The success of Asadata Dafora and his production *Kykunkor* in 1934 eclipsed that of Winfield and Guy and preceded Dunham's triumphs in New York City in the late 1930s. If Winfield and Guy achieved recognition for their participation in contemporary innovations in American concert dance, Dafora brought African dance to New York stages with an exuberance and theatricality that received greater notoriety.

Born in 1890 in the colonial society of Freetown, Sierra Leone, Asadata Dafora continued a prominent lineage that included his great-great-grandfather, the first African to be knighted by Queen Victoria and the first black mayor of Sierra Leone. Dafora's mother and father met while in England, he studying at Oxford and she, the piano. Following this tradition of European schooling, Dafora received a British education at the local Wesleyan School in Freetown and went on to study music and dance in Italy and Germany. Seeing more opportunity in the United States, Dafora moved to New York City in 1929 to pursue singing but also continued drama and dance. He combined all these elements in his 1934 production *Kykunkor*. Only sixty people showed up the first night, but after John Martin's favorable review in the *New York Times* on 9 May, 425 people appeared that evening, 200 of whom had to be turned away because of an overflowing theater. The show moved from smaller theaters to larger ones throughout Manhattan for a four-month run, most often to sold-out audiences.[31]

The story of a tribal wedding ritual in West Africa, *Kykunkor* appealed to many senses (see figure 3.1). Continuous drumming, according to audience members and critics, provided relentless aural accompaniment to a visual feast of "semi-naked black men and women, posturing, writhing, crazily whirling, dancing insanely—vitally."[32] Dafora's African dance consisted of vigorous movements, often at a rapid tempo, that included flat-footed stomping, isolated actions of hips, torso, and shoulders in rhythmic patterns, and bodies bent forward from the waist on deeply bent legs with protruding buttocks. Vastly different from the linear and tightly held backbones of ballet and even modern dance, African dance stimulated interest merely in its exuberant use of the body. Compared to the austerity and starkness of Graham and Humphrey-Weidman concerts, the African dance of Dafora offered different pleasures. A story added a frame of reference and narrative progress unlike modern dancers' evocation of one emotion, such as in Graham's *Lamentation*. *Kykunkor* depicted the flirtation of romance and mating rituals with vibrant group dances and pantomime solos. The bridegroom selected his bride from young women who performed a maidens' dance; dances of welcome occurred between the two families. Kykunkor, a witch woman, cast a spell on the groom for a jealous rival eager to marry the bride himself. A male witch doctor saved the groom from death, and the wedding and celebratory festival closed the drama on a note of gaiety. Dafora's group of eighteen men and women filled the stage with bright costumes, colorful backdrops, and live music and gave no heed to the modern-

FIGURE 3.1. Kykunkor *by Asadata Dafora. Dafora is stage front, on the right. Photograph by Maurice Goldberg. (Jerome Robbins Dance Division, The New York Public Library for the Performing Arts, Astor, Lenox and Tilden Foundations)*

ist creed of stripping the stage of adornments that Graham and Humphrey followed.

In its disavowal of certain modernist theatrical principles and its embrace of other Africanist ones, Dafora's vibrant performance fit neatly into contemporary conceptions of white critics and audience members of so-called primitive and black peoples that exalted their closeness to nature, to animals, and to the basic functions of living—especially sex. The story of mating rituals abetted movement that depicted sexual attraction between men and women. The explicit heterosexual base of the story, and the overt masculinity of the male dancers especially, countered the common association of effeminacy and dance. In fact, white male modern dancers such as Ted Shawn plundered African and Native American dance traditions for heroic images to display in their own choreography that would affirm the masculinity of male dancers. The sexual play of *Kykunkor* elicited an ease in reviews as white intellectuals praised elements that they understood as distinctly black and primitive, with the well-respected critic Gilbert Seldes in *Esquire* naming it "a real sexual drama." He added that this show was "proof that Harlem still draws on its racial memories for its typical shouts and steps."[33] Linking all the cast by their innate racial talent—dancing barefoot to pounding drums on African ground—white critics proclaimed that the American-born performers could "trace their lineage back to the tribes from which their forbears [*sic*] came."[34]

Audience members came to the theater with preconceptions. A photograph of Dafora and his dancers promoting a performance of *Kykunkor* in Asbury Park, New Jersey, in 1934 displays nothing specific about the dance but is rich in meaning about the context in which these performers were seen (see figure 3.2). Ostensibly, the dancers are publicizing a performance by making music as a truck drives them around town. The truck, with its slogan "We sell good coal," holds a driver, a white man who looks unswervingly at the camera. A young white boy can be seen looking through the driver's window and into the camera, giving a kind of generational comment on the ways in which young people learn how to see from those who are older. A white woman, replete with a flowing dress and a parasol, distracted and apparently uninterested, gazes behind the truck and frames the photograph on the right. The woman could be an icon of white womanhood under threat from the unquenchable sexual desires of black men. In its overwhelming contextual clues, the photograph renders symbolic the racial preconceptions that clouded the ways in which white people saw black people.

Beyond the sexual elements of racial conceptions, Dafora's performance also fortified interest in Africa, a fascination of many white modernist artists and intellectuals in Europe and the United States. Proclaimed for its authenticity in representing the rituals of the African jungle, the show attracted "scientists and explorers of Africa" as well as leading theatrical managers of New York and other artists and intellectuals including George

FIGURE 3.2. *Asadata Dafora's group of musicians and dancers in Asbury Park, New Jersey. Photograph by Policestro Studio. (Jerome Robbins Dance Division, The New York Public Library for the Performing Arts, Astor, Lenox and Tilden Foundations)*

Gershwin, Sherwood Anderson, Theodore Dreiser, Virgil Thomson, Carl Van Vechten, and modern dancers Charles Weidman and Helen Tamiris.[35] Edmund Giligan, a white novelist, was so impressed by the performance that he wanted the cast of *Kykunkor* to appear in a film version of his book, *One Returns,* which told the story of the sole survivor of a journey by white explorers into the African jungle.[36] Adding to the claims of authenticity, Dr. James Chapin, the curator of the American Museum of Natural History, declared that "the drum rhythms and most of the singing rang so true as to carry me back to the dark continent."[37] Chapin's comment exhibited the tendency of many white viewers and critics to lump all Africans together as inhabitants of the "dark continent." White anthropologists and artists supplanted the dislocations created by a rapidly changing society with an imagined Africa that was unadulterated, unspoiled, and a clearly utopian vision of simplified nature.[38] *Kykunkor* was a re-visioning of a place, a transferring of Africa to American ground where it still stood apart, as the use of witch doctors and dances of welcome between families reinforced. For white viewers, Dafora's *Kykunkor* confirmed the distance and distinctiveness of Africa, and, by extension, of the black peoples there and elsewhere that it featured.

African American critics also praised *Kykunkor* but had different considerations. "Here it is, at last, Godmother—as you have dreamed and prophesied—and though it will not take root immediately—it is here and cannot be denied," Alain Locke wrote in 1934. Godmother was Locke's white patroness, Charlotte Osgood Mason, and the realized prophesy was Asadata Dafora. Mason had long pressed for more primitive work from African American artists of the Harlem Renaissance; she had given financial support for the folklore investigations of Zora Neale Hurston, for example. Locke often resisted Mason's appeal, wanting to encourage the mastery of what he deemed more sophisticated art. But in Dafora's *Kykunkor* Locke finally saw an African art arrive on American stages with the stylistic purity that he had extolled in *The New Negro*.[39] For other African American critics, *Kykunkor* refuted the frightening, maniacal picture of the jungle in the popular play *Emperor Jones,* which had been turned into a movie with Paul Robeson in 1933. "*Kykunkor* Gives the Lie to Fantastic White Beliefs/Beauty and Charm of Native Life Shown in Presentation," a June 1934 article in the *New York Amsterdam News* announced. The article went on: "[H]ow different the customs of the land appear on the stage from the depressing tales which missionaries bring back! No unclothed savages preparing a juicy stew of some hapless fellow man. No listless natives wallowing in filth. Instead here are a beautiful black and brown people, colorfully clad in gay raiment of brilliant hues—gold, green, crimson and white—riotously dazzing [*sic*] against the background of their dark bodies."[40]

The brilliancy of the colors and action overwhelmed African American critics as it did white ones, but in their praise for African authenticity these black critics did not include all dark-skinned peoples as indistinguishable "natives" and saw instead variations of "black and brown." They made particular mention of the different West African tribes depicted in the drama, the Mendi and Temne; they distinguished between the "Harlem origin" of some of the dancers and the "native-born African artists"; and they credited Dafora with a presentation "devoid of New World influence."[41] One article exposed the attempt by some dancers to prove their authenticity, noting that "[a]lthough many of the actors are obviously of Harlem origin, the theatre program lists them in the cast with beautifully euphonic African names." Francis Atkins became Musu Esami; Alma Sutton, Mirammo.[42] Most black critics pointed out connections *and* variations between African American culture and the native picture Dafora presented.

Kykunkor signaled the arrival of black choreographers commanding artistic authority on American stages and an increase in theatrical presentations of Africa and the Caribbean. Dafora and Clarence Yates, the dance director of the Negro Unit of the WPA's Federal Theatre Project, choreographed dances for Orson Welles's Haitian version of *Macbeth* in 1936, often called the "Voodoo Macbeth." That December the project produced *Bassa Moona* with choreography by Momodu Johnson, a Yoruba from Nigeria. In Chicago, Katherine Dunham created *Haitian Suite* in 1937, first appealing to William Grant Still to write the music for a large historical piece about the Haitian revolution. Still was quite intrigued by the idea and eagerly questioned Dunham about music she had heard in Haiti, asking, "[W]ill you advise me as to the characteristic use of the rada drums, i.e. whether they are played intermittently or constantly[?]" and "[W]ill you describe as fully as possible the sounds of native instruments other than drums?"[43] Although he soon had to pull out of the project because of demands for movie scores, Still's questions and Dunham's pursuits suggest that both of them were mining sources in the Caribbean in new ways.

In the mid-1930s, at the same time that African American dancers turned more resolutely to Africa and the Caribbean, more white modern dancers began to decry racial discrimination within the dance world. As fascist policies became widespread in Europe, American modern dancers looked more closely at the ethnic and racial prejudices in their own society. The success of a few African American dancers such as Winfield, Guy, Dafora, and Dunham also brought new attention to all black dancers, whose plight had been easily ignored before. The first National Dance Congress, held in New York City in May 1936, passed a resolution stating, "Whereas the Negro people in

America have been subject to segregation and suppression which has limited their development in the field of creative dance, be it resolved that the Dance Congress encourage and sponsor the work of the Negro People in the creative fields."[44] At the congress itself, Lenore Cox, a "Negro Dancer and Instructor," gave a talk entitled "On a Few Aspects of Negro Dancing," in which she called for more training of African American dancers in concert dance techniques. Edna Guy danced a solo in one of the evening performances that accompanied the days of meetings and lectures.

Guy and Cox were instrumental in maintaining this heightened attention and organized a Negro Dance Evening on 7 March 1937, at the Kaufman Auditorium of the 92nd Street Young Men's Hebrew Association, the most prominent new theater for white modern dancers. The occasion proclaimed the formal inclusion of African Americans into the largely white concert dance scene and illustrated much of what had occurred since Guy's discouraging attempts to train in the mid-1920s. The organizers, Guy, Cox, and Allison Burroughs, were prominent African American dancers who had gained recognition among white concert dancers: Guy through her contact with Ruth St. Denis, Cox at the National Dance Congress, and Burroughs in Communist Party functions. But this concert was a call to independence. The organization of the program revealed their intentions "to make immediately apparent to the audience the roots of the dancing in the Americas today." Beginning with dances of Africa, the program then moved across the Atlantic Ocean to North America, featuring slave dancing and spirituals. The final section began with contemporary social dances, such as the lindy hop and truckin', which "help to brighten drab moments . . . [a]nd then comes the contribution of the contemporary Negro artist," the modern dance pieces.[45] Providing a history of the dancing of dark-skinned peoples, the Negro Dance Evening reinforced the importance of dance to African Americans in the past and the present by crossing the globe, from Africa to the Americas, moving from African rituals and depictions of chattel slavery to the high jinks of Harlem. The variety of dance styles, and particularly the inclusion of more abstract modern dance, went beyond stereotypes of the natural dancing ability of African Americans—most commonly associated with tap and social dancing—although the dancers and choreographers of the evening did not deny these traditions either. Instead, they provided a narrative of African American identity through and in dance that presented African dance as the foundation of later concert and social dance styles and foretold the emergence of a combined style of African and modern dance.

The Negro Dance Evening in 1937 presented Katherine Dunham from Chicago to New York City, and it was Dunham who would build on the contributions of Winfield, Guy, and Dafora and secure long-term fame by creating a distinctive African American modern dance style. Born near Chicago in 1909, Dunham was the daughter of a light-skinned woman of French Canadian and Native American ancestry who died when Katherine was only a few years old. Her father remarried, ran a laundry business, and promoted the educational achievements of Katherine and her older brother, Albert. Her father's volatile rage and fluctuating finances, however, tore the family apart, and Dunham went back and forth between her father's home and that of her stepmother's relatives. Directing a cabaret for a church social, track, basketball, and the Terpsichorean Club in high school offered some relief. At eighteen she left home, began taking classes at Joliet Junior College, and received a job in a Chicago library on the basis of a civil service exam. She participated in theatrical productions of the Cube Theater, co-founded by her adored older brother, and eventually followed her brother to the University of Chicago, where she took sociology and anthropology classes from Robert Redfield beginning in 1928 and from which she graduated with a bachelor's degree in 1936. She also began taking dance classes with the Russian ballet teacher Ludmilla Speranzeva, white modern dancer Diana Huebert, and the leading Chicago ballet dancers Bentley Stone and Ruth Page.[46]

College inspired Dunham to pursue both anthropology and dance and offered a way to combine them. Anthropology interested her because it was the "study of man," with the purpose of recognizing "universal emotional experiences," but dance and art pulled her too, for similar reasons: "Every person who has a germ of artistry seeks to recreate and present an impression of universal human experience—to fulfill either human needs or wants." She thought that looking at the intersection of art and anthropology would lead to greater understanding of both fields. More specifically, she wanted to know "why [people] dance as they do."[47]

Anthropologists who began exploring these kinds of questions in the

FIGURE 3.3. *Katherine Dunham. Photograph by Roger Wood. (Roger Wood Collection, Jerome Robbins Dance Division, The New York Public Library for the Performing Arts, Astor, Lenox and Tilden Foundations)*

first part of the twentieth century promoted the belief that cultural traits were acquired, not innate. By the 1920s and 1930s this idea began to affect understandings of male and female roles, most famously in the work of Margaret Mead. It also led to studies of the differences between nations; Ruth Benedict applied this approach to the study of North America in her 1934 *Patterns of Culture.*[48] Franz Boas, one of the founders of the field and still influential in the 1920s and 1930s as a mentor to many graduate students at Columbia University (including Mead, Benedict, and Zora Neale Hurston), inspired important work on the cultural roots of racial distinctions. This represented a radical leap in regard to common understandings of race: refuting the biological determinism of eugenics, cultural relativity overturned the idea that skin color signified fundamental dissimilarities (and, for many, inequalities) among people.[49]

Melville Herskovits, a white Jewish student of Boas, became one of the most well-known anthropologists exploring the heritage of dark-skinned peoples. Herskovits contributed to *The New Negro* with an article affirming "The Negro's Americanism," in which he argued that the Harlem community of New York represented "the same pattern [of other American communities], only a different shade."[50] Historian Sterling Stuckey has noted that Herskovits began to emphasize the survival of African traits in the diaspora (despite "The Negro's Americanism") in the mid-1930s when he started to do more field work in the Caribbean.[51] From then on Herskovits's work increasingly charted the behavior and abilities common among dark-skinned peoples. In his 1941 book, *The Myth of the Negro Past,* he looked at different black peoples, judging the extent of interaction with white or European cultures and describing the resulting syncretism. Dance "carried over into the New World to a greater degree than almost any other trait of African culture," Herskovits argued.[52]

Herskovits's views of dance were certainly impacted by the field work of Dunham, who contacted him at Northwestern University in 1932. Seeking his opinion as an expert in the field, she wanted to know if he thought a "comparative study of primitive dancing," beginning with Native Americans and moving onto "such primitive groups of American Negroes as remain" was a worthy topic of research.[53] Dunham never accomplished this comparative project, but she tackled parts of it. Through Herskovits's advice and help in obtaining grant money from the Rosenwald Foundation, Dunham traveled to the Caribbean in 1935 to conduct field work. She spent most of her time in Haiti and Jamaica, going between the social dancing scene in Port-au-Prince and the ritualistic dancing in smaller villages.[54] When she returned, she created *Haitian Suite* (1937) and traveled to New York City through a snowstorm in March 1937 to appear in the Negro Dance Evening at the 92nd Street Y. Graduate work in anthropology pulled her, but she chose performance and choreography and never completed a graduate degree. She put her anthropological work on theatrical stages.[55]

L'Ag'Ya (1938), which premiered on 27 January 1938, as part of the Federal Theatre Project's Chicago unit, showed how Dunham's studies affected her choreography. Program notes and photographs from these early productions and a later filmed version show that *L'Ag'Ya,* named for a Martinique

FIGURE 3.4. L'Ag'Ya *by Katherine Dunham. Photograph by Roger Wood. (Roger Wood Collection, Jerome Robbins Dance Division, The New York Public Library for the Performing Arts, Astor, Lenox and Tilden Foundations)*

fighting dance, presented a variety of Caribbean dances, such as the Creole mazurka, the beguine, the Cuban habañera, and the Brazilian majumba, all performed to music composed by University of Chicago music professor Robert Sanders. The first scene gave a sense of a Caribbean market, with pantomime, gesture, costuming, and lighting slowly exposing the daily rituals of a small fishing village. The second scene took place in the jungle, where animal cries accompanied a steady drum and slow dancing. Dunham repeatedly used a dance step from the Maroons in Jamaica: a male dancer moved back and forth, right and left, in a deep second position, legs wide and turned out, knees bent, and hopping—a grounded, portentous, but open stance (see figure 3.4). The final scene depicted a festival day, with the revelry more persuasive because of its contrast to the even routine of the first scene. The energetic mazurka and beguine matched the bright light and vibrant costumes. But a jealous lover entered, moving in the menacing second position from the jungle scene, and conducted a fighting dance, L'Ag'Ya, which resulted in a death.[56]

Dunham created a full picture of a Caribbean village, with joy and pathos and even the tedium of life. Although she combined dances from various places in the Caribbean, many of the steps used were taken directly from her own observances of those particular dances. *L'Ag'Ya* joined Dunham's anthropological sensibilities and her choreographic and dancing skills; it was neither an exact rendering of the dances as she had seen them, nor a flashy spectacle of constant skirt tossing and whirling moves, nor a wholly accurate picture of Martinique. Instead, Dunham designed a sense of a place, where gesture, sound, and color existed in a variety of ways, and dance was a sensory experience among many. As dance scholar VèVè Clark argues, Dunham created a diasporic vision.[57]

Dunham's anthropological field work strengthened her belief in the forceful ties binding the peoples of the African diaspora together. In the language of anthropology, she was a true participant-observer, entering deeply into the societies she observed. Part of the ease with which she did this was due to the fact that she was a black person investigating other black people. For Dunham's trip to Haiti in 1935, Herskovits wrote many letters of introduction to people there; Dunham wrote back that she discovered she did not have much need for the letters because she met people easily and they led her around. Closer to Haitians because of similar skin color and finding her way quite comfortably, she acknowledged that she may have used some unconventional methods, but "there are ways and ways of doing field work, I find." Her great-grandparents were Haitian, and she thought this won her friends too. The Haitians at first thought she had spiritual powers because of her dancing ability, and at the end of her time there she was initiated as an obi, a sort of spiritual guide, which symbolized her acceptance into that society.[58]

Anthropology also attracted the writer Zora Neale Hurston, who primarily investigated the religious beliefs, folklore, and language of black Americans in the South in the 1930s and wrote both fiction and nonfiction based on this research. The pull to anthropology of Hurston, Dunham, Syllvia Fort in Seattle (who later was a member of Dunham's company), and Pearl Primus (the next leading African American modern dancer) was a way for black women to uncover their past and explore the heritage of peoples of the African diaspora. These women received legitimacy for their artistic endeavors through higher education, a common path for African American women. Anthropology itself attracted many women, foreigners, and Jews who because of their marginal status in America felt compelled to examine the roots of that marginality.[59] Under the rubric of cultural relativism, they defended other cultural patterns and held out hope for changing the lives of people who had secondary status in the societies of which they were a part. Hurston and Dunham relied on ethnography and their personal experiences as black participant-observers to validate their conceptions of the black peoples they surveyed. They transferred their knowledge and experience of African diasporan cultures to an African American setting and, in the process, rejuvenated notions of blackness. Dunham found that movement, the cultural patterns of gestures and action, stretched past the American South to the Caribbean and Africa, preserving a racial heritage that extended beyond words.[60]

In a 1938 interview Dunham rejected the notion of dance as a "more natural medium of racial expression," but she tied dance and racial identity together again when she wrote that same year, "[T]o predict the future of the Negro in dance would be, in a large measure, to predict the future of the Negro as a social entity. It is impossible to separate the two concepts."[61] Dunham rightly bound together the place of African Americans in society with their place in the dance world, flattening the distinction of art as a rarefied realm of insight and experience that existed above or outside larger societal beliefs. Her training as an anthropologist led her to put art into the broader category of culture, the social repository of a group's values and beliefs. Dunham, Margaret Mead, Ruth Benedict, and Zora Neale Hurston promulgated an anthropological definition of culture that encompassed social stratifications in art and made visible the relative nature of definitions of high and low culture within modernism. During the 1930s anthropologists began uncovering the dramatically different meanings ascribed to race, gender, sexuality, and class around the world. They promoted a malleable view of these categories, pushing against restrictions and prejudices based upon preconceptions. But limitations remained. Societal beliefs steered women to dance, and racial, sexual, and class characterizations underlay the division between high and low culture in modernism—despite Dafora's and Dunham's attempts to circumvent them. Within these constraints, Dunham's path to success lay in making high art in the United States from African and Caribbean sources, capitalizing on a heritage of dance within the African diaspora and raising perceptions of African Americans' capabilities.

Dunham faced obstacles in surmounting racial prejudices embedded in modernism that were exacerbated by being a woman. Critics easily deflated the artistic import of her work because of its sensual overtones. In the 1930s Josephine Baker represented the archetypal success for African American women performers. On stage and off, Baker's playful embodiment of an erotic "primitive" formed the foundation of her celebrity. In Paris, Baker thrilled audiences at the Théâtre de Champs-Elysées in 1925 and the Folies Bergères in 1926 and reigned thereafter. Her U.S. appearances were rare; she appeared in the Ziegfeld Follies of 1936 in New York to reviews that discredited her singing and dancing talent and upheld the notion that her primary talent was what lay beneath her banana skirt.[62] Dunham wandered into this maelstrom of varying sexual play, from the seductive banter of Baker to the sexlessness that white women modern dancers successfully deployed. In confronting audience expectations of sexual provocation and the association of artistic legitimacy with sexlessness, Dunham remained steadfast in her inclusion of African dance traditions that featured more forthright acceptance of sexual elements in dance.

Dunham's determination, combined with her worthy talent and education, provoked a variety of responses. White critics almost never missed an opportunity to comment on both her anthropological studies *and* the sensual, sometimes even sexually explicit, movements she included in her choreography. "As an anthropologist the gist of Miss Dunham's report seems to be that sex in the Caribbean is doing all right," was how John Martin, the influential *New York Times* critic put it. "Did you ever see a Degree in Anthropology dancing?" another critic asked.[63] Reviewers slighted the seriousness of Dunham's academic study by continually using it to justify the sexy movements, while at the same time anthropology legitimated these so-called primitive movements in the sanctified realm of the theater for white critics. In either case, as an anthropologist uncovering primitive dances or as a black woman rotating her hips, Dunham decidedly affirmed white critics' conceptions of all black peoples as inherently more sexual.

Criticism of Dunham that focused on her over-use of the hips prompted attacks of vulgarity, lack of artistry, and sensationalism.[64] Critics described Dunham as hot and performing in a sexually taunting, splashy, and theatrical style. She was the originator of the role of Georgia in the Broadway version of *Cabin in the Sky* (1941), about which John Martin proclaimed, "She is 100% seductress."[65] The city censor of Boston even forced Dunham to drop a part of her *Tropical Revue* on a 1944 tour because it was too sexually explicit (prompting a friend of Dunham's to comment that Boston was "more like a Clothing Convention than an Art Center").[66] Dunham did choreograph more revue-like dances that played up the steel drums and flashy colors of Caribbean culture, perform in bigger theaters as a part of a line of shows that had more popular appeal, and appear in Hollywood movies in the 1940s. But some of the splashiness came from the encouragement of the impresario Sol Hurok. For *Tropical Revue,* the show that received the heaviest criticism for its sensual allure, Hurok persuaded Dunham to leave out *L'Ag'Ya,* thinking it too heavy, and include the more lively *Rites de Passage.* This apparently appealed more to Hurok's sense of what would sell, at least outside Boston with its well-known puritanical attitude toward theater. Boston critics attempted to save Dunham's reputation, once again, by pulling out her anthropological background to legitimize the sexual moves. To counter the city censor, Elinor Hughes of the *Boston Herald* listed Dunham's work toward a master's degree, her winning of research fellowships, and her brother's position on the faculty of Howard University. Still, Dunham provoked censure while Shawn and His Men Dancers, performing as nearly nude as possible on Boston stages, did not. The sexual allure of black women caused more consternation than that of white men.[67]

The rise of another African American woman, anthropologist-cum-dancer Pearl Primus, elicited comparison with Dunham in the 1940s. Critics often noted differences between Dunham and Primus and their use of sexual movements. Primus's body more broadly conformed to the stereotypical male or female "Negroid": broad nose, large expressive eyes, dark pigmentation, and muscular thighs and buttocks (see figure 7.3). Although only five feet two inches tall, she was described as strong and sturdy rather than petite. Perhaps largely due to her distinguishable physical character-istics, descriptions of her dancing generally pointed to how well she per-formed the "primitive rhythms." White reviewers described the muscular and barefooted Primus as a "strong, rhythmical, wild creature," a "young filly" romping over the pasture, showing all the signs of being a "thorough-bred," and looking out from "jungle distances" as, in Martha Graham's words, a "panther."[68] Identifying Primus as a member of the animal king-dom reinforced prejudices about African Americans' sexual nature and their place on the evolutionary scale. Put a different way, one audience member of the 1940s I spoke to said she did not know until she saw Primus that women could move with such weight, strength, and masculinity.[69]

The difference in the criticism that Primus and Dunham received might suggest that Primus—because of her easily identifiable "Negro" features— reinforced expectations and stereotypes and provoked less discomfort than Dunham. Dunham was "always lovely to the eye," but Primus's "technical equipment" apparently overwhelmed her sex appeal.[70] Primus was sexual without being sexually attractive. With her lighter color, taller and leaner build, and narrower facial features, Dunham more closely fit white ideals of dancers and beauty and may have triggered a more hidden and festering rea-son for the derisive comments: she reminded Americans of the truth of their racial heritage—miscegenation. Dunham sometimes consciously flaunted her erotic appeal but perhaps unconsciously aggravated this nagging impli-cation. And her marriage to a white man, set and costume designer John Pratt, may have added to the unease on this topic. In contrast, Primus—of "unmixed African descent" and with a stockier build that helped her "out-jump any man"—generated less criticism.[71]

Dunham and Primus mediated sexuality within their artistry in a different way than Graham and Humphrey but garnered enough praise to challenge some white critics to rethink assumptions about the capabilities of African American dancers and the difficulties they faced. Lois Balcolm, writing in the more intellectual of the dance periodicals of the time, *Dance Observer,* reported comments she overheard during a concert by Primus in October 1944 that reflected contradictory beliefs: "[She's] at her best when she is most Negro" and "[She's] at her worst in the primitives—just a modern dancer's approximation." Most audience members were seemingly more comfortable seeing Primus dance jazz. Balcolm, on the other hand, advised Primus to continue to explore the more "serious" avenue of modern dance, seeing neither "tribal ritual" nor "Harlem high spirits" as expressing the "things of most importance."[72] Franziska Boas, the daughter of pioneering anthropologist Franz Boas, and who also was involved in modern dance, urged the African American dancer to steer clear of African and Caribbean dance material as it encouraged the "mistaken notion that this is the well-spring of his inspiration and he must return to it from time to time." Boas argued that black dancers needed to step beyond the folk-dance level and continue to explore the aesthetic principles of modern dance, thereby challenging the expectations of the white audience.[73]

If Boas and Balcolm illuminated some of the preconceptions of a predominantly white audience, they also betrayed judgments about the difference between entertainment and art that haunted African American concert dancers.[74] They believed African and Caribbean dances ("folk dance," according to Boas) and "Harlem high spirits" lacked aesthetic elements; these judgments upheld distinctions between entertainment and art based on class and racial prejudices and often refracted in sexual terms through denigration of erotic appeal. They rejected Dunham's and Primus's attempts to imbue the popular dances with artistic intention—by choreographing, not improvising, them and by performing the numbers on stage alongside other kinds of choreography. Boas and Balcolm insisted on the superiority of the higher art form created and sustained by white critics and dancers as the path to pursue in breaking down the discrimination facing African American artists.

Commentary about Dunham and Primus amongst African American critics manifested similar elements. Peggy Galloway of the *Chicago Defender* advocated pursuing ballet because "it does possess great possibilities towards polishing our cultural aspirations," thus tying black achievement to success in traditionally white fields.[75] More generally, black critics focused on how Dunham and Primus represented "the race." The New York African American community quickly embraced Dunham upon her triumphant show in 1940; she graced the cover of *Crisis* in March 1940 and was hailed as "the leading colored dance artist in the country."[76] As with white reviewers, Dunham's *Tropical Revue* provoked some discomfort among black critics and revealed that sexual allure was a component in measuring racial authenticity. One critic recognized the lack of authenticity in *Rites de Passage* and *Primitive Rhythms* but rationalized that "the inadequacies of material are surmounted for the sophisticates by the beauty and vitality of the production and for the barbarians by the hip-swinging that is a hallmark of the show." While the comment re-created a dichotomy between sophisticates and barbarians, it also recognized that both types might be in the audience. In the end, the reviewer strongly endorsed the show, saying that "hip-wriggling is relegated to its proper place," in contrast to white reviewers' toilsome efforts to justify such movements with anthropological insights.[77] In fact, most reviews of Dunham in the black press gave only passing comments on the sensuality of the movements, as in the above remark, although Dunham's attractiveness did affect her success. An African American soldier wrote *Yank* magazine in 1944 claiming, "[T]here are four or five battalions, three or four regiments and two or three division of fellows around here who would like for you to put in a photo of Katherine Dunham," following one of Lena Horne.[78]

Primus's rise in the early 1940s prompted analysis about both dancers in the African American press that stressed authenticity and political purpose rather than sexual attraction specifically. As with white reviewers, Primus fared better, being designated as a "strictly classic dancer" and "an artist of the people."[79] While the reviewer Nora Holt declared comparisons "odious," she ranked Primus as one of the best dancers of the era and congratulated her for expressing a "deep and sincere understanding of her people, of the Negro's struggles, his frustration." What Dunham first displayed so brilliantly, "the natural dancing technique of the Negro," Primus expanded upon, "leaping from the heart of a dark continent and spreading its symphonic beauty through an unbounded universe in a story of freedom . . . unstemmed and thunderous."[80] The critic Don Deleighbur worried that Dunham had let Hollywood and commercial success inspire a taste for "the glitter and glamour of the extravaganza and mimicry."[81] The worry masked a concern that Dunham had fallen sway to white ideals of entertainment, copying their idea of dance for African Americans—with its emphasis on sexual provocation—and losing the racial originality she had possessed earlier. Dunham's flashier style, her mulatto appearance, and perhaps her white husband brought her racial authenticity into question. In these ways, the attributes of womanhood folded into the argument of authenticity and supported the critical favor Primus received.

From the 1920s to the 1940s questions of racial representation and artistic responsibility burdened African American critics and dancers. Responses to these artists and artworks reinscribed the questions so that "Negro art" was never free from the tentacles of representing "the race." For white reviewers, African Americans' natural dancing ability confirmed their closeness to so-called primitive societies, unsophistication, nature, bodies, and sex; white critics had difficulty acknowledging African American dancers' contributions to an aesthetic project that included philosophical ideas about art. For African American critics, the debate between high and low art transformed into one of art and propaganda; they recognized that aesthetics were inextricably linked to racial perceptions within society at large. Black critics satisfied the demands of both propaganda and art by heralding the innate dance talent of African Americans as a unique cultural offering and as a racial tradition among peoples of the African diaspora.

In the project of modern dance, African American concert dancers had a marginal but critically defining role. Racism limited their involvement in modern dance as training, monetary support, and performance opportunities were scarce. Questions of race, however, were crucial to the definition of modern dance as a new art form. In the performances of the National Dance Congress in 1936, Edna Guy danced on a program of "Variety and Theater Dance" rather than a program of modern dance. White modern dancers set themselves against the low art of the dance halls, the revue shows, and the sensual play black dancers aroused. Recognizing their slighted place in the United States, African American concert dancers celebrated the traditions of Africa and the Caribbean. Graduate work in anthropology lent credibility and helped Dunham, and later Primus, mold and legitimate an African American aesthetic in a dance field mostly populated and supported by white Americans. Dafora, Dunham, and Primus enhanced the importance of dance when they stressed its function as ritual in African and Caribbean societies. In this they contributed to changing ideas of art in the 1930s, forcing a bleeding into the larger category of culture that emphasized the distinctive social grounding of values and beliefs. As much as African American dancers expanded definitions of culture, however, when they performed in American theaters they remained bound by traditional notions of art as Culture. The path for African Americans to segregated theaters through side doors, back stairs, and balcony seating was a spatial representation of the circuitous way critics reviewed and affected the careers of African American dancers. African American concert dancers involved in artistic and anthropological realms strengthened the significance of dance, but more important, they exposed the enduring constancy of race as a foundational element in structuring ideas of art and culture within modernism.

4 : men must dance

In the late 1920s Ted Shawn, the male half of the dance pair and institution Denishawn, began to speak out about the state of dance in America. He predicted a gathering of different dance trends into a new American dance form but quickly dispelled the notion that jazz—the social dance craze of the time—should be incorporated. Shawn conceded that the savage, simple, "innocently sensual" dances of African Americans might someday be refined into a "negro ballet," but his persistent racist attitudes, more overt than those of other modern dancers, demonstrated the enduring nativist elements of the 1920s that lingered in the 1930s.[1] These public denouncements differed from other white modern dancers' call for racial justice in their dances and point to the peculiar position Shawn held in the burgeoning modern dance movement of the 1930s. Later known as Papa, Shawn nurtured the Denishawn careers of Martha Graham, Doris Humphrey, and Charles Weidman in the 1920s, and his all-male troupe, Shawn and His Men Dancers, toured to acclaim around the country in the 1930s. But his visions of artistry were more romantic and traditional than those of other modernists, and his concern with legitimizing modern dance as a high art form revealed the strains of prejudice about African Americans, women, immigrants, and the working classes that other modernists challenged—if not wholly or successfully. Shawn's mission to champion the artistic worth of modern dance, though, also sprang from his particular place in society. His romantic view of this new art form was based on an idealization of male homosexuality.

Men modern dancers, like women, faced assumptions about masculine and feminine characteristics both on stage and off. While Graham and Humphrey accumulated descriptions of their dancing as masculine and ugly, accusations of effeminacy and suspicion of homosexuality dogged male dancers. At this time the delineation between "queer" and "straight" signified an inversion of gender roles more than particular sexual acts or partners. Queers were men who exhibited perceived female traits and behaviors such as a high-pitched voice, a languid, swivel-hipped walk—and an interest in the arts, especially dance.[2] The lack of financial security in a dance career was also more problematic for men because of their traditional roles as breadwinners, a particularly acute source of concern in the economic hard times of the Great Depression. The precarious place of men— and the growing assertion of women who were holding families together and playing a larger role in the workforce and politics—sparked fears of feminine men and masculine women. Behavior that defied conventional gender roles threatened an already feeble society, worn down from poverty. Women such as the leading modern dancers worked within and against these conventions, but most Americans tolerated little challenge to the traditional image of men as strong and sufficient—manly. In the 1930s severe crackdowns increased on gay bars, drag balls, and theatrical pansy acts in New York City, as did legislation prohibiting the representation of homosexuality.[3]

All these factors led to a dearth of men in modern dance. The leading men who ended up in dance at this time—Ted Shawn, Charles Weidman, José Limón, and Lester Horton—embraced virile dance in response. As gay, predominantly white men (Limón was born in Mexico), they advocated for more men in modern dance as a way in which to legitimize a predominantly female art form in the predominantly male arts world seething with the innovations of modernism. Homosexual allure often molded their dances, but it remained an undercurrent, an allusion most often picked up on only by other gay men. Led by Shawn, male modern dancers' emboldened masculinity attracted both men and women, refuted the effeminacy associated with dance, and eventually steered them to leadership roles.

Edwin Meyers Shawn was born in Kansas City, Missouri, on 21 October 1891, the second son of Elmer Ellsworth Shawn, a journalist for the *Kansas City Star,* and Mary Lee Booth Shawn. Shawn's mother traced her lineage back to "a nobleman serving under William the Conqueror when he invaded and conquered England"; his father came from less aristocratic

German folk who had emigrated to the United States in the 1840s. The Shawns moved to Denver in Ted's early childhood, and there Ted decided to become a Methodist minister, attracted to the moral ideals of a religious life. During his third year as a pre-theology student at the University of Denver, Shawn contracted diphtheria, a bacterial infection that caused difficulty in breathing, high fever, weakness, and, in Shawn's case, temporary paralysis of his legs. To rebuild his stamina and physical dexterity, he sought out dance lessons.[4]

Shawn had displayed an interest in theater before his bout with diphtheria. In 1911 he wrote a two-act play entitled *The Female of the Species* for his fraternity, Sigma Phi Epsilon. A satirical look at women's suffrage, the play depicted a postsuffrage future (in 1933) where men dressed in "ruffled trousers, laced waists, ear-rings," and women wore "men's full dress coats and shirts"; women ran the government as commissioners of the "Bargain Counters" and "Manicurists and Beauty Parlors," and the only man ran the tiny department of "Municipal Affairs." "Horrified and shocked beyond expression" at this futuristic scene, the rabid feminist character swore "to renounce suffrage."[5] In reinforcing traditional roles for men and women, the play foreshadowed Shawn's own path through the dance world in opposing the changing social and artistic roles for women in modernism.

Shawn's theater experience and ballet and ballroom dance lessons eventually led to his leaving the University of Denver by choice, just before expulsion. A publicity photo with his dance teacher, Hazel Wallack, elicited a denouncement by the university chancellor for their sensuous activity, evident in the photograph by the slit in Wallack's gown that exposed her leg almost up to her hip.[6] Shawn left school to launch a lifelong career in dance. Although he gave up his ideas of becoming a minister, Shawn, like Isadora Duncan and Ruth St. Denis at the same time, believed that dance joined mind and body in a spiritual union. He found affirmation in *The Making of Personality* by the poet Bliss Carman, who described dance as "that perfect fusion of sense and spirit, without which no art is possible and no life is fortunate," a view that prompted Shawn to write the poet for advice about making a career in dance.[7] Shawn sought out Carman in early 1914, and that meeting led him to Ruth St. Denis, whom Carman believed best embodied the union of "sense and spirit." After an introduction in New York, St. Denis's and Shawn's mutual admiration soared as they exalted shared idols such as Ralph Waldo Emerson, Mary Baker Eddy, and François Delsarte. St. Denis asked Shawn to accompany her on an upcoming tour; he quickly accepted. Their passionate conversation continued, and, after much beseeching, Shawn convinced St. Denis to marry him later that same year, in August 1914.[8] St. Denis did not want the hindrances of marriage, but she also felt that Isadora Duncan had damaged the reputation of dance with her notorious love affairs and illegitimate children. So St. Denis married Shawn, but she refused to obey: she had the word stricken from the ceremony.[9] St. Denis gained a dance partner with entrepreneurial acumen; Shawn benefited from St. Denis's prominence and her devotion to and success in creating a new form of dance.

Their alliance initially prospered. In 1915 they established the Denishawn school in Los Angeles, interrupted by Shawn's service in World War I (never overseas) in 1917. Other schools followed, first in New York City in 1922, then in Rochester, Boston, Wichita, and Minneapolis. Touring constantly, they garnered international acclaim, acquired glorious costumes made up of fabrics and accessories from various countries, and earned some wealth, which they consistently reinvested in their productions and their dream of a permanent Greater Denishawn school and company in New York City. But their personal relationship was fractious. Professional envy (most often, Shawn's jealousy of St. Denis) and extramarital love affairs by both continually riled them. By the late 1920s they spent more and more time apart, eventually splitting personally as well as professionally. The Denishawn school and company ended in 1931, and although they did not divorce, Shawn and St. Denis never lived together after 1930.

While St. Denis dallied with men during her marriage to Shawn, most of them younger than she, Shawn also pursued the affection and love of men. Their mutual affection for one man contributed to their permanent separation. Shawn and St. Denis met Fred Beckman in 1927 in Corpus Christi, Texas, while on tour. In early 1928 Shawn invited Beckman to become his personal representative, and eventually his lover. Although the dissolution of St. Denis and Shawn's company and marriage was imminent, a secret liaison between St. Denis and Beckman doomed the partnership when Shawn found a romantic letter from St. Denis to Beckman.[10]

Shawn fled to solo tours in Europe. German newspapers praised his

American "freshness, youth, even boyishness," which contrasted sharply with the Russian male dancers who toured in Germany and were "sluggish, degenerate . . . [and showed the] weariness of civilization."[11] The generous flattery soothed Shawn's ego, bruised by the betrayal of St. Denis. In the wake of Denishawn's crippling debts Shawn needed money, so he toured the United States from 1931 to 1932 with a small company known as Shawn and His Dancers. He soon headed resolutely to the wooded retreat he had bought in 1930 near Lee, Massachusetts, named Jacob's Pillow. Jacob's Ladder was the highest mountain in the Berkshires; a large sloping rock on Shawn's property thereby became Jacob's pillow. At the restful farmhouse in the woods Shawn turned his full attention to a mission he had publicized as early as 1916: men must dance.[12]

On his 1931–32 tour Shawn devised lecture-demonstrations for university and college audiences that advocated dance for men. During the winter of 1932–33, he found a way to implement his ideas. Nearby Springfield College (then the all-male International Young Men's Christian Association College) had a strong physical education program, and with the enthusiasm of the college president, Shawn offered a class in dance. Determined to overcome the charge that male dancers were sissies, Shawn stipulated that the class be mandatory, thus ensuring that all suffered the stereotype and that peer pressure would not arouse further divisions among the male students. Shawn gave them strenuous exercises the first day, pushing them to recognize the physical stamina dance required. He learned that simple descriptive words about action—leap, turn—translated better to his class than the French ballet terms such as ballon and pirouette. By the end of the term, he "had his disciples."[13] More important, he had fellow performers. In quick response to an offer to perform in Boston, Shawn pulled together men from his Springfield College classes and performers (including women) from his touring company. On 21 March 1933, at the Repertory Theatre, Shawn and his dancers debuted to rave reviews, with the all-male pieces receiving the most praise.

The success of the Boston performance inspired Shawn to arrange a formal company, Shawn and His Men Dancers, and he immediately set about training, choreographing, and touring. From 1933 to 1940 the company of either eight or nine men (including Shawn) held 1,250 performances in more than 750 cities in the United States, Canada, and England.[14]

FIGURE 4.1. *Noontime sunbathing at Jacob's Pillow, ca. 1936. (Barton Mumaw Collection, Jacob's Pillow Dance Festival Archives)*

Throughout the seven years of touring, Jacob's Pillow was home and sustenance. Living there each summer, the troupe built cabins, a studio, and eventually a theater; took daily dance classes; refurbished older works and created new ones; and each noon hour sunbathed nude as Shawn read from Havelock Ellis, Ouspensky (a disciple of the theosophist Gurdjieff), and the philosopher Alfred North Whitehead. (A 1936 catalog for "Shawn School of Dance for Men" described this last daily ritual as a "required course in the principles of applied anatomy, body mechanics, corrective exercises and massage . . . held, as a rule, during the noon-hour sun-bathing period" [see figure 4.1].)[15] At the suggestion of F. Cowles Strickland, a friend of Shawn's and director of the Berkshire Playhouse in nearby Stockbridge, the troupe began hosting "teas" to make a little money. Shawn invited the dowagers of western Massachusetts to the Pillow in the late afternoon. The "boys" would serve tea, then retreat to the woods and emerge, stripped to tan trunks, and perform. These teas blossomed into the Jacob's Pillow Dance Festival that continues today.

Shawn's commitment to promoting men in dance, and especially the ideal of an all-male company, encompassed his idealization of homosexual love between men. Shawn looked to the musings of Walt Whitman, and to the British writers Edward Carpenter and Havelock Ellis, the standard reading list among gay men of the era, to fortify his belief in the higher ideal of love between men.[16] Shawn sought out Carpenter and Ellis during a 1924 tour to London, and Walter Terry, Shawn's friend and biographer, suggested that the meeting eased Shawn's mind about his own homosexual inclinations.[17] In his book *Love's Coming of Age,* Carpenter wrote of the "intermediate sex" that combined a balance of masculine and feminine characteristics in one person and included a same-sex love object. Love between men or between women was not a "result of disease and degeneration" in Carpenter's view; in fact, "it is possible that in this class of men we have the love sentiment in one of its most perfect forms." Among men the "intermediate sex" man who unified masculine and feminine traits exhibited superior artistic talent, and Carpenter named as examples Michelangelo, Shakespeare, and Marlowe.[18] This was a vision of homosexuality—and artistry—that Shawn could espouse. In yearning for legitimation of his artistic talent, he clung to this ideal that incorporated his own social standing as a white man with a wife and a male lover.

It was Plato who best captured Shawn's thoughts about homosexuality. To Barton Mumaw, his lover from 1931 to 1948 and the principal dancer in his company, Shawn recited this passage from Plato's *Symposium:*

> The whole soul, stung in every part, rages with pain; and then again remembering the beautiful one, it rejoices. . . . It is perplexed and maddened, and in its madness it cannot sleep at night or stay in any one place by day, but is filled with longing and hastens wherever it hopes to see the beautiful one. And when it sees him and is bathed with the waters of yearning, the passages that were sealed are opened, the soul has respite from the stings and is eased of its pain, and this pleasure which it enjoys is the sweetest of pleasures at the time.
>
> Therefore the soul will not if it can help it, be left alone by the beautiful one, but esteems him above all others, forgets for him mother and

brothers and all friends, neglects property and cares not for its loss, and despising all the customs and proprieties in which it formerly took pride, it is ready to be a slave and to sleep wherever it is allowed, as near as possible to the beloved; for it not only reveres him who possesses beauty, but finds in him the only healer of its greatest woes. Now this condition, fair boy, about which I am speaking is called Love by men.[19]

This kind of heroic love guided Shawn's relations with Mumaw as well as his next long relationship, with John Christian, which lasted from 1949 until Shawn's death in 1972. This embrace of homosexual love did not include the "fey actions" (presumably effeminate or campy gestures), as Mumaw put it, of other homosexual men. "[It] makes me sick. It's all wrong. That's the kind of thing that brings discredit on what is essentially a noble thing. Our kind of love . . . must be lived on a higher plane than the other or it sinks to a lower level," Shawn wrote to Mumaw.[20] Shawn's vision of a higher love borrowed heavily from Edward Carpenter and from Havelock Ellis's *Studies in the Psychology of Sex.* In six volumes, published from 1897 to 1910, the British sexologist defended sexual passion, including homosexuality, and attributed spiritual qualities to sex. Shawn was his ardent disciple, even idealizing his love of St. Denis when in 1948, after eighteen years of separation, he carefully noted that the marriage "has survived the passing of the physical tie and has emerged a greater thing than it ever was on that plane."[21] For Shawn dance emerged from this spiritual and idealistic view of sex and love; Ellis's *The Dance of Life* was "the dancers' bible," and Shawn rarely missed an occasion to extol it.[22] His group of men dancers, then, was more than a sales campaign for dancing as a career for men. It was also a philosophical and artistic ideal—which included homosexuality—in action.

This purpose was clear to other gay men. Lucien Price, the gay male novelist and music critic for the *Boston Globe,* first saw Shawn dance his *Thunderbird* in 1931 and "was in an agony of desire to see it right over again."[23] Price also attended the 1933 Boston performance that included all-male dances and became an indefatigable champion of the troupe and a constant correspondent with Shawn throughout the 1930s. Price recognized that they "serve[d] the same dieties [*sic*]—beauty and brotherhood."[24] Price commended and emboldened Shawn's effort to re-create a Greek ideal in his group of men dancers, combining athletic grace, philosophical import, and the quest for beauty through the male body: "I think the combination of high intellectual content and genuine spiritual feeling in the dances, together with almost complete nakedness of the male body are letting people feel, if not see, for the first time that there need be no conflict between flesh and spirit, and that an ennobled sexual attraction can be a vehicle for religious feeling."[25] Price praised the combination of intellectual stimulation and physical prowess possible among men, but he also exalted the closeted nature of homosexuality: "Uncomfortable as one's position may often be, it has the comfort of not being exposed to this mass-exploitation by theater, movie, literature, and every crude device down to the roadside advertising signs."[26] In the next paragraph of this letter, however, Price asked to see recent photographs Shawn had received from Denmark, most likely a reference to the Danish pornographic magazine *Eos*. Certain forms of sexual commodification, then, Price valued.[27] This pornography (circulated by subterfuge to avoid criminality under U.S. postal laws) apparently did not contradict Price's belief that gay male sexuality, unlike heterosexuality, remained free of corruption by mass culture. Price's views were perhaps less about commodification than about the freedom in, and specialness of, shared secrecy. Unlike women or African Americans, whose marks of difference were physically evident, white homosexual men could operate within the world of male privilege *and* create another covert, ennobled one.

Price saw Shawn and His Men Dancers as an example of the latter, and the troupe inspired him to write *The Sacred Legion,* a series of four novels that chronicled love between men, some of whom were dancers, and that he chose to publish privately to escape censorship problems.[28] "In you and the boys I had watched [the ideal] being lived," Price recalled. He had even been attracted to one member of Shawn's troupe, John Schubert, an interest that Schubert apparently returned. Schubert died in World War II, however, and his death, along with that of another lover in World War I, contributed to Price's romanticized vision of homosexual love.[29] Shawn and His Men Dancers also propelled other gay men to be a part of the dance world. Walter Terry took dance classes with one of Shawn's former students at the University of North Carolina and roomed with Foster Fitz-Simons, who was to become a member of Shawn and His Men Dancers. Terry had decided on the career of a dance critic rather than dancer, and Shawn encouraged him, helping Terry gain his first post at the *Boston Herald* in 1936 (he moved to the *New York Herald Tribune* in 1939). Similarly, Arthur Todd approached Shawn about writing his biography, a task that Shawn had already promised to Terry. Todd ended up working primarily in the fashion world but photographed Shawn and wrote about dance in *Dance Observer* and *Dancing Times.*

John Lindquist, a cashier at Filene's department store in Boston, stopped by the Pillow one summer afternoon in 1938 out of curiosity. An amateur photographer, Lindquist became entranced by capturing dancers on film, especially naked male dancers. He came back every summer from then on, becoming the official photographer of the Pillow as well as the unofficial photographer of male dancers posing nude in the woods outside the studio and theater areas. The commercial photographer George Platt Lynes also photographed ballet dancers for public and private use.[30] For gay men at this time, it was a boon to have a photographer as a friend. Lindquist personally developed film that was considered criminal and distributed these photographs fairly widely to a circle of gay men that included Shawn and other male dancers.[31] Not all gay men in the dance world were a part of Shawn's circle, though. Neither John Martin, dance critic of the *New York Times,* nor Lincoln Kirstein, writer on dance and supporter of George Balanchine, endorsed Shawn's vision. Although both engaged in homosexual affairs, both were married—and thus were perhaps less inclined to glorify Shawn's fraternal ideal—and both were more critical of Shawn's artistry.[32] For some gay men, though, Shawn and His Men Dancers was a triumphant model of a brotherhood enacting a nobler ideal of love and artistry.

Shawn's conception of dance for men relied on an emboldened masculinity. In his attempt to dispel the popular link of dancing and effeminacy and to counter the dominance of women in the concert dance field, he upheld distinctive, essential differences between men and women and heralded masculine traits. Female modern dancers also took on masculine movements in an attempt to broaden the movement vocabulary and the kind of dance often performed by and expected of women; they challenged ideas that women could not make serious art and followed the modernists' penchant for breaking with old patterns. Shawn reified differences between masculine and feminine movement, however, and denigrated feminine influence to ensure a place for men in dance.[33] Even some women believed that the role of men was crucial to the legitimation of the art form: "[O]nly in the event of increasing and enthusiastic male participation, can dance hope to vindicate itself as a major art form," argued Ruth Murray, a prominent dance educator.[34] Walter Camryn, a dancer and teacher in Chicago, articulated the conceived end to this idea: "[U]ltimately [a male dancer's] career should lead into teaching, directing or choreography"—men at the helm of the art form.[35]

The path to leadership began with the promotion of masculine movement. Shawn wrote that "[t]he dancer has one fixed limitation that must be faced: the human body is the instrument and medium of the dancer, and human dances are either male or female."[36] Male and female bodies engendered different postures. Men's posture was "widespread, feet and legs apart, pelvis forward, chest forward, a broad stance"; women's was "the concave receptivity."[37] Shawn pronounced that men and women had always held different roles in society that would naturally lead to different kinds of movement: "[W]omen's movements are conditioned by cooking, sewing, tending babies, sweeping, etc., small scale movements which use comparatively little stress through the trunk of the body and a greater use of the small arm movements, with resultant greater flexibility of wrist and elbow." Men, on the other hand, inherited "movement impulses from forefathers who wielded scythe, axe, plough, oars, etc., and the masculine movement uses stress from the ground up through the entire body, culminating in big arm movements from the shoulder out, and with much less flexibility of elbow and wrist joints."[38]

Limp wrists, flamboyant dress and colors (especially a red tie), and an exaggerated walk sparked assumptions of homosexuality and also served as signals that constituted a system of divulgence and communication among gay men.[39] The emphasis on wrists in Shawn's description of movement— and the lack of their flexibility in masculine movement—was another attempt to disassociate male dancers from this sign of homosexuality. Some reviewers picked up on this attempt, praising Shawn for freeing the dance "from the purple tints which usually hover around male dancing" and commenting on his "expressive hands and muscular wrists."[40] Charles Weidman and Lester Horton also drew incisive attention to wrists. Horton danced "with a firm wrist," and Weidman lamented men who were doing "darling little things with their wrists" when he first began teaching.[41] Shawn condemned men dancers "with pinked toes and wisps of white chiffon [who] writhed and skipped to our mingled amusement and disgust."[42] Similarly, claimed Shawn, "[T]o most normal people masculine movement in a woman dancer is just as repulsive as feminine movement in a man dancer."[43] The goal was to achieve the unity between men and women dancing in their respective "anatomically, functionally, emotionally, and . . . inherited movement impulses . . . eternally different—opposed and yet complementary."[44]

After defining masculine movement Shawn retraced the history of dance, proclaiming it an occupation originally "limited to men alone." Citing the societies of Western civilization such as Greece and Rome and the so-called primitive societies of Native Americans and Latin America, Shawn claimed that only men had performed in theatrical works and rituals.[45] No art form could succeed if "dominated by one sex," and, more important, "the dance in its fullness . . . demands strength, endurance, precision, perfect coordination of mind, body and emotion, clarity of thinking, all distinctly masculine qualities."[46] Instead of breaking with the past as other modernists were doing, Shawn wanted to reinstate an older model of the arts, one in which men not only controlled the arts but were the only participants. In the current state of dance, he believed that it was best to isolate men thoroughly, "away from any chance to mimic feminine gestures."[47] Shawn advocated that men study with male dance teachers; he even let go his female accompanist in favor of a male accompanist and composer, Jess Meeker.[48] Thus the male idyll at Jacob's Pillow was born.

Shawn believed that athletics best prepared men for masculine movement and preferred that his dancers have athletic training and no dance background. The 1936 application for the Jacob's Pillow summer school included the questions "At what athletic games are you proficient?" and "List athletics for which you have received awards." Wilbur McCormack was a "former track man, wrestler and gymnast" from Springfield College; Frank Overlees was a swimmer and all-around athlete; Dennis Landers held the record for pole vaulting for northeastern Oklahoma.[49] Athletics suffused Shawn's choreographic ideas, too, and culminated in *Olympiad* (1937), for which individual members of the company choreographed their own solo

FIGURE 4.2. *Shawn and His Men Dancers in* Olympiad. *Photograph by Shapiro Studio. (Ted Shawn Collection, Jerome Robbins Dance Division, The New York Public Library for the Performing Arts, Astor, Lenox and Tilden Foundations)*

or group dances. Wilbur McCormack choreographed a "Boxing Dance"; Fred Hearn did "Fencing"; Foster Fitz-Simons danced the "Decathlon"; and the piece ended with a basketball "dance." The offstage apparel of the troupe also gave the impression of an athletic team: terry cloth bathrobes worn immediately before and after performances, like boxers, and knit sweaters that sported a large S, like members of a college tennis team (see figure 4.2). Most reviews of the troupe mentioned the athletic backgrounds of the troupe members, often comparing the performance of the male dancers with that of athletes. A sportswriter for a Springfield, Massachusetts, paper compared Shawn to a wrestler and concluded that he was "far more the master of a far more flexible craft [who] makes the liveliest wrestler seem like a petrified tree stump."[50]

Dances emerged from the physically active regimen at the Pillow. *Labor Symphony* (1934) offered four portrayals of men's work: in the fields, in the forests, on the sea, and in a factory, wherein movement mimicked actual work motions. In "Labor of the Fields," a dancer lurched forward, chest toward the ground, as if pushing a plow through the fields. Planting seeds followed with long swinging arm gestures, and the section ended in a harvest, with full knee bends and scooping motions. The next sections matched this pantomimic approach: two men cut down a tree with the broad back-and-forth torso movements of wielding a long saw; a crew rowed as one man guided a rudder and another threw out a net and hauled it in; and circular alternating arm motions of the group in a rhythmic pattern created a human gear shift in the final section.[51]

For Shawn, physical labor and athletics prepared men for masculine movement, but dancing nude best communicated such movement. While female modern dancers covered their body in long tubular dresses, in effect downplaying their curvier physical attributes with little display of the legs, Shawn and His Men Dancers most often performed as close to nude as permissible.[52] Quoting Whitman and Ellis, and noting the example of Greek civilization that stressed the divinity of the body, Shawn protested that clothes always restricted the dancer and, moreover, limited what a dancer could communicate: "There is no way of representing invisible form, the idea of Man, except by the nude human body. We cannot associate the cosmic Man with clothes, because clothing suggests classification — clothes would place him as to race, nationality, period of history, social or financial status — and Man would become man."[53] His 1923 *Death of Adonis* drew on Greek ideals in a portrayal of a Phoenician god as the epitome of beauty of the human body. Shawn performed the piece in a powdered wig and body and wore only a fig leaf G-string. The work was mostly poses, flowing from one into another, embodying a fluid sculpture.

But it was the beauty of the *male* body that particularly interested Shawn. In describing the moderation and good health that would come about if all had to walk around naked, Shawn picked an image of a woman as the example of excess: "To look at a nude woman whose breasts are flabby and discolored, whose body is gross and fat, produces only nausea and disgust."[54] The male body enchanted Shawn, as photographs of nude male dancers taken at the Pillow by John Lindquist, the noontime nude sunbathing hours, and his later hobby of carving wood sculptures of male nudes conveyed. Shawn's 1935 solo *Mouvement Naif,* inspired by a Whitman poem, personalized this fascination. The piece was a discovery of the motions of one own's body through isolated moves of shoulders, torso, ankles, arms.[55] In the same year that Graham presented women as representative pioneers in the solo *Frontier,* Shawn reinstated universal Man in *Mouvement Naif.*

Unlike other representations of the archetypal man, however, Shawn's vision featured sexual enticement. This quality made some in the audience uncomfortable. One reviewer commented that "in the opening group of dances the particular thing reminding me of the fan dance was the absence of a fan."[56] John Martin of the *New York Times* picked up on the homosexual allure, commenting about a 1934 performance that "Mr. Shawn's present program . . . is highly personal and its costuming scant to the point of non-existence—a combination not conducive to comfort on the receiving side of the footlights." Martin worried that this approach would negate Shawn's effort to attract young men to dance, but Martin may also have been uncomfortable with the public display of his own desires.[57]

Women reacted positively and with great enthusiasm. As the wife of a friend of Lucien Price's remarked (in Price's recounting): "The show was wonderful. I tell you it was simply wonderful. Why, the young men had next to nothing on. Next to nothing on. You might say they were naked."[58] Barton Mumaw claimed that often the curtain would raise to gasps and then stunned silence, the men's sexualized bodies arousing the audience into watching them.[59] Charles Weidman, too, attracted women who asked for private lessons and sought him out after performances.[60] Katherine Drier, in her book on Ted Shawn, may have had sexual imagery in mind when she wrote that Shawn "stands for a power of rhythm which refills one with fresh vitality."[61] After a 1940 slide show at a women's luncheon, a publicist for Jacob's Pillow commented to John Lindquist that his pictures were a "KNOCKOUT. Every time I showed a single of Barton they applauded and insisted on the film being held in the projector."[62] For these women and the dowagers who supported Jacob's Pillow, Shawn and His Men Dancers offered a rare spectacle of male sexual exhibition.

The ironies of social attitudes about male and female bodily display on stage emerge in looking at reactions to Shawn and His Men Dancers. Although the company danced close to nude, the dancers rarely received admonitions for their performances, even in Boston, where Katherine Dunham drew censure in the 1940s. Price attributed Shawn's success there to the fact that Shawn did not accompany his performances with "frank discussions" (presumably about sex or the divinity of the body), although no other modern dancers did either.[63] Nudity was partially censored in the art projects sponsored by the WPA—officials allowed the use of nudity in paintings and sculptures in allegorical settings but excised it from artistic portrayals of contemporary life. Barbara Melosh suggests that this policy targeted female nudity, ostensibly because it was more sexualized and represented a greater "affront to public decency," an idea that apparently applied to the dance world as well.[64]

Newsreels and Farm Security Administration photographs of saddened, resigned men in battered shacks and long unemployment lines were perhaps the most prominent images of men during the decade. Artistic images countered this documentation, with partial nudity of dynamic men as part of the strategy to inspire national strength. Many popular WPA murals and paintings featured the bare muscular torsos of laboring men. This celebration of manly strength in portrayals of manual laborers was reminiscent of National Socialist art in Nazi Germany and Soviet realist art of the 1930s.[65] Bernarr Macfadden, the entrepreneur behind the magazine *Physical Culture,* picked up on this trend of the 1930s and advocated the combination of virile bodybuilding and active citizenry. *Physical Culture* featured pictures of Shawn as well as occasional articles by Benito Mussolini, who extolled healthy, aggressive bodies as the basis for his Fascist "citizen army."[66] Unlike partially nude women, partially nude men in magazines and paintings and dancing on stage projected an inflated masculinity and strength that was accepted and even promoted if used in the cause of workers or nationhood. Bare, bulging muscle men flattened and obscured images of emaciated, shrunken specters.

Although homosexuality inspired Shawn's plying of nudity, the almost hypermasculinity of his troupe diminished the homosexual implications of the bare bodies because it did not fit into the societal framework of homosexuality as fey, effeminate inversion. Dance scholar Ramsay Burt argues that the pressure to conform to heterosexual images of men prompted Shawn's heroic masculinity and that he did not, therefore, challenge conventional norms of male heterosexuality.[67] Although this may be true, Shawn's visions were also about an idealized male homosexuality. These manly men may have conformed to heterosexual norms, but they were challenging common homosexual images of sissies. In this way, Shawn helped change the definition of homosexuality from gender inversion to same-sex object choice through visual display of the male body itself. Dance abetted this change. Visual display of the body is a central component of dance, and Shawn exploited this characteristic to reveal the male body as an object of audience gazes and sexual enticement. The physicality of dance mirrored the physicality of sex; for gay men, choosing to engage in sex with a man meant choosing a male body over a female one. Through dance Shawn highlighted the centrality of the body (and particularly a muscular, hardened male body) in this choice.

But different audience members picked up different messages. Shawn countered notions of male effeminacy in dance more frankly than he posited love and sex between men. Shawn refuted the feminization of dance with muscular bravado and replaced any fluidity of gender roles that modern dance may have inspired with the rigidity of separate roles for men and women emanating from different physical bodies. This vision depended upon a heightened machismo *and* on Shawn's closeting of his homosexuality. Shawn asked both St. Denis and Mumaw to remain silent about his sexual practices, because he thought the truth would cause more harm than good.[68] Charles Weidman and José Limón sought out equal pairing with women on stage and off to deflect attention from their relationship; they both lived with Doris Humphrey and Pauline Lawrence, even after Humphrey married, until Weidman became involved with another male dancer in 1939.[69] Either as a group of robust men dancing in tight trunks or paired with women, these male dancers epitomized a kind of manliness on stage that was far removed from common notions of queer effeminacy. But the offstage reality of homosexuality alters the image. Shawn's dances, in particular, detached masculinity from heterosexuality and began to unravel the definition of homosexuality based on gender inversion.

By the mid-1930s other parts of the dance world also began to promote male dancers and masculine movement. In May 1935 *New Theatre* magazine and the New Dance League sponsored a dance recital of men only. Shawn and His Men Dancers did not appear, but most men active in the dance field in New York City did, including Charles Weidman, the ballet dancer William Dollar, and the African American dancer Add Bates. The concert included Weidman's *Dance of Sports,* and the only ballet dancer on the program elicited a great many hisses, reflecting the leftist slant of the sponsors and the audience, and perhaps the view that ballet and masculine movement did not mix. Gene Martel, another concert participant and modern dancer, took up Shawn's cause, writing an article entitled "Men Must Dance" in *New Theatre* the following month. He scorned ballet more strongly than Shawn by bringing out its elitist past: "The Ballet was born and flourished during the era of doublet and hose, lace cuffs, perukes, and snuff. These furnishings parallel its superficiality, its lack of wholesomeness and strength—a reflection of the court life of the period." Martel went on to embrace the distinction between feminine and masculine movement that Shawn had defined, pushed for more male teachers, and claimed that dance was men's "natural heritage."[70]

In March of the following year the New Dance League sponsored a second (and final) Men in the Dance program featuring a greater variety of dance, including African dancers (led by Momodu Johnson, who would choreograph *Bassa Moona* for the Federal Theatre Project in December 1936), the white jazz dancer Roger Pryor Dodge, the Russian ballet dancer Vladimir Valentinoff, and a final section by modern dancers, headed by Charles Weidman and José Limón. The variety of dance styles illustrated the necessity of grouping all men dancers together for the unified cause of promoting dance as a career for men. Female dancers could afford to maintain a righteous distinction between ballet and modern dance (and even between the different groups within modern dance); male dancers recognized the bigger social barriers and, on these two occasions at least, overlooked aesthetic battles.

John Martin deemed that the thrilling opening of the 1936 performance by the African dancers "made what followed seem a bit pale and lifeless in spots."[71] Martin's comment reinforced the trend among male dancers and critics to plunder ethnic and racial stereotypes for models of masculine movement and imagery in dance. Such models played on preconceptions about these societies' closeness to nature and sex and reinforced the association of heterosexuality with masculine movement.[72] Reviewers often praised José Limón, of Spanish, Mexican, and Native American heritage, for his virility, and Limón took up the cause, writing an article in *Dance Magazine* in 1948 on "The Virile Dance."[73] The stories of heterosexual romance in Asadata Dafora's dance dramas also abetted common stereotypes of the primal sexuality of African and African American men. Perhaps believing that these men would add manliness to the cause, Martin praised the inclusion of black male dancers in the 1936 Men in the Dance concert.

But the leading modern dance companies that included men at this time did not regularly employ any African American men, nor were portrayals of Africans by white male dancers common. Native Americans, however, held particular appeal for white male dancers, especially Shawn and Lester Horton, the leading modern dancer in Los Angeles. They both extolled the sacredness of dance in Native American traditions, and Shawn promoted the prominence of men in Native American dances to support his view of dance as a natural manly function. Shawn and Horton, like Martha Graham, also upheld Native American dance as the basis for any American concert dance. In a 1929 production of his *Hiawatha,* Horton wrote in the program notes that "one of the purposes of the production . . . is to inculcate in the minds of young Americans a sense of duty to the original owners of their country."[74] Especially for Horton, celebrating Native American dance combined interest in creating a new American art form of concert dance and a political concern for groups ignored or discriminated against in social policy.

Shawn had a decidedly different political bent. He was more conservative than other modern dancers, and his definition of an American pioneer barred women from the role just as Graham and Humphrey were seizing it. As the "ideal type of young representative American manhood," for Shawn a pioneer embodied fortitude, athleticism, outdoor living, and entrepreneurial spirit.[75] The young men in Shawn's troupe were self-sufficient (including financially), responsible, and active. Shawn and His Men Dancers even incorporated, sharing ownership of two cars, costumes, and sets and splitting profits from the tours. Their robust independence and dynamism was a rebuttal to Depression-era resignation and governmental assistance — and a reinstatement of the leadership of men.

Shawn's social conservatism mirrored his political conservatism, which

FIGURE 4.3. *The Humphrey-Weidman Group in* American Saga. *Charles Weidman is in front of José Limón and Bill Matons. (Jerome Robbins Dance Division, The New York Public Library for the Performing Arts, Astor, Lenox and Tilden Foundations)*

was at odds with the widespread embrace of Communism and socialism at this time. Despite this, Shawn cultivated a populist basis for his fame. An apparent draft of a press release declared that, given his Kansas City birth and Denver upbringing, "no beginning could have been purer U.S.A. — just as his consequent career and entire personality is of the flavor of the hardy and staunchly patriotic early American pioneer."[76] Horton, too, acclaimed his childhood in small-town Indiana, and Weidman publicized his growing up in Lincoln, Nebraska, and choreographed some of his most successful Americana works based on his family, including *On My Mother's Side* (1940) and *And Daddy Was a Fireman* (1943). Weidman's all-male 1936 *American Saga* best combined his midwestern roots with an attention to American manliness (see figure 4.3). Re-creating the tale of Paul Bunyan, *American Saga* yoked the story of America to a husky lumberjack of the Great Lakes and Pacific Northwest.

Shawn did not rest on paeans to midwestern roots, however. He claimed that he brought the new American dance to the "hinterland of the States," where intense prejudice still existed against male dancers and against dance as an art form.[77] In a 1934 interview he chastised New York artists for their elitist attitude, claiming that "New York is not as American as even other big cities," and announced that his group intended to appeal to real Americans elsewhere.[78] The dances created from the back-breaking outdoor labor at Jacob's Pillow "have a quality of verity about them," Shawn argued, "that convinces audiences out in Texas and Montana and Wyoming."[79] Reviewers around the country picked up on this populist appeal and praised Shawn for it. A writer in the *Dallas Times Herald* in 1937 commended Shawn for shunning "the glib way of the high-pressured press agent," organizing his own tours, and demonstrating tenacity in his annual long winter tours throughout the United States. "His business has been to dance, and to dance, he has not been ashamed to appear in obscure halls, school auditoriums and many strange and humble places."[80] Walter Terry, Shawn's champion, named the populist appeal of Shawn's dance as his greatest feat: "[H]e brings the most understandable art to the greatest number of people."[81]

Shawn's populism contained a disavowal of modernist principles embraced by women modern dancers. A high point of his *O, Libertad!: An American Saga in Three Acts* (1937) was "Depression," of which the first part, "Modernism," featured Shawn as "a hag in robes, ringlets and a frightening mask." One reviewer caught the parody, calling it "a pitiless burlesque of the Martha Graham manner, a courageous step that made her followers gasp and sent more rational observers of the dance into hilarity."[82] Shawn responded to "Modernism" with "Recovery—Credo," his own autobiography in dance form. "Credo's" plunges, extended arm movements, and leaps swallowed the bent-over, grave, and insistent stamping of the previous "Modernism." Lester Horton also poked fun at the earnestness of women modern dancers in his *Flight from Reality* (1936), about which a reviewer wrote: "[T]he sterile isolation of the bloodless aestete [*sic*] is lampooned in delicate satire that brought long continued applause."[83] Performing to audiences outside New York City, Shawn and Horton exposed the elitism of the New York moderns, but they could also risk parody of women because of their sanctioned place as white men within society and traditions of art.

Shawn's populist appeal confirmed his idealization of art as best realized by an elite group of white gay men, and *Kinetic Molpai,* which ended *O, Libertad!*'s final section, "The Future" (but which was often performed separately), relayed this idea.[84] Shawn drew on the work of Gilbert Murray, author of *The Classical Tradition in Poetry,* who described the Molpê (the singular form of Molpai) as an ancient Greek art form that included poetry, singing, drama, and rhythmic movement, but "in its essence it was only the yearning of the whole dumb body to express that emotion for which words and harps and singing were not enough."[85] *Kinetic Molpai* began with Shawn's entering and circling the stage with pounding steps, and his role as leader shaped the narrative of the piece. The piece climbed to a crescendo with men whirling in the section "Surge," creating a wavy fugue with four alternating lines, falling to the floor and rising, and repeating the pattern in side motions in three lines. In a dramatic depletion of the frenzy, the dancers dived to the floor and formed a circle, each head to another's feet, as bodily links in a circular chain. Into this calm the leader came forth from offstage, reviving the men. Holding onto one man's arm, he ran around the circle, successively pulling up all the men and creating a simple but dramatic explosion of energy (see figure 4.4). The finale, "Apotheosis," moved to a waltz beat and featured big balletic steps of tour jetés, arabesques, and even a set of fouetté turns for Shawn. Shawn finished *Kinetic Molpai* with a fierce run forward to the audience in a straight line spanning the stage, a drop to the knees, and broad side arms that pointed to center stage. He stood there, regal, arms stretched upward and then sideways, as if in an embrace of the kneeling men.

Kinetic Molpai melded masculine movement and Greek heroism to form a triumphant vision of "the Athletic Art of the Dance as a field of creative endeavors for the American man," "with the athlete, the artist, the philosopher combined in one man—the dancer."[86] And Shawn envisioned himself as that dancer. His idealistic, even egotistic, vision sold in small towns across America where the economic hard times of the Depression had corroded hope. In a crisis of American manhood, where men lost jobs more often than women did, suffered from not being the breadwinner for the

FIGURE 4.4. *Shawn and His Men Dancers in* Kinetic Molpai. *Photograph by Shapiro Studio. (Jerome Robbins Dance Division, The New York Public Library for the Performing Arts, Astor, Lenox and Tilden Foundations)*

family, and witnessed women successfully obtaining jobs, the heroic masculinity embodied by Shawn and His Men Dancers soothed their wounded spirits. Even if the present was a time of struggle, the hope for the future of America lay in its kinetic, heroic men.

But Shawn devised very little new movement, relying instead on balletic steps and pantomimic gestures, and conceived of art in romantic terms in which a small cohort of talented men enlightened rural townspeople. In many ways Shawn's career was a reversal of the path of the white women and African American men and women in modern dance who fought against social conventions and prejudices in creating difficult, confrontational, and inventive dance. While these dancers challenged ideals of femininity and blackness, Shawn recycled movement with little ingenuity and cultivated a group of white gay men to define his sense of artistry. His reification of heroic masculinity may have upset stereotypes of homosexuality (particularly for those who knew or suspected Shawn was gay), but it also reaffirmed the dominance of white men. Shawn recognized the paradoxical place he had in modern dance by the end of the 1930s, when he began to complain that he not received enough credit for nurturing Martha Graham, Doris Humphrey, and Charles Weidman, by then the acknowledged innovators who had trained at Denishawn.[87] This was another attempt to gain artistic sanction for his dances that most critics were reluctant to give.

What Shawn received consistent praise for was his promotion of men in dance. His social standing as a white gay man—even a closeted one—marked his contribution to dance modernism more than his movement ideas. Shawn and other gay men found in modern dance a way to both display and conceal their circumscribed lives and, in so doing, further substantiated the coded association of the arts with male homosexuality. The intertwining of bohemian and artistic enclaves with gay male urban culture in New York's Greenwich Village and Harlem in the early part of the twentieth century encouraged sexual experimentation, eccentricity, and flaunting of norms, characteristics often taken as indications of artistic talent and originality, especially within a modernism that celebrated breaks with tradition and the uniqueness of individual expression. In this atmosphere gay men may have been less intimidated by the stigma of effeminacy assigned to the arts, more inclined to pursue their artistic proclivities, and more likely to benefit from friendships with other gay men (in the 1940s, Shawn heavily promoted Mumaw's solo career, and Weidman advanced his new lover, Peter Hamilton, over older members of his company).[88] In general, artists tolerated difference, and once gay men filtered into the arts, other gay men followed. In a society that criminalized homosexual acts, the arts provided a place of relative comfort, acceptance, and community.

While all the arts depended on expressiveness, the performing arts offered a way to live and embody that expression, even if for transient moments on stage.[89] The stage liberated possibilities because of its delimited, alternative, artificial status. And for people living secretive or coded lives, a performance gave them center stage and rapt attention. In camp and female impersonation, performances allowed gay men to flout the social conventions of the day and, especially, expose the instability of gender and sexual categories that defined their lives. Drag queens symbolized the most threatening representation of the social stigma of homosexuality—choosing men as sexual partners *and* a wholesale (if playful) adoption of a female persona—and thus often suffered condemnation from both the gay community and the heterosexual one.[90] Gay men in the performing arts may have received the same satisfaction from role-playing on the stage, and yet they could more easily escape the stigma associated with drag queens; the highbrow status of art shielded them.

In the 1930s white gay men succeeded in modern dance due to the strategy Shawn devised to heighten virility and thereby diminish the perceived threat of homosexuality. Masculine movement suited both male and female modern dancers' vision of a new American art form and operated in a variety of ways: as an example of America's potency; as a sign of essential differences between men and women; and as an ideal of homosexual love between men. Shawn's choreographic proclivities for nearly nude male bodies nourished the need for symbols of vigor during the Great Depression, and the attention to bodies may have attracted gay men to dance over other genres of art. Even in their small numbers, men helped sanction modern dance as a high art form—and eventually assumed the helm.

5 : organizing dance

Ted Shawn once remarked to Walter Terry, half jokingly, that he was "probably the only living American who thought Herbert Hoover was our greatest president."[1] More likely, he was the only person in the dance world who held any respect for Hoover. For some radical modern dancers, even Franklin D. Roosevelt did not push society far enough to the left. Modern dancers walked picket lines, formed associations, choreographed political statements, held technique classes that were then followed by classes on social and political theories, and appealed to the government to change policies about the arts and about issues that had nothing to do with the arts at all. The political causes in which modern dancers were involved, the kinds and purposes of organizations they formed, and their dealings with the federal government all illustrate their activism. Political causes attracted modern dancers, most notably in the battle against Franco's regime in Spain beginning in 1936, but also in protests against war and fascism in general. Organizations ran the gamut from a repertory theater of different companies to dancers' unions and, most conspicuously, a National Dance Congress in 1936. In the mid-1930s the Federal Theatre and Dance Projects of the WPA initiated formal government interaction with, and aid to, modern dancers for the first time. Unlike many modernist artists who divorced their aesthetic revolution from political action, modern dancers designed a political presence and incorporated political ideals into their artistic revolt.[2]

The political thrust of modern dancers encompassed theories of government as well as the weaving of modern dance into institutions such as colleges and universities. As a new art form, modern dance needed funds, some kind of network to support its endurance and enhancement, and legitimation—which men dancers argued that they added. In 1930, when the critic Margaret Gage praised "the communal presentation of idea" that modern dance offered, she did not reckon with the many forces that had to happen offstage for that presentation to occur onstage. Writ large, the qualification that Doris Humphrey added to Gage's belief—that is, the tension between individual expressiveness and group action—often stood as an obstacle in institutionalizing the movement. Modernists in other genres fell back on established institutions and distributive networks even though they were presenting aesthetic challenges in their works. Painters had art galleries and museums, including the Museum of Modern Art established in 1929; writers published their work in a flurry of new magazines like the *New Yorker,* begun in 1925; musicians and theatrical workers confronted similar problems of expense in putting on performances but had a range of options, including smaller venues and commercial possibilities. While modern dancers occasionally choreographed for vaudeville, variety, and Broadway shows, the art form eluded commodification. Combined with the marginal social status of the people involved, modern dance's tussle with politics and institutions contributed to its cleaving to the rim of the arts and society. In its conjunction of social, governmental, and institutional politics, modern dance gave American modernism its radical edge.[3]

In the late 1920s modern dancers' confrontational stance against ballet encompassed a class attack against elitism in the arts. As dance historian Linda Tomko has shown, humanist concerns drove aesthetic dance in the Progressive Era, so that settlement workers and dance teachers sought to include as many people as possible in classes and performances. The politics of modern dance was rooted in this tradition. Children of eastern European Jewish immigrants living on the Lower East Side of Manhattan—Helen Tamiris, Anna Sokolow, Sophie Maslow, Edith Segal, Miriam Blecher, Lily Mehlman, Lillian Shapero, Nadia Chilkovsky, Fanya Geltman—received their first dance training at Henry Street Settlement House and first performance experience in productions at the Neighborhood Playhouse.[4] From initial classes at Henry Street, daughters of Jewish immigrants found their way to classes by Graham, Humphrey, and others, and then into their companies. These women led the way in choreographing and dancing political statements and prodded other modern dancers to be responsive to the realities of employment, funding of the arts, class struggles, and the need for social change. Helen Tamiris worked effortlessly to group dancers together

FIGURE 5.1. *Tamiris's Group. (Jerome Robbins Dance Division, The New York Public Library for the Performing Arts, Astor, Lenox and Tilden Foundations)*

in various organizations; Anna Sokolow choreographed fluid statements as powerful in their politics as their artistry. With the exception of Sokolow, heralded for her choreographic talent, and Jane Dudley, who came from a middle-class Protestant background and also contributed to the infusion of politics in modern dance, Tamiris and other Jewish women from the Lower East Side were the political leaders of the modern dance movement without being considered its most talented progenitors. Their status in the dance world in the 1930s, and particularly their elision from dance history until recently, reveals the class dynamics at play in the formation of modern dance as a new art form.[5]

In the late 1920s and 1930s radical political organizations embraced dance in the effort to use culture and art to serve working-class battles for better wages, conditions, and recognition. In 1930 Edith Segal, born on the Lower East Side to Russian Jewish parents and trained in dance at Henry Street, choreographed *The Belt Goes Red* for the Lenin Memorial sponsored by the Communist Party at Madison Square Garden. Re-creating an assembly line with dancers in "stiff, straight postures" representing the machine, the dance ended triumphantly as the dancers overtook the machine, covering it with a red cloth. "They took it because they had built it," Segal declared.[6] Segal was a mainstay in New York Communist Party functions in the 1920s and 1930s, with her Red Dancers group performing in various pageants. She also taught at Kinderland, a camp in Dutchess County devoted to fusing secular Jewish culture with radical politics.[7] Back in New York, Segal worked with Lily Mehlman and Nadia Chilkovsky at the New York Workers International Relief, offering dance classes to workers for ten cents, and Mehlman led the International Workers Organization Dance Group. Workers danced, as the dance scholar Ellen Graff has shown.[8]

Out of this interaction between dance and radical politics the Workers Dance League and the New Dance Group emerged in 1932 with the more specific intention to blend the aesthetics of modern dance with an adherence to political goals that went beyond Party propaganda. In the wake of the death of Harry Simms, a young union organizer who was shot and killed by the police in New Jersey in 1932, dancers who marched in a parade commemorating his death decided to create the New Dance Group. "The philosophy we agreed on was to provide dance instruction for everybody, for the masses," recalled Chilkovsky, a founding member.[9] From Communist Party functions Segal, Chilkovsky, Anna Sokolow, and Miriam Blecher formed the Workers Dance League at a *Daily Worker*–sponsored May Day celebration and Recognition Rally of the Friends of the Soviet Union at the Bronx Coliseum in 1932. They planned to provide an umbrella organization for different performing troupes in order to increase communication among groups and create a larger place for dance within workers' movements, with the goal of using "dance as a weapon in the class struggle."[10]

In the subject matter of dances and in the political causes they supported, members of the Workers Dance League and the New Dance Group concentrated on the plight of workers. Particular kinds of movement enforced that theme. A photograph of Tamiris and her group in *Revolutionary March* (1929) best captured the movement used in these instigative dances. The dancers

FIGURE 5.2. Revolutionary March *by Tamiris. Photograph by Soichi Sunami. (Jerome Robbins Dance Division, The New York Public Library for the Performing Arts, Astor, Lenox and Tilden Foundations)*

lunged deeply, feet planted to the floor as if nothing could force them to move. Hard, straight, fisted arms pierced the air, shooting upward and diagonally. With heads lifted and chests full, they were defiant (see figure 5.2). These stark movements (often in agit-prop style), the overt use of red in costumes and sets, and a revolutionary narrative filled the Communist- and socialist-inspired dances. But neither the theme of workers' rights nor the forceful movements were that different from those of modern dancers not closely associated with radical political movements. "Martha Graham's technique is eminently fitted for working class motifs," a writer for the *Daily Worker* confirmed.[11] And both Graham and Humphrey choreographed the theme of workers' rights. In the 1929 *The Life of the Bee,* Humphrey considered the relationship between a leader and a horde; Graham's *Immigrant,* composed in 1928, had two sections, "Steerage" followed by "Strike." In the late 1920s and early 1930s most modern dancers advocated the rights of workers in showing the inequality of hierarchical factory systems, the divisions in society it fostered, and the dehumanizing effects of routinized labor. In theme and technique, class struggles figured prominently in shaping the new art form.

Although there was sympathy for workers' causes among most modern dancers, differences remained and festered. Nadia Chilkovsky, writing under the pseudonym Nell Anyon in *New Theatre,* disparaged Humphrey's *The Life of the Bee,* saying, "American dancers consider their art as above their actual lives. Thus we have dance of 'the life of the bee' and none of the lives of working men."[12] In periodicals such as *New Masses, Daily Worker,* and *New Theatre,* critics and dancers waged a battle over "revolutionary" versus "bourgeois" modern dance that showed the extent to which political ideals were shaping the art form. Attacking modern dance as "steeped in pessimism, mysticism, exoticism, diversified abstractions, and other flights from reality" (referring to Graham, Humphrey, and others), Chilkovsky and other revolutionary dancers and critics aligned themselves with Communist Party policy that art "must come from the collective spirit of the masses" and promote a revolutionary class struggle.[13] Even in recognizing the appropriateness of Graham's technique for "working class motifs," the *Daily Worker* went on to criticize Graham: "It is unfortunate that Martha Graham herself misuses [the technique] for religious ideas, serving the needs of the decadent bourgeoisie."[14]

One subject revolutionary dancers embraced was the fight for racial justice. The Workers Dance League concert at the Brooklyn Academy in 1934 showcased a variety of dance groups, including the Modern Negro Dance Group, and advertised a talk by Asadata Dafora on "The Negro Dance" a few months before Dafora became famous through *Kykunkor.*[15] Beyond content such as racial justice, revolutionary dancers believed they could meld content and form for political purpose. Jane Dudley, a member of the New Dance Group who later joined Martha Graham's group, linked thematic attention to workers to form, advocating "mass dance" in an article for *New Theatre* in December 1934. With large groups of lay dancers, Dudley began with simple exercises such as walking and moving in particular directions together, in unison: "[T]he unity of every one's movement should be worked for." Then she described a possible dance entitled "Strike," with three groups divided as picketers, militia, and workers.[16] Here, form and content merged in the ideal revolutionary art: workers—untrained dancers —dancing in a piece about workers' struggle using simple, accessible movements and triumphing in a class revolution.

The revolutionary dancers' movement never achieved the unity, accessibility, and triumph for which its members clamored. Acrimonious debates among radical dancers filled the pages of leftist periodicals. Michael Gold of *Daily Worker* and Edna Ocko, who wrote predominantly in *New Theatre* and *New Masses,* fought over the progress of the revolutionary dance movement and the role of criticism from 1933 to 1935. Gold attacked the 1934 Workers Dance League Festival for its depressing subject matter and especially its lack of inspiring dancing. Ocko defended the festival and the movement as progressing solidly toward a powerful revolutionary art form that "takes time" and castigated Gold to "[g]ive them a chance."[17] The use of bourgeois technique also drew passionate opinions from critics in the radical publications. Some, like Ocko, believed that the technique of Graham and others could be adapted to suit revolutionary purposes. Others, like Gold, felt that the bourgeois technique ruined any chance of creating an effective workers' art. Harry Elion in *New Theatre* supported Gold's view: "The workers' dance must free itself from this influence [bourgeois technique] and create a dance form that is expressive of the workers' needs. This form will come as a result of the revolutionary content, providing the dancers free themselves from the idea that all that has to be done is to give the bourgeois dance working class content."[18] Elion expressed the problem as the chicken-and-egg debate: which came first, content or form? Revolutionary dancers believed that political content would lead them to a more truly political form. Most modern dancers and critics, though, accepted the interaction between revolutionary and bourgeois dancers' concerns, without getting caught up in the ideological purity of their positions. Critics Paul Douglas of *New Theatre* and Horace Gregory of *New Masses* praised Tamiris as the dancer who most successfully combined form and content and utilized bourgeois technique for revolutionary purposes.[19] Ocko, however, even challenged Tamiris on this, accusing her of changing a dance to "play down" to a workers' audience. Tamiris retorted hotly that she had made a technical change in *Conflict* that "in no way affected the basic ideology of the composition—and certainly was not dictated by a desire to insult the intelligence of a workers' audience by 'playing down' to it."[20] Rarely were definitions and issues agreed upon even amongst those critics and dancers who advocated a revolutionary purpose for modern dance.[21]

This vociferousness apparently did not inspire the same passion in audiences. "We had major problems in trade unions when we danced. They all loved tap dancing, and here we came in our rags, in our safety pins, always being starving workers, and the real starving workers wanted ballet dancers in tutus, or tap dancers," Ocko remembered.[22] The combination of Communist politics and modern dance never attracted a substantial following among workers. Despite the failure of that goal of many of the revolutionary dancers, the practical, philosophical, and political concerns of workers in fact shaped modern dance. Michael Denning argues that the interaction of three groups brought about an incorporation of socialist and Communist ideas in American culture during this period. Moderns conveyed formal innovations; European émigrés contributed a fuller treatment of Marxist ideas about art and culture; and plebeians brought to the arts their personal experiences as second generation immigrants.[23] Modern dance brought together all these groups. The formal innovations of moderns like Graham and Humphrey mixed with the collectivist ideas of German dancers Mary Wigman and Hanya Holm and the working class immigrant backgrounds of Segal and Tamiris. The dissension among these groups demonstrated the extent to which they were decidedly interconnected. Particularly in the fledgling years, revolutionary dancers brought modern dance attention—in classes, audiences, and periodicals. Dancers performed with Graham or took classes with Humphrey and *also* participated in the Workers Dance League and New Dance Group. The currents fed off each other and, in their distinctions and their conflict, infused modern dance with passionate purpose. Early modern dancers debated class issues in America, questioning who gets to participate most fully in art and society.

In 1934 the modern dance student Helen Priest Rogers wrote in her notes from a course by Louis Horst that "the modern dance has been revolutionary but the revolution is over. The modern dance must have form now."[24] Horst was a longtime advocate of musical and choreographic structure, but the push for form by the mid-1930s went beyond the studio and the stage. In 1934 Horst helped start a periodical devoted to modern dance, *Dance Observer,* that became the house organ of modern dance. Featuring reviews of dance concerts around the country, interviews with leading dancers, and ongoing debates, *Dance Observer* recorded the growing flourish of groups and organizations that created the surge of a movement. Much of this energy was not specifically political. The inchoate institutionalization gave a new solidity to modern dance that eventually marked a shift away from radical politics.

Dance Observer capitalized on the organizing momentum that started with the Dance Repertory Theatre, Tamiris's idea to have the leading modern dancers rent a theater for a week and perform on alternating nights, avoiding competition for audiences, theaters, dates, and Louis Horst's talents as accompanist. In 1930 Tamiris, Doris Humphrey, Charles Weidman, and Martha Graham performed; in 1931 Agnes de Mille joined them. But the Dance Repertory Theatre did not last beyond that season. It espoused no overt political goals; its existence grew from the recognition that in the face of intractable financial difficulties modern dancers would be more likely to receive artistic legitimacy together. Writing in 1938, John Martin of the *New York Times* remarked that the Dance Repertory Theatre failed because it was a cooperative movement without any authority.[25] With no overarching political goals or commitment to work together, dancers maintained a strict adherence to their individual artistic agendas—a dilemma seared into the foundation of the art form.

Occasional political causes in the early 1930s gained the support of all modern dancers, however. Circumventing the New York state blue laws that forbade any entertainment on Sunday, including "cock fighting, bearbaiting and boxing with or without gloves," was one of them.[26] Dancers wanted to take to the stages on Sundays because they could rent theaters more cheaply then than on popular weekend nights. Theater owners, too, could earn a bit more money, so they allowed dancers to rename their performances "sacred concerts."[27] But dancers had to contend with moral guardians, organized as the Sabbath League, who roused the police to badger them. Despite the fact that more salacious dancing arguably occurred in other venues such as burlesque theaters and nightclubs, concert dancers were an easier target and did not have the money to pay off the police.[28] Dancers banded together as the Concert Dancers' League to fight the blue laws and won a permit in 1932 for "concert and recital dances on Sunday after 2:00 p.m. if authorized by local authorities."[29] The league then quickly dissolved.

A more noteworthy and longstanding grouping of the modern dancers occurred at the Bennington Summer School of the Dance in Vermont. Beginning in 1934 Bennington College hosted influential summer programs that brought together the New York leaders with young women from around the country. Beyond the summer program, the formation of the college itself, which opened to students in the fall of 1932, fused the ideals of modern dance and changing opportunities for women in a college setting. Bennington solidified this trend begun in 1914 when Bird Larsen formed the first dance program at Barnard College. A few years later Margaret H'Doubler finished her master's degree at Teachers College of Columbia University and returned to the University of Wisconsin, where she established the first dance major in 1926. In April 1930 the National Society of Directors of Physical Education for Women devoted their entire meeting to dance; in 1931 the larger American Physical Education Association created a National Section on Dance; in 1932 Barnard College hosted a college dance symposium that included representatives from Barnard, New York University, Smith, Vassar, and Wellesley. Dance educators from the University of Michigan, Wayne University, Michigan State, Western State, and Kellogg School of Physical Education gathered at the University of Michigan the same year. These events augured the boom of modern dance in college physical education departments in the 1930s.[30]

The founding of Bennington College perpetuated the association of women with dance and other arts that had grown out of the belief that artistic interests produced cultured girls and women. But Bennington established women as practitioners of the arts rather than just amateurs or patrons. When discussions began among Bennington's founders in the 1920s about starting a new college, more women than ever were attending institutions of higher education.[31] The founders pondered questions of whether women should be educated in single-sex or coeducational institutions, eventually agreeing that the pastoral location provided an ideal setting for

women students as a means of getting away from urban settings, probably an attempt to decrease the sexual temptations young women may have
faced in a city. But the founders also wanted to implement new educational ideas, especially those of the American philosopher John Dewey, who
favored "learning by doing" and advocated experiential methods rather
than rote memorization. Robert Leigh, the first president of Bennington,
who had taught at progressive Reed College and originally wanted both
men and women at Bennington, explained the decision to try this approach
in a new women's college: "[P]arents would be less willing to take risks
with their sons' educations than with their daughters'."[32] Low societal expectations of educated women freed the Bennington founders to institute
an experimental educational model. Bennington began with four divisions
(arts, literature, science, and social studies), required no entrance exam, and
admitted students primarily on the basis of recommendations and school
record. The students who came to Bennington, white women from afflu-
ent, mostly New England Protestant families, reflected that part of the
population with the most opportunities to take advantage of these aims.[33]
Ultimately, Bennington offered structured rebellion and experimentation
within its relatively loose educational format.

Modern dance was a fundamental part of this mission and a part of
Bennington's physical education curriculum from its first semester. In the
second year of the college, 1933–34, dance so dominated the physical education department that the director of sports left, the president hired a second dance teacher, and the initial dance teacher, Martha Hill, set up a trial
dance major.[34] The success of the modern dance program at Bennington
prompted Hill to suggest that the college facilities be utilized in the summer for a school specifically for modern dance. Blossoming under the inspiration of Hill and the administrative proficiency of Mary Jo Shelly, a
prominent physical educator of dance at Columbia University, Bennington
Summer School of the Dance took over the campus in the summers from
1934 to 1938.[35] The summer school offered classes, lectures, workshops, and
performances to modern dance students from around the country. In its
first summer, 103 students—all women—attended, ranging in age from fifteen to forty-nine and representing twenty-six states, the District of Columbia, Canada, and Spain. Two-thirds were teachers, many of them university
and college physical education teachers who came to learn the fundamen-

tals of modern dance. The total number of students grew over the next four summers, reaching a high of 180 in 1938. Certain characteristics prevailed throughout the first five years of the program: there were almost no male students enrolled (the highest number was in 1936, when Charles Weidman offered a Men's Workshop that had eleven participants, six of whom were in his New York performing group); teachers outnumbered students aiming for a stage career; only one African American woman attended (and many considered her to be passing as white); and, while all of the states were represented, the vast majority of students came from the East (50 percent) and the Midwest (35 percent).[36]

Students took classes with the New York leaders of modern dance: Martha Graham, Doris Humphrey, Charles Weidman, and Hanya Holm, but not Helen Tamiris. Beginning in 1935 the summer sessions ended with performances, which featured one group per year for the first three years (Graham's in 1935, Humphrey-Weidman's in 1936, and Holm's in 1937). This tradition culminated in a large production of all three groups in 1938, before the summer school relocated to Mills College in California the following year. Some summer school students performed as adjuncts to the companies for the Bennington festivals, but the leading dancer-choreographers primarily seized the opportunity to choreograph for their own groups, away from the constant hassles and financial struggles of New York.

The bucolic and restful atmosphere beckoned, occasional picnics occurred, and classes sometimes took place on the rolling lawns, but people mostly remember dancing *all* the time. "After the first few days our muscles were so sore we went up and down the stairs on our bottoms," as the Bennington student Elizabeth Bloomer (better known as Betty Ford) put it.[37] Students were up at 8:00 A.M. for a dance history or criticism class taught by John Martin, the *New York Times* dance critic. Classes in technique, composition, music for dance, and production followed, with rehearsals for performances squeezed into free moments. "You slept dance, you ate dance, you drank dance," a Bennington participant explained.[38]

Out of Bennington grew the "gymnasium circuit," the label given for the touring routes of modern dancers in the mid- and late 1930s. University and college gymnasiums housed many of the first modern dance concerts around the country, and most often the Bennington Summer School of the Dance provided the connection. Humphrey-Weidman toured in January

FIGURE 5.3. *Doris Humphrey and students at Bennington Summer School of the Dance. Humphrey is seated, center, looking toward the camera. (Jerome Robbins Dance Division, The New York Public Library for the Performing Arts, Astor, Lenox and Tilden Foundations)*

1935; Helen Tamiris gave concerts in the Midwest in 1936; Hanya Holm and Group traveled across the country performing in 1936; Graham gave a solo transcontinental tour in 1936 followed by a tour with her group the following year; and out of the 140 venues where Shawn and His Men Dancers had appeared in two years of touring in the mid-1930s, 114 were associated with higher education—thirty-eight state teachers' colleges, seventy-two universities and colleges, and four teachers' conventions.[39] At the summer school session at Mills College in 1939, Humphrey ruefully conceded the importance of the "despised physical education department": "[It] is something like a combination of a circus and a drugstore. It keeps you healthy and occasionally provides amusement."[40]

Humphrey's comment betrayed modern dancers' worry about relying on gym teachers, who might not appreciate the difference between volleyball and dance, to be responsible for disseminating their nascent creation. Art existed far from sweaty athletes and competitive physical exertion, Humphrey believed, formulating another distinction critical to placing modern dance within traditions of high art. But university and college physical education departments created a vital base for modern dance. Women physical educators sustained the New York moderns—teaching adherents, creating audiences, and providing needed salaries with performance and class fees. Modern dance, in turn, suited the demands of physical educators. Deemed an appropriate option of physical exercise for women, modern dance had intellectual roots and a seriousness of purpose that university and college educators could uphold. At Bennington modern dance fit well the agenda set for women students, which emphasized the significance of the arts and aimed to develop individual initiative, creativity, and independence.

Despite the bringing together of the leaders of modern dance at Bennington, artistic collaborations rarely occurred there. Some Bennington participants remember that the "Graham crackers" (as Graham devotees were called) never spoke to Humphrey-Weidman dancers and that each group congregated under a particular tree, dividing the campus into camps under leafy fortresses.[41] Although the question remained as to how much collectivity the modern dance movement could sustain, political theories and ideas were present even at Bennington. The visits of husbands and boyfriends prompted some political talk. Leo Hurwitz, the husband of New Dance League member Jane Dudley, was an influential radical filmmaker who showed "Pie in the Sky," a 1934 film he directed with Elia Kazan that was "a satire on all the orthodoxies."[42] Some students wrapped tin foil into big balls to "send to Spain for the cause," in support of the democratic forces fighting against Franco's fascist regime. But the atmosphere at Bennington was more communal than political.[43] Dancers from the revolutionary branch of modern dance participated at Bennington if they were a part of the companies of Graham, Humphrey-Weidman, or Holm. Others most likely could not afford it. The absence of Tamiris and other revolutionary dancers, coupled with the appeal of modern dance to college educators, marked a move away from the earlier tie to working-class concerns.[44] In its communal rather than political spirit, Bennington provided needed structure through its teaching program and touring network but also inched the art form upward in its rise to the high end of the cultural spectrum.

Revolutionary and bourgeois dancers—and the ideas that concerned them—mingled at Bennington and merged in New York in the mid-1930s by rooting politics in things American. Changes in Communism contributed to the shift. In 1935 the Congress of the Communist International called for a Popular Front to combat the rise of fascism. Seeking to embolden Communist Parties within nations (and improve those nations' relations with the Soviet Union), the Popular Front took a broader approach to doctrinaire Communist policies. It fostered an Americanization of Communism with an emphasis on cultural questions and issues rather than Party policy and discipline. Echoing the Popular Front strategy, modern dancers with radical or proletarian sympathies moved from a revolutionary international emphasis to a cultural American one; the struggle between nations eventually eclipsed the struggle between classes.[45]

In this spirit the Workers Dance League renamed itself the New Dance League in 1935. The effort to re-create the organization and pronounce its difference as "New" meant taking the "Worker" out of the name. That year even the radical political devotee Nadia Chilkovsky admitted that the "Fundamentals of Class Struggles" course offered by the Workers Dance League (with one hour on economic theory and another hour on revolutionary culture) was "very poorly attended," though she reiterated the need for "mass dance."[46] Diminishing the association with Marxist-influenced politics, the New Dance League hoped "for a mass development of the American dance to its highest artistic and social level, for a dance movement that is against war, fascism, and censorship."[47] More significantly, however, the reformed group called for members "regardless of other political or artistic differences."[48] The new organization centered more narrowly around dance. No longer was political ideology the defining, agreed-upon principle, with dance as a means toward a political end. Now that line was being subtly shifted to make dance itself the primary priority.

Institutional support reflected this shift too, as the 92nd Street YM-YWHA emerged in the mid-1930s as the New York home of modern dance. Originally built in 1874 by a group of German Jewish philanthropists, the 92nd Street Y first offered English classes, vocational training, and only occasional cultural events. In 1934, under the new leadership of Dr. William Kolodney, the 92nd Street Y took on the role of a smaller home of the arts for the whole city to enjoy. Modern dance immediately took up residence. In 1935 a subscription series for dance concerts was started, and classes, lecture-demonstrations, and public interviews with famous dancers and choreographers soon followed. Dr. Kolodney explained the appeal of modern dance to the Jewish community: it fused "the intellectual and spiritual needs of that element of the population which found its recreation primarily in the world of ideas." Coinciding with the background and beliefs of many Jewish women involved in modern dance, the 92nd Street Y's program emphasized American cultural traditions primarily and Jewish ones only secondarily.[49] The rise of modern dance in the 1930s paralleled the change in its Jewish institutional homes: from Henry Street, the Jewish-founded community center in the midst of the tenements, to the 92nd Street Y, a predominantly cultural Jewish institution in a middle-class neighborhood. The Y's teaching opportunities, public forum, and affordable performing space literally meant survival for the nascent art form and placed it on par with longer-standing artistic genres.[50]

The 92nd Street Y's role as modern dance's headquarters was clear when it hosted the National Dance Congress in late May 1936. The congress included days of talks and nights of performances, with each night devoted to a kind of dance: folk, modern, ballet, experimental, and theater dancing. Fourteen hundred people attended; two hundred performed. Although criticized for its rushed organization, inadequate publicity, and New York City focus, the congress displayed a broad spectrum of dance. In addition to the variety of performances, lectures ranged from "The Economic Status of Dancers" to "The Museum as a Dance Center," "The Dance in Sweden," and Lenore Cox's "On a Few Aspects of Negro Dancing." A contemporary focus and an insistent purpose to improve the status of dance and dancers pervaded all the lectures and reflected the organization and leadership of modern dancers, including the activists Helen Tamiris, Anna Sokolow, Edna Ocko, and Miriam Blecher.[51]

In forming the congress dancers followed artists of other genres who were grouping together in congresses at the same time. In May 1935 the first National Writers Congress met; in February 1936 the first American Artists Congress convened in New York City and the first National Negro Congress met in Chicago. (In fact, the first National Negro Congress featured Edith Segal's *Black and White, Unite and Fight,* about workers' unity, and her *Southern Holiday,* about lynching. Two years later, Anna Sokolow performed at the second National Negro Congress in New York.)[52] Instead of joining explicitly political organizations, such as the cultural branches of the Communist Party, artists formed organizations defined by their art form or race and worked for the betterment of their status. Sometimes this goal included specific political issues. The Dance Congress supported policies against discrimination on the basis of race, color, or creed (and specifically encouraged African American dancers). It refused to endorse any organization believing in fascism, war, or censorship but stated that it would hold "no political affiliation at any time."[53] By this time most modern dancers had left behind strictly propagandist notions of using art only to relay a political message, but they still incorporated social relevance within their mission as artists.

Despite the generality of these political goals, two leading dance critics attacked the political activism they felt distorted the activities of the Dance Congress. John Martin of the *New York Times* and Margaret Lloyd of the *Christian Science Monitor* scolded the leftists, with Lloyd warning, "And if the left-wingers continue to run the whole show, as they did this one, they will only succeed in turning the remaining liberals into fascisti."[54] Battles often mixed differing political views with dance issues. Lloyd coyly stated that at a lecture entitled "Ballet Today," Anatole Chujoy, the lecturer, "was nearly mobbed by objections not always closely related to the subject."[55] The battle with ballet incorporated a variety of complaints. Ballet could be condemned as elitist and catering to wealthy patrons interested in escapist, fantastical flights from reality, but for some Communist sympathizers, the strong tradition and love of ballet by all levels of society in the Soviet Union complicated the condemnation of elitism. When Anna Sokolow traveled to the Soviet Union in 1934 and found only ballet offered, "she disapproved, of course, as any modern revolutionary dancer would." Sokolow's modern dance performances, however, "bewildered" Soviet audiences.[56] The popularity of ballet in the Soviet Union and Stalin's official ban of modernist influences from Russian art contributed to the heralding of modern dance by politically minded dancers under the Popular Front.

Broader definitions of political beliefs inspired by the Popular Front policy loosened up categories so that Communists and socialists could embrace those they condemned earlier. In modern dance this was most notable in the praise of Graham's new political awareness in the mid-1930s. The Americana subject matter of such dances as *Frontier* (1935) and *Chronicle* (1936), which was a consideration of war as catastrophe that ended with a "prelude to action" and a plea for unity, allowed Communist sympathizers to place Graham behind the banner of the Popular Front. In 1936 the *Daily Worker* alluded to Graham in this endorsement of contemporary modern dancers: "[A]ll outstanding modern dancers in America today, who for years had been championing the cause of abstract and pure art forms, have joined forces with progressive culture and elected to deal in dance terms with matters of social import."[57] Edna Ocko praised Graham's 1935 *Panorama* for its social commentary, but, still forceful on class issues, she also recognized that the concentration on Americanism overwhelmed radicalism. *Panorama*'s final movement, the "Popular Theme," "sought to remain too conscientiously within national confines. To feel, at this time, that a peoples' theme which has broad, universal implications must end on a distinctly national note is unprophetic, or else evasive."[58]

Almost all modern dancers, including Graham, coalesced in opposition to fascism that the Popular Front had begun in the mid-1930s. In late 1935 the Committee to Boycott the German Dance Festival formed to counteract the German government's International Dance Festival, an accompaniment to the Berlin Olympics in the summer of 1936. The boycott successfully stopped American dancers from participating. In a letter of March 1936, Graham decried the persecution of German artists and found it "impossible to identify [herself], by accepting the invitation, with the regime that has made such things possible." "Some of my concert group would not be welcome in Germany," she wrote, acknowledging the Jewish members of her company.[59] More politically active dancers went further than Graham in berating Mary Wigman and Rudolf von Laban, the innovators of modern dance in Germany. They did not view Wigman and von Laban as "persecuted," as Graham did, but saw them as willing organizers of the dance festival and supporters of the Nazi cause. Wigman's seeming complicity with Nazi policy prompted her protégé Hanya Holm to change the name of her New York school from the Mary Wigman School to the Hanya Holm School in November 1936.[60]

In 1937 the New Dance League joined with the educationally focused Dance Guild and the workers' rights–focused Dancers' Association to form the American Dance Association (ADA). Under a national name and identity, politically radical groups merged with others more devoted to dance education. One of the first acts of the ADA was to continue the fight against Nazism by condemning the German modern dancer Harold Kreutzberg for representing the Nazi government at the Paris Exposition in the summer of 1937. The ADA sent a telegram informing Kreutzberg of its resolution against fascism and lamenting his position as a representative of the German government, and the New York chapter of the ADA asked its members to boycott his performance.[61]

These political statements of the mid-1930s peaked in denunciations of the Franco regime in Spain. Joining writers, painters, and musicians, modern dancers performed in benefits to raise awareness and money for anti-Franco forces. The ADA sponsored two concerts entitled "Dances for Spain," from which a percentage of the proceeds went to the Medical Committee to Aid Spanish Democracy. Edna Ocko raised money for ambulances for Spain as head of the Dancers Committee of the Theater Arts Committee, which formed to aid victims of fascism. Instead of debating practical policy points, artists championed humanitarianism and highlighted the human destruction inevitable in war. Graham choreographed three solos—*Imperial Gesture* (1935), *Immediate Tragedy* (1937), and *Deep Song* (1937)—that portrayed grief over the loss of lives and individual freedom. Anna Sokolow's *Excerpts from a War Poem* (1937) contained no battle scenes or preaching, but its five sections, organized around lines from a poem by the Italian poet F. T. Martinetti, contrasted the heroics celebrated in the poem with the chaos, despair, and suffering caused by war. To the line "because it realizes the long dreamed of metalization of the human body," Sokolow choreographed a picture of physical contortion in the third section of the piece. Dancers moved spasmodically, crumpled by pain, frantic in chaos. A critic in *Dance Observer* praised the choreographic picture of distortion "in which human values are crushed by the very symbols which pretended to idealize those values," decreeing that Sokolow had created "a final stern and passionate indictment of the madness bred by fascism."[62]

Utilizing the formal abstraction and malleability of their art form, modern dancers gave a physical presentation of cruelty, suffering, and pain—weighty emotional topics that suited their gravity-laden, forceful technique. European fascism offered modern dancers a way to fuse content and form. In content, the dancers held up America and its version of democracy as the ideal by showing that fascism was nationalism gone awry; in form, they pulled earlier simple outlines of collective action into more abstract and personalized cries of protest. Radical political statements that highlighted class struggles faded as modern dance techniques and principles solidified and attention to nationalism grew in the volatile situation of world affairs.

Trumpeting America's democratic tradition was the political position that modern dancers melded most harmoniously with their modernist aesthetic principles.

The organizing spirit and political purpose of modern dance coalesced under the auspices of the federal government in the mid-1930s, a conjunction that added another layer of solidification to the art form. The $4.8 million appropriated for the WPA in early May 1935 included designations for four federal arts programs—Art, Music, Writers', and Theatre. Dance first landed in two places in the WPA: as a teaching activity in the Recreation Project, offering classes in social, folk, and square dancing in communities around the nation, and under the Theatre Project in theatrical productions that included concert dance. The "always embattled dancers," as they came to be called by Hallie Flanagan, the national director of the Federal Theatre Project, immediately demanded their own project.[63]

Although dance in the Recreation Project provoked complaints by local dance teachers who felt their business was being taken away by the free Recreation Project classes, the concert dance faction raised the far noisier ruckus. From the beginning of the Federal Theatre Project (FTP), concert dancers asked that dance be recognized as an independent art form worthy of its own project. Eventually, in January 1936, the New York City Municipal Theatre Project granted dance its independent status. The New York–based Dance Project lasted only a little over a year, from early 1936 to mid-1937, until dance lost its own bureaucratic structure and was folded back into the control of the New York City FTP. Its contentious year revealed the larger political battleground upon which modern dancers fought to expand and institutionalize their new art form.

The Dance Project gave concert dancers a regular paying job, a place in a larger organizational structure, and even a union to join. They were workers in their chosen profession. Previously paid only an average of $10 per performance (despite numerous hours of classes and rehearsals), now they received $23.86 per week regardless of whether they took class, rehearsed, or performed. Before the Dance Project, concert dancers had been involved in unions only by association with the Communist Party or in their own attempt to organize in late 1934, when Helen Tamiris put together the Dancers Union to find work for unemployed dancers in the newly formed

Civil Works Administration, the precursor to the WPA.[64] In the WPA, those workers not covered by other professional unions created the City Projects Council (CPC), devoted to protecting white-collar workers. Concert dancers received guidance and organizational support to argue for workers' rights —their own—for the first time.

They did so with zeal. Numerous issues angered the dancers on the project, but they united in the fight to oust the director, Don Oscar Becque, a dancer with ballet training and some choreographic experience but little repute. Becque's supposed incompetence was really due to the inefficiency endemic in this newly formed and new kind of bureaucracy. Delayed productions, continual budget cuts, and changing rules about personnel procedures were constant problems. In response, dancers walked picket lines outside his office shouting, "Our project's a wreck with Don Oscar Becque." Becque remembered that they threw desks out of the fourteenth-floor window of his office, and a record of Hallie Flanagan's daily memoranda included a typical complaint: "The dancers acting up again—Mr. Becque says he can't stand it."[65]

One rancorous controversy occurred over the auditioning of dancers. Because money came and went sporadically according to federal government subsidies and cuts, the hiring and firing of dancers caused most of the problems on the project. After initially hiring eighty-five dancers off the relief rolls in the spring of 1936, Flanagan and Becque instituted an audition policy and required those dancers already on the project to audition as well—opening up the possibility of their losing their jobs. Dancers erupted in protest. They interpreted the policy as a way to get rid of the political troublemakers on the project and felt it also gave Becque too much control. With guidance from the CPC, dancers picketed the New York City FTP offices and demanded meetings with Flanagan and Philip Barber, the New York City FTP director.[66]

Auditioning continued despite the protest, and Becque remained under fire throughout the fall of 1936 for that policy and many others. Dancers called for his removal; he, in turn, called for the removal of the choreographers Gluck-Sandor and Tamiris because of their supposedly insubordinate behavior. The disputes themselves also concerned political issues outside the dance world conflicts of audition policies and production delays. The dancers and choreographers employed on the project included many of

"Lookit, I'm paying 55¢ for standing room and a week ago I could have seen the same dancers on the picket line for nothing."

--Don Freeman

FIGURE 5.4. *Political cartoon by Don Freeman commenting on dancers and labor relations.* (Federal Theatre, *14 June 1937*)

those involved with the politically active Workers Dance League of the early 1930s and its later reincarnation, the New Dance League. Fanya Geltman, Nadia Chilkovsky, and Tamiris led the struggles against the Dance Project leadership, with training and goals from the revolutionary dance movement and the CPC.[67] Tamiris and Geltman, teamed as the "long and the short of it" because of Tamiris's height and Geltman's lack thereof, stormed Federal Theatre offices in Washington, D.C., and New York City demanding Becque's removal.[68] Geltman and Tamiris's political credentials coincided with those of most others on the project. Becque's perceived incompetency, on the other hand, probably came from his lack of radical political credentials rather than his inefficient management.[69] (A couple of years later, Becque wrote to Ted Shawn seeking fellowship with him in ostracized conservatism and hoping to gain his support in revealing the "palace intrigue" that had led to the ascendancy of Tamiris, Graham, and others.)[70]

Government attention to the arts at this time went beyond the WPA-sponsored projects and finally included dance. Martha Graham appeared at the White House in February 1937 for the first performance of dance there. That same year, two arts bills came before the House of Representatives: the first, in January, proposed an executive department of "Science, Art, and Literature" with an officer on the president's cabinet; the second, in August, more popular and feasible, asked for the establishment of a Bureau of Fine Arts with a commissioner to be appointed by the president and six directors to head divisions of theater, music, literature, graphic arts, architecture, and dance. Neither bill got very far, but the inclusion of dance in these bills demonstrated its rising status in the American arts. And it was modern dance, not ballet, that led the dance category. The modern dance–led American Dance Association claimed in February 1938 to be the "present headquarters of the dance division of the Federal Arts Commission," and Ruth St. Denis was recommended to head the proposed national division of "Dance and Allied Arts."[71]

The inclusion and prominence of modern dance in these legislative proposals and in the Federal Theatre Project gave it new legitimacy. The WPA promoted American art and artists, and modern dance was the kind of dance the government supported in the 1930s. This happened because of the political maneuvering and vocal protests of modern dancers themselves but also because modern dance was seen as the most significant dance form of the era. That legitimacy, however, also furthered racial divisions in dance and society: African American dancers were relegated to the Negro Unit of the FTP, housed at the Lafayette Theater in Harlem. Add Bates danced in one Dance Project performance, Charles Weidman's *Candide* in 1937. In late 1938 the possibility of a "Negro Dance Group" arose, and the Dance Audition Board, which included Tamiris and Humphrey, rated fifteen dancers, giving Edna Guy a B.[72] A Negro Dance Group never materialized, though, and final dance productions did not employ African American dancers. The government legitimation of modern dance thus extended the racial separation that defined its aesthetic principles and social composition.

By the end of the 1930s federal government support of the arts turned to criticism. The House Committee on Un-American Activities (HUAC), also known as the Dies Committee, attacked the WPA, accusing the Writers' Project and the Theatre Project of Communist infiltration. The outspoken, politically active dancers contributed to the radical image of the Theatre Project. Hallie Flanagan wrote to John Martin of the *New York Times* in January 1939 praising an article he had written that beseeched project dancers to contain their political stridency: "Your article in urging our young dancers not to confuse their politics with their pyrotechnics comes at a time when it may be enormously helpful."[73] These pleas, however, did not persuade the dancers still on the project to diminish their political advocacy. In 1939 Tamiris choreographed *Adelante,* a piece inspired by poetry written in Spain during the civil war; narrating a story about the execution of a peasant soldier, the dance ended "with a courageous, spirited, triumphal march of the peasantry."[74]

Tamiris's call to class revolution, though, was anomalous by the end of the 1930s. In fact, the steadfast commitment to class issues and political activism of Tamiris and other Jewish women from the Lower East Side pushed them from the forefront of the dance scene just as the first histories of modern dance began to be written. By the end of the 1930s Martha Graham, Doris Humphrey, Charles Weidman, and Hanya Holm were in place as the "Big Four," the sanctioned founders of modern dance. This grouping signaled the triumph of aesthetic over political principles. Although the divide between politics and artistry was never neat, the bourgeois branch of modern dance eventually trumped the revolutionary branch by the end of the 1930s because the revolutionary dancers were unsuccessful in upsetting the class structure of the high/low cultural hierarchy. The Big Four represented the most aesthetically minded dancers and choreographers and the least politically involved part of the movement.

The experience of dancers in unions in the late 1930s and early 1940s reveals the odd place to which their political activism had led them. In 1939 representatives from the American Guild of Musical Artists (AGMA), a union that primarily protected singers and instrumentalists in the opera and concert fields, attempted to organize concert dancers under its aegis. L. T. Carr, the union organizer, disclosed his plan for dance concerts: an AGMA closed shop, $45 per week for dancers during performing weeks (with extra pay for more than eight performances per week), $20 per week for thirty-five hours of rehearsal per week with overtime pay for additional rehearsals, and a ban on motor transport on tour in favor of railroads. These were the goals that dancers had sought for over a decade: to be recognized as professionals and to earn livable pay. Ballet dancers quickly joined AGMA, but modern dancers did not. Ballet companies had wealthy patrons, such as Lincoln Kirstein, and a place in institutions, such as opera houses; with ballet dancers, the union more often had someone on the other side of the bargaining table who had money to meet the demands of the AGMA contracts. Modern dancers, on the other hand, resisted AGMA representation. Editors of *Dance Observer* noted in October 1939 that the threat of AGMA representation had reduced concerts, curtailed productions, and postponed bookings "because the financial return from dance recitals is not sufficient to pay the salaries Mr. Carr demands." The editorial lamented the loss of opportunity in training and performance experience this posed for younger dancers and accused AGMA of risking the "future of the American dance."[75]

More than in the institutional apparatus of unions and large concert halls, the "intellectual strip tease" of modern dance, as the caricatured fan dancer Sally Rand termed it, found its long-standing home in the physical education departments of colleges and universities. There it dominated. Modern dancers trained by the Big Four wrested control of college and university dance departments in the 1930s.[76] A 1939 survey of dance in California colleges and universities indicated that modern dance received "twice the emphasis of any one type of dancing," far surpassing attention to ballet, tap, and folk dancing.[77] In a broader survey conducted in the mid-1940s, modern dance was taught at 66 percent of the coed schools and 100 percent of the women's colleges, again perpetuating the association of women and dance.[78] Women's dominance of the art form in the 1930s led to its institutionalization in higher education, where modern dance fit the intellectual and physical demands and class ideals of the growing number of women students.

Radical politics mixed with the social composition of modern dance to situate the art form on the edge of American modernism in the early

1930s. Modern dancers created a form malleable to many kinds of bodies and political agendas, almost ensuring that dances would be confrontational. Many modern dancers took the opportunity to work against bourgeois notions of art, attempting to appeal to working classes and audiences who had few traditions in seeking out art. Largely unsuccessful in that goal, they also fought to enhance their own status as workers. Modern dancers protested mightily for economic support for dance throughout the 1930s but were unable to secure large sources of funding beyond the federal government, and companies were unable to employ dancers on a regular payroll. With the dissolution in 1939 of the one major institution that had provided support, the Federal Theatre Project, modern dancers went back to lone occasional concerts, unconnected to each other and no longer buffered by a weekly paycheck for dancing. The ascendancy of modern dance in universities, however, allowed modern dancers to adjust their aims to highbrow art and social, if not radical political, change. Set off from mainstream audiences, modern dance refined an esoteric air in universities and colleges that encouraged formal aesthetic innovations over political content and calls for a class revolution.

6 : dancing america

Modern dancers explored theories of government, the relationship between workers and artists, and the political meanings of different kinds of dance. But the politics of modern dance extended beyond those issues. "It wasn't so much the political scene of Presidents and Vice Presidents, as blacks and whites and women," Welland Lathrop, a participant in the Bennington Summer School of the Dance, remembered about Helen Tamiris and the politics of the art form.[1] Both kinds of politics—systems of government and labor and the battles among social groups—coalesced in choreographic pictures of America. These dances ranged from depictions of Native Americans and indigenous religious groups to the settling of the West and the fight for racial justice. While combining formal politics with social politics, these Americana dances integrated many of the gender, racial, sexual, class, and political issues embedded in the development of modern dance. The changes in these dances from the 1930s to the 1940s reveal shifts in the issues, and in definitions of what it meant to be an American, as the country moved into the Second World War.

Walt Whitman was modern dancers' guide in configuring America in dance. Following Isadora Duncan's embrace of Whitman, Ted Shawn thought American dance would be big and democratic like Whitman's sprawling *Leaves of Grass*.[2] Tamiris created the fullest exposition in movement of Whitman's poetry in *Walt Whitman Suite* (1934), with sections of the dance named for particular poems—"Song of the Open Road," "I Sing the Body Electric," "Halcyon Days," and the most popular one, often performed separately, "Salut au Monde." Whitman's passionate patriotism mirrored that of modern dancers. In his sensuous embrace and explication of bodies, sexuality (including homosexuality), and the rights of women,

Whitman offered modern dancers a literary model of American physicality to exploit on stage. "I Sing the Body Electric," with its declarations "And if the body does not do fully as much as the soul?" and "If any thing is sacred the human body is sacred," gave modern dancers an explicit celebration of bodies articulated in words. Whitman's embrace of individualism with a concomitant belief in the masses also paralleled modern dancers' credos. Recognizing the possible conflict between individual expression and communal action, Whitman set about the task "to reconcile them."[3] And it was this notion of a democracy that was incontrovertibly American that modern dancers attempted to choreograph.

Groups moving together in harmony or conflict provided another way of seeing this theme, which was also invoked in literature, painting, and other performing arts. Literature and the visual arts gave thematic attention without live enactment; theater included language to mediate the debate; and music offered an abstract rendition through instruments. Dance presented live bodies themselves shoving, gyrating, and interacting in motion, less exact in message than theater but more material than music. Masses became visible as a large group of women rushed forward toward the audience in running jumps in Martha Graham's *Panorama* (1934), for example, manifesting both threat and power in the unifying activity of a crowd.

By challenging the relationship between the audience and performers, modern dancers added another layer to this theme of the individual and society. Not content to be like ballerinas remaining on a lofty pedestal of otherworldliness, neither did they want everyone coming up on stage, joining them in leaps across American vistas. Modern dancers strived to carve out a new kind of cultural event, utilizing the theatrical conventions of ballet performances but deriving the meaning of their work in sparking a more active involvement of the audience. Spectators were a necessary part of the performance, as Graham explained: "It is for the audience to finish what is essentially a conversation between the dancer and itself [the audience]. The dancer must be magnetic. She does not throw roses to the audience like a ballerina. She draws the public to her, so that their emotion can complete her work. That is the essential—that the audience should enter in and feel what the dancer is trying to express."[4] Lester Horton recognized the art form's difficulty in presenting ideas that were "stark and severe" and not "isolat[ing] itself from the audience on which it depends."[5] Modern dancers generated contradictory and confused reactions that fostered hostility from some audience members, but those responses did not abrogate the dancers' intentions. They wanted debate, not amusement, and accepted the risk that such a challenge could result in dislike. In their attempt to reconfigure modernism to be both confrontational and participatory, authorial and populist, modern dancers' greatest successes were in dances of America where they put forth this participatory theatrical process as an enactment of democracy.

In a letter to her parents in September 1930 Doris Humphrey laid out her fascination with the Shakers: "I'm interested in doing a danced [*sic*] based on religious cults—the general theme being Shakerism. They did a dance, you know[,] with definite formations and gestures and music. The subject is fascinating to read about—but is chiefly important as a starting point for the composition. The subject never is the point—you know. I agree with Roger Fry who insists that Cezanne's apples are as important as Raphael's Madonnas."[6] This comment framed modern dancers' interest in particular subject matters within the aesthetic world in which they operated. Humphrey's reference to art critic Roger Fry underscored modern dancers' belief in emphasizing abstraction over a mimetic rendition of a subject. Fry praised Cézanne's break from realistic representation and advocated that other artistic genres follow Cézanne's lead and concentrate on using form to express ideas and emotions, a defining element of modernism.[7] The point was not the apple or the Madonna, as Humphrey wrote, but rather the way in which formal elements composed meaning.

Modern dancers believed that the new ways of moving they were developing expressed the most important point, the emotion or idea. Graham's landmark solo *Lamentation* (1930) was not a depiction of a woman in sorrow—it was grief itself. Dance scholar Susan Leigh Foster persuasively explains the meaning of art underlying this phase of modern dance as communication. Modern dancers understood expression as the revelation of an individual's inner thoughts and emotions, and the body of the dancer as the instrument of this holistic expression. The choreographic subject was a universal statement most often derived from a personal, subjective experience; the purpose was to evoke empathy in viewers by their identification of the universal principle within the personal disclosure. The individual dancer represented, and could then comment upon, society.[8]

Beyond Foster's generalizations, and Humphrey's claims to the contrary, subject matter counted on its own terms and also as a reinforcement of broader issues that concerned modern dancers. Dance modernism in the United States encompassed an interest in principles that could be understood as both national and universal at the same time, a "cosmopolitan modernism" as dance scholar Amy Koritz defines it.[9] The task was to find a topic that could speak to national concerns through a universal framework. Religion interested many modern dancers for the universal principles that they believed lay beyond scriptural doctrines. Spirituality and, more specifically, the human body and its movements in spiritual practices attracted them, and it was religious expression in America that garnered attention in contrast to Isadora Duncan's celebration of Hellenic ideals and Ruth St. Denis's fascination with Asian religions.

Humphrey turned to the Shakers because of the inclusion of dance in their rituals. This feature, combined with the pronounced equality between men and women, the founding of the sect by a woman, and the commitment to chastity (as an eldress of the sect said, "[W]e make everything except babies"), intrigued her.[10] In fact, the interplay between dancing as a bodily pleasure and the requirement forbidding sex formed the dualistic tension in Humphrey's *The Shakers* of 1931. The Shakers believed "[Y]e shall be saved, when ye are shaken free of sin": bodies retained sinfulness, but body movement through dancing absolved sin.[11] These *good* effects of dancing probably appealed to Humphrey because some Christian religions had promulgated the evils of dancing by tying it to licentiousness. Humphrey's portrayal of the Shakers offered ways to link religiosity with the joys of body movement, neither denying the connotations of sex nor confining body movement only to that interpretation. Instead, she gave expression to both possibilities through modern dance.

A work for thirteen dancers, seven women and six men, *The Shakers* maintained the rigid separation of men and women that characterized the sect.[12] Women stayed on stage right and men on stage left, and the Eldress often remained far upstage on a bench, between and above each group. The split down the middle of the stage was like a cleanly cut wound in the skin, both repellent in its painfulness and magnetic in its clarity. The dance evolved around this incision. Toward the middle of the approximately nine-minute composition, the groups of men and women on their respective sides of the stage each formed a circle. Walking in drudged steps slightly pitched forward, their bodies rigidly straight like a long plank of wood, the dancers pounded one fisted, locked arm against the side of their bodies as if punishing themselves for desires of the flesh, hoping for pain to replace longing. The inevitability and doom of desire laced the heavy reluctant walk, downward stare, and angled lurch of the body. The circles of men and women worked in unison, straining toward one another, but remaining separate and not touching. The dancers then formed a line along the boundary, a woman facing a man, and peeled off in arcs to opposite sides of the stage in an awkward and agonizing back bend with a steady gaze at their partner across the divide. Humphrey depicted carnality in anguish (see figure 6.1).

The Shakers also expressed a rapturous religiosity alongside this torment, suggesting that joy came from this distress. As if inspired and pulled by something above, high, bounding, seemingly spontaneous jumps with legs splitting to the side exploded intermittently throughout the piece. The jumps occurred throughout the dance, building to a crescendo toward the end. The Eldress started the final series with small hops, and all the other dancers eventually joined her, finishing in a circle facing the victoriously tall Eldress on her bench, their backs to the audience. *The Shakers* ended with the entire company bursting skyward in these jumps of release and joy and concentrated energy.

Like the jumps, words punctured the piece. Experimentation with spoken words or texts happened fairly frequently in the dances of the 1930s because some topics begged for clarity and accessibility. Both the political dances of the Communist-inspired dancers and the Americana dances carried this import for many. Following the pattern of Shaker worship that often inspired spontaneous shouts of "Hosanna" and "Alleluia," Humphrey included this tradition but added more pointed exclamations. "My life, my carnal life; I will lay it down because it is depraved," a man burst out; "The Lord hath declared that thou shalt be saved—thou shalt be shaken clean from sin," a woman declared.[13] Redemption followed the declaration of sin. Words echoed movements as the recognition of the sin of desire gave way to physical outbursts of religious ecstasy.

FIGURE 6.1. *The Humphrey-Weidman Group in* The Shakers. *Photograph by Soichi Sunami. (Jerome Robbins Dance Division, The New York Public Library for the Performing Arts, Astor, Lenox and Tilden Foundations)*

The Shakers formally premiered in the Dance Repertory Theatre season of 1931 and garnered unanimous praise.[14] The restraint of movement and concise choreographic form showcasing the bursting passion underneath chastity, order, and control prompted critics to herald the choreography's precision in blending content and form. The subject matter signified the work as American since the Shakers were ensconced in New England and were well known for the furniture and products they made, if not for their religious doctrine or communal customs. Humphrey relayed the simplicity of design and functionality of form in her sparse, powerful choreography. The conflict of Christian physicality—desire and sin—also categorized the piece as American and placed tortured relations sprouting from sexual desire between men and women at the center of communal concerns. A woman, the Eldress, wielded power in setting up and controlling the groups of men and women, although the activity and dilemma of the dance centered on the groups themselves. *The Shakers* thus pushed to the forefront the essential issue shaping modern dance: the leadership of women and the social dimensions of bodies.

Other modern dancers also investigated religiosity, primarily Native American rituals that incorporated dance and sanctified bodies as fleshly dwellings of spirituality. Graham's *Primitive Mysteries* (1931) substantiated women's roles in a piece danced entirely by women and evolving around one woman—an abstraction of the Virgin Mary, performed by Graham. Graham's interest in Native Americans had started at Denishawn under the tutelage of Ted Shawn, who began using Native American imagery in his 1914 *Dagger Dance* and continued his interest in *Xochitl* (1921), the ballet that featured Graham. He created a number of solos depicting Native American rituals for himself, but in 1934 he choreographed a new piece for five men, the *Ponca Indian Dance*. Shawn believed that Native Americans relayed in their dance the "cosmic forces" suffusing all humanity, and this ennoblement of body movement attracted him, as it did other modern dancers.[15] He also emphasized the forcefulness of dancing Native American men.

Ponca Indian Dance featured a tribal leader and four followers moving to music composed by Jess Meeker, the accompanist who lived at Jacob's Pillow. The group and the leader stayed separate throughout the dance, with the four men creating a square pattern on stage and the leader most often on the opposite side of the stage, occasionally weaving himself in and around the group. The group moved in small steps, bodies bent at the hips with the torso and head directed toward the ground, thighs squat and steady, alternating legs sliding forward only from the knee. From this heavy stance, members of the group turned around themselves in small jumps, arms thrust up and one leg elevated forward, bent at the knee, flexed at the foot. They then returned to earthward shuffling steps and small parallel hops. The soloist, on the other hand, more often danced with body upright, sometimes doing the same movements as the group but not at the same time. All five men moved together, executing the same steps only once

FIGURE 6.2. *Shawn and His Men Dancers in* Ponca Indian Dance. *(The Harvard Theatre Collection, The Houghton Library)*

in the short dance, in a kind of face-off circle around the stage, the leader parrying the group (see figure 6.2).[16]

Shawn's tribal leader replicated Humphrey's Eldress in *The Shakers,* but whereas the Eldress remained a kind of overseer, Shawn's leader occupied center stage alone and drew attention with more active steps. The group of followers had no real distinction in steps or story, nothing comparable to the riveting anguish of the groups of men and women in *The Shakers.* And instead of carnal desire in theme and designed movement, the men in *Ponca Indian Dance* revealed naked legs and torso, covered only by a G string with a flap panel in front and feathers on their head, back, and arms. Shawn showcased, rather than choreographed, male strength, and the design of the dance best conveyed the importance of a forceful leader in corralling a group. *Ponca Indian Dance* exemplified Shawn's belief in the worth of his own leadership role.

On the West Coast Lester Horton, too, gravitated to Native American dances, although little remains of his dances. Horton was more convinced of the necessity of using this tradition to substantiate an American art form rather than to display manly fortitude. "A dance can be built upon these art forms that would be truly representative of this great country, something new and fundamental," he said of Native American dancing, reiterating Shawn's and Graham's beliefs.[17] While Native American dance incorporated religiosity, manly vigor, and American heritage—central themes for most modern dancers—Native Americans themselves did not generally appear on concert stages. Molly Spotted Elk, a Penobscot from Maine, found success in vaudeville, Wild West shows, and movies but yearned to "dance solely for art!" Her desire led her to Europe and back; on her return she mostly received modeling gigs and dancing spots at Greenwich Village clubs. She collaborated once with Charles Weidman and his dancers but found them "too immature to do well real Indian work." She returned to Paris in 1938, frustrated by the limited opportunities available to her in the United States.[18]

If the subject of Native American lives and spirituality found greater acceptance in modern dance than Native American dancers themselves did, the reverse was true in the case of Jews. Naum Rosen, a critic writing in *Dance Observer* in 1934, added the Jewish tradition to Graham's naming of the African American and the Native American traditions as indigenous American material to be utilized in creating the new art form. Perhaps prompted to do so by the large number of young Jewish women filling modern dance classes and companies, Rosen argued that Jewish tradition could inspire modern dancers. For him the universal element underlying each of these religious traditions, as well as their geographical convergence and longevity in the United States, determined their Americanness.[19] But the subject of Judaism or Jews in America surfaced only occasionally in modern dance and then most often in the Communist-inspired dance groups like the Workers Dance League, whose member Miriam Blecher choreographed works on Jewish themes, such as *East Side Sketches* (1937), which portrayed the teeming world of the Lower East Side.

The paradoxical prominence of Jews in modern dance companies and schools and the lack of thematic attention to them reflected the precarious process of assimilation in which Jews were involved in the 1930s. In 1928, when Ruth St. Denis wanted to re-form the Denishawn company to reduce the number of Jews to 10 percent of the school, many Jewish women at Denishawn left to join Doris Humphrey and Charles Weidman in their new company because "they stuck up for us," as Gertrude Shurr, a Latvian Jewish immigrant, declared.[20] Both Humphrey and Graham praised the emotion that they thought Jews brought to modern dance, a trait particularly well-suited for the new dramatic modern dance.[21] This positive interpretation still came from stereotyped understandings of Jews, however. Humphrey remarked on the large number of Jewish girls in her classes, happy to fuel their passionate commitment but also judging the success of her school on their presence, since she believed that Jews strove to get the best bargain.[22] Judgments of emotional intensity vied with miserliness and bled into the ways in which Jewish dancers were seen. St. Denis's comment that the art form needed to be recognized by other countries as American implied that Jews had a visual, physical identity that would not fit into a picture of America. Seemingly more important than an American way of moving was a particular type of static, physical appearance. Whether referring to facial characteristics, darker hair, or skin color, St. Denis's picture of America resembled her own fair-skinned and high-cheekboned features.[23]

Similarly, a former member of the Humphrey-Weidman Group of the 1930s remembered hearing that Humphrey and Weidman had commented on the audition of a Jewish woman who did not have a "WASP face," showing concern about whether she would fit into the company. Despite this reservation, they accepted her.[24] Modern dance was much more welcoming to Jews than other realms of society, such as higher education with its quota system, and Humphrey, Weidman, Graham, and others refuted the anti-Semitic beliefs that St. Denis and Shawn held.[25] But in the ways that people distinguished one another, differences remained between Jews and others. Physical characteristics mattered in this inevitable process, and Jews garnered particular comments. "You could be Jewish [and have an easier time] if you didn't look Jewish," a Jewish modern dancer of the Humphrey-Weidman Group summarized.[26]

In searching for an American religious tradition to uphold, modern dancers idealized Native American spirituality in the absence of Native

American concert dancers and disregarded Judaism in the presence of many Jewish modern dancers. And modern dancers made distinctions between bodies, deciding who could best portray dances of America. More often than not, the group was made up of individuals who looked like one another. (Graham collected most of the notice that her company members looked like her, leading to the nickname "Graham crackers.")[27] Even as they were committed to abstractions—emotions, ideas—the leading modern dancers put together pictures of America with a lingering attention to what people looked like and whether they qualified as looking like Americans.

This tendency was even more obvious in the way that modern dancers dealt with African Americans and the fight for racial justice in their dances of America. Dancing to African American spirituals, as Ted Shawn and Helen Tamiris did, combined white modern dancers' interest in religiosity with the enduring question of the rightful place of African Americans in America. The dancer most identified with choreographing spirituals was Tamiris, who felt more inclined to explore this part of the American vista than that of her own Russian Jewish immigrant heritage. *How Long Brethren?* (1937) was the peak of Tamiris's accomplishments in the modern dance world, combining her interest in African American oppression with her commitment to leftist politics. Put together under the auspices of the short-lived Dance Project, *How Long Brethren?* became the project's biggest success, revived twice the same year. Tamiris choreographed a dance for twenty women to seven African American spirituals, songs that had been collected through travels into the South by a white writer and composer, Lawrence Tibbet. As white women wearing dark veils danced on stage, an African American chorus sang, barely visible to the audience at the side of the stage or in an orchestra pit. Lengthy, with differing sections, and accompanied by an orchestra and chorus, *How Long Brethren?* presented a full theatrical story of the plight of African Americans in the United States (see figure 6.3).

As in Tamiris's earlier solos to spirituals, the weighted body was the central movement motif.[28] In *How Long Brethren?* heavy, slow steps, with feet barely off the ground, displayed the gravity of burden and oppression. Arms followed the legs, swaying from the shoulder joints downward, hanging

FIGURE 6.3. *Tamiris and Group in* How Long Brethren? *(Jerome Robbins Dance Division, The New York Public Library for the Performing Arts, Astor, Lenox and Tilden Foundations)*

listless. The head was often the only body part given movement upward—in a beseeching gaze, yearning for answer and relief. The piece moved "from desperation to a certain amount of defiance," from muted light to a march into a "red dawn."[29] Photographs, the only extant visual documentation of the 1937 version of the work, depicted defiance too: arms in an angular circle held over the head with elbows jutting out of the circle, legs elevated with a break at the knee, and bodies pitched forward or torsos leaning backward from a kneeled position on the floor. In contrast to the continuity of a straight line or a curve, the angles signified conflict. The break in the body itself held the eye and was the source of tension in the movement—

unlike the sense of equanimity projected by a straight line out to space or contained in the space of a circle. "Opposed lines," most explicit in a right angle, "always suggest force," Humphrey explained.[30]

Tamiris depicted the growth of defiance in the face of injustice as proto-typically American. In its messages and body movements, *How Long Brethren?* displayed not the internal struggle of sin of *The Shakers,* but the psychological toil of oppression, showing that the cause of the struggle came from externally imposed restrictions rather than self-imposed constraints. Even more than in *The Shakers,* words reinforced and clarified this message through the songs sung by a chorus. In the title song the choir asked, "How long, brethren, how long / Mus' mah people weep an' mourn?" In the end, inner strength and the joining together of the oppressed won freedom and justice. Influenced by leftist organizations banding together under the Popular Front, Tamiris depicted the necessity and power of collective action in obtaining political and social change in America.

This staged struggle became a real protest on the night of 20 May 1937, when the dancers asked the audience to stay with them in the theater after the performance in a sit-in to decry budget cuts of the WPA. Given the political thrust of the work and of the Federal Theatre Project, this kind of activity could be seen as part of the same collective action *How Long Brethren?* dramatized and celebrated. The protest ultimately did little good in stemming the WPA's declining budget, but it exemplified the activity modern dancers wanted to spark in their participatory theatrical interaction.[31]

The economic struggles of the WPA dancers did not compare to the story of slavery in *How Long Brethren?,* however. If freedom from oppression was the more general American theme that Tamiris emphasized, she placed that abstraction in the specific American case of racial discrimination and slavery. *How Long Brethren?* acknowledged social and political segregation by skin color as an indelible part of the American past, but the absence of any African American dancers in the production reinforced the continued presence of racial segregation in American life. Even more ironically, Charles Weidman's *Candide,* which appeared on the same program directly following *How Long Brethren?,* featured the African American dancer Add Bates. Well-known for his political activity on the WPA and an admitted Communist, Bates performed a number of important roles as an actor and dancer in the Federal Theatre Project, in several of its divisions, including the Living Newspapers and the production unit housed at Harlem's Lafayette Theater. Fanya Geltman Del Bourgo, a cast member of *How Long Brethren?*, remembered Bates as the "token black" in FTP productions.[32] Tamiris had not yet included men in her group so it may not have been reasonable to expect Bates to be part of the cast, but African American female dancers, including Edna Guy, were also a part of the project.

How Long Brethren? appeared just two months after the Negro Dance Evening at the 92nd Street Y, which had included Guy's performance to many of the same spirituals Tamiris used. Nothing specific remains from Guy's rendition of these spirituals, but the Americana offerings of Katherine Dunham at this time emphasized a different part of African Americans' legacy in the United States. Although Dunham would choreograph a moving account of lynching in 1951, *Southland,* her dances of the late 1930s showcased the lively social dances of rural and urban blacks, from back-breaking work in *Field Hands* (1938) to the mimicking strut of plantation owners in *Cake Walk* (1940), and her use of spirituals stressed despair over Tamiris's call to justice.[33]

A central Americana piece, Dunham's *Barrelhouse Blues* (1940) featured a romantic shimmy between a man and a woman and other signature movement elements in Dunham's technique.[34] Set in a bar on a cold Chicago night, the piece began with the swagger of the man across the stage, long strides initiated by a circular roll in the hip that lengthened out the leg, torso leaning back, arms held up and to the side in a drawn-out presentation of himself. The couple loosely held one another, at one point thrusting their hips forward to each other with gazes averted knowingly to the audience. Snapping fingers, bumping butts, low honeyed kicks, and rolls rippling through shoulders, torso, and hips all expressed flirtation and fantasy, the joys of bodily pleasure in a cold merciless world (see figure 6.4).

As with the dances of Asadata Dafora, *Barrelhouse Blues* celebrated the heterosexual play that dance could relay. Lenore Cox suggested that the effect of these appealing dances was to make an "active participant" of the audience, "electrified by every movement, every sound."[35] Predictably enough, white critics conjoined the lustiness of the piece with African Americans themselves. "As performed by these young artists, the unrestrained cavortings resolve themselves into healthy, yet extremely lusty, folk dances, and if these dances are usually considered cheap, it is undoubtedly

FIGURE 6.4. *Katherine Dunham and Vanoye Aikens in* Barrelhouse Blues. *(Jerome Robbins Dance Division, The New York Public Library for the Performing Arts, Astor, Lenox and Tilden Foundations)*

because they are cheapened by white performers," the dance critic Walter Terry explained.[36] As an anthropologist, Dunham recognized the importance of restoring and highlighting these dances as a crucial part of American identity. Instead of thematic pieces about the plight of black people in American society that concerned white modern dancers, Dunham focused on the cultural contributions of African Americans themselves. Abstract choreography of injustice and oppression were less important than demonstrating the continued presence and offerings of African Americans—especially dances—that Dunham believed held artistic worth.

Dunham and Tamiris shared common ground in the promotion of the significance of African Americans in American history and contemporary society, but their choreographic pictures of this significance differed. Hallie Flanagan, the director of the Federal Theatre Project, highlighted the racial interaction of *How Long Brethren?,* with its African American songs collected by a white man, sung by a black chorus, and danced to by white women: "You cannot tell where black voices become white bodies." This exemplified Flanagan's goal of creating an American theater through the FTP, "an epitome of that freedom from racial prejudice which must exist at the core of any theatre for American people."[37] Tamiris's leftist political stance coupled with her own background as a daughter of poor Jewish immigrants gave at least some credence to her empathy and identification with African Americans' oppression. "I understand the Negro people so well," she declared.[38] But *How Long Brethren?* perpetuated racial prejudice in its absence of black dancers and its use of white women to symbolize African Americans. The work was another example of the role white woman claimed in modern dance—to represent all humanity. This artistic stake in universality legitimized white women's place among modernist artists.

While representation may have occurred, however, it went only one way. Susan Manning argues that "whereas the white body could represent a universal body, the black body could represent only a black body," and Tamiris and other white modern dancers thus extended the minstrelsy tradition of blackface in a metaphorical way.[39] Instead of representing white people in her dances, Dunham deepened the portrayal of black people, particularly in sanctioning a range of dance practices on the concert stage. Her exploration of black peoples—from Africa, the Caribbean, American dance halls and plantations—exposed the breadth of her vision and the limits imposed upon it. Given its inextricability from bodies, dance in American modernism conveyed the indelible role of race in defining individuals, the ways in which they interacted in American society, and the persistence of racial stereotyping, segregation, and discrimination.

In 1937 and 1938 several longer works about America pulled together the subjects of earlier shorter works. Shawn's *O, Libertad!* (1937) emphasized Mexican and Native American heritage and ended in a heroic American revival of Greek civilization's manly strength and leadership in *Kinetic Molpai*. Regional Federal Theatre Projects sponsored Americana works, too, including *How Long Brethren?* in New York City and an American Dance Evening in Chicago in January 1938 that featured *An American Pattern* by ballet dancer Ruth Page and the Caribbean visions of Katherine Dunham in *L'Ag'Ya*. In a Festival of American Dance in 1937 for the Los Angeles division of the FTP, Myra Kinch put together three sections of dances. The first, "Divertissements," included a range of world dances from "Song of Judea" to the tango. "Dance Satires," the second section, presented concert dance styles from different time periods—romantic ballet in 1840, aesthetic dancing of the 1910s—ending in a "coronation" of today's modern dance. The final section, "Theme of Expansion," included the dance "An American Exodus," which depicted Americans' trek westward, "looking for something better than they had," establishing homes, and celebrating harvest.[40]

Lester Horton also choreographed Americana dances for audiences in Los Angeles. He first conceived of a long work about different religious traditions in America, including Penitents, Shakers, and Holy Rollers, but felt that other modern dancers had already been "definitive" on the subject (particularly Humphrey with *The Shakers*).[41] He turned to a more political chronology of American history in *Chronicle* (1937), which moved from a "colonial" section to a period of "self-ruling" and ended with a powerful dramatization of a lynching. Bella Lewitzky, who played the lynching victim, remembered the anxious attempts at escape that halted "at the very last moment [when] somebody caught my hand and pinned me in space and all the figures stayed still and I swung from that hand and the curtain came down" to a deafening roar from the audience.[42] This finale captured the attention of most critics, who praised Horton for his social consciousness and success in giving a "scrutiny of American forces" rather than the "costume-befuddled pageants of high schools and Elk conventions."[43] Even so, the brown veil over Lewitzky's head could not mask the persistent absence of African American dancers on stage in this production, as others, even on the subject of their oppression.

Martha Graham's *American Document* (1938), the most well-known of these longer expositions of America, replicated this configuration of race and brought together other typical Americana themes. On the humid, languid night of 6 August 1938, in the makeshift theater of the Bennington, Vermont, armory, dancers entered a stage walking in a procession, one following another, stopping when the whole company faced the audience. After they took bows in canonical fashion, a man stepped forward and spoke to the audience: "Ladies and Gentlemen, good evening. This is a theatre. The place is here in the United States of America. The time is now—tonight." He introduced the group of dancers, himself as the Interlocutor, and the principals Erick Hawkins and Martha Graham. The music resumed, the company exited as it arrived, and a short "Duet of Greeting" between Hawkins and Graham ensued. The performance space had been defined generically as a theater, specifying that the nation was more important than the exact locale. As in Thornton Wilder's *Our Town* of the same year, the gap between the audience and the players had been bridged by direct contact with the audience by an intermediary. So *American Document* began.[44]

The work's title proclaimed its purpose. Drawing upon specific texts and providing a script for the dance, Graham hoped to remind Americans of their heritage. *American Document* was a relatively long work by modern dance standards of the time, running about twenty-five or thirty minutes. "Patterned freely after an American Minstrel Show," Graham's version of a walk-around, a parade of the company strutting with uplifted knees holding onto the middle of their skirts to let their legs move up and down in a processional march, added structure to the whole dance by providing an obvious transition from one section to another.[45] The promenade set off but also incorporated each episode into the whole document. Graham chose the minstrelsy format and the interlocutor role to make the piece more accessible. Unlike other times when a certain ambiguity might have been her intention, Graham wanted *American Document* to be clear: "I want the audience to feel no obscurity or doubt at any time about what is happening on the stage."[46] She intended to design a readable and understandable document of America available to a wide audience.

After the spoken introduction of the Interlocutor, a similar introduction occurred in movement, first with the duet between Graham and Hawkins, then with the company in a "group movement of strong, affirmative action using leaps to enter and exit." Immediately after this vibrant display, the Interlocutor proclaimed the Americanness of various immigrants, from Spain, Russian, Germany—only naming Europeans. According to the libretto, qualifying as an American was a question of belief, and "Declaration," the first episode, defined just what Americans believed. Graham chose text from the Declaration of Independence, and when the words "Declaration 1776" were spoken, four panels at the back of the stage flung open and four dancers in blue appeared "like visual trumpets."[47] Moving from the ideological foundation of the country, the second episode, "Occupation," evoked the land itself. Accompanied by words from Red Jacket of the Senecas, Graham danced as a "Native Figure" lamenting the loss of land. Her long, straight hair, slicked down the sides of her face covering her ears, and a downward focus of the eyes and head conveyed drawn-out loss. Slightly bent legs grounded the movement to the earth as Graham's body moved slowly and with deliberation, ending in a pose of accepted resignment, kneeling center stage facing front.

"The Puritan" followed, reinforcing the theme of repression that Graham felt the Puritans exemplified (and which she felt she had experienced in her childhood). More judgmental than Humphrey's *The Shakers*, here Graham condemned what she interpreted as the sexual and physical restraint of the Puritans. The words of Jonathan Edwards began the sentence of sin in an episode spoken by the Interlocutor "as though delivering a judgment." A sensuous duet by Graham and Hawkins provided a bodily counterpoint to the impassioned words of Edwards that alternated with phrases from the biblical "Song of Songs." Newly in love with Erick Hawkins, Graham employed a man for the first time, and this scene departed from her previous style. She used the physical differences between a man and woman for some lifts and represented romantic love with more entwined movements. Graham slid around Hawkins's body, landing at his feet on the floor as he stood resolute, like "Grant Wood's Americana gentleman," as the choreographer Alwin Nikolais put it, a reference to Wood's

FIGURE 6.5. *Martha Graham and Erick Hawkins in* American Document. *(Jerome Robbins Dance Division, The New York Public Library for the Performing Arts, Astor, Lenox and Tilden Foundations)*

famous 1930 painting *American Gothic.*[48] Graham laid bare women's sexual desire. Suspensions punctuated the duet, conveying tension between man and woman, between repression and desire, and their dependence as partners. In a poignant moment Graham held up both arms, face turned into Hawkins's chest, leaning one hip into his, while Hawkins captured an arm, steadying her and allowing her to deepen the bend. Love won out. The two dancers left the stage together to the words from "Song of Songs," "I am my beloved's / And his desire is toward me" (see figure 6.5).

Turning from relations between men and women to the political arena of the nation, the next episode, "Emancipation," rooted the recent controversial trials of the Italian anarchists Sacco and Vanzetti and African American men accused of raping white women in the Scottsboro case in a pattern of injustice in the United States. Photographs show off-balanced movements: a jump with the torso pitched forward and the arms reaching backward, perhaps portraying in its awkwardness the hypocrisy of a system of slavery within a system of democracy. Recalling and then refuting the legacy of slavery, Graham ended this section with a semicircle of dancers, arms reaching out to the side embracing freedom and unity as the Interlocutor spoke words from Lincoln's Emancipation Proclamation.

The final episode, "After Piece," used the same framework of opposing scenes to comment upon the present day. Beginning with a "lament for the living," three women in red (originally members of Graham's company known for their leftist sympathies) danced the sorrow of the Depression. They glided one leg on the floor from front to side with arms spread sideways and curved and the torso and head arching backwards, in a full-bodied plea. In the following solo, Erick Hawkins embodied communal hope as "one man," "one million men," and "you," a man who had "faith . . . fear . . . [and] need," to a drum beat that built to a crescendo. In the final declaration, the whole cast came together in a "mass chant and call," trumpeting faith in Americans joining together to realize democracy.[49]

American Document premiered in a small Vermont town on a makeshift stage in the State Armory. Trappings of Americana and America's government could not have been more obvious. Turning a military building into a theater fit the piece in emphasizing the creative and unifying aspects of democracy rather than the militaristic elements of government. Progressing from Occupation to Emancipation and Invocation, Graham presented a cycle through shameful as well as proud episodes in American history and ended on a triumphant note of hope about democracy. Solos, duets, and group numbers, linked through the intermittent walk-around, symbolically connected the individual to society in harmonious and enriching ways, with democracy allowing individual freedom for all and communal unity.

In its view of the past, *American Document* invented a version of history that conveyed a balance between injustice and justice not necessarily present in American history.[50] Graham's view of the past incorporated elements overlooked in other American historical narratives, such as a critical view of the Puritans and the conquest of Native Americans, thereby revising her innocent vision of the pioneer's resolve in the earlier *Frontier* (1935). Via texts and themes she acknowledged the ethnic and racial diversity of America. But the performance in 1938 also continued discrimination. *American Document* utilized the minstrelsy form that evoked caricatures of black Americans and narrated episodes in Native American and African American history that lacked the presence of Native Americans and African Americans on stage. Graham's view of the American past reflected contemporary racial segregation and appropriation.

Graham's usable past also differed in important ways from the era's other artistic representations of U.S. history. Barbara Melosh argues that New Deal art and theater presented a domesticated version of pioneer life with women as pacifist mothers and the complementarity of male and female as representative of genial collectivity.[51] Modern dancers, on the other hand, placed women in the workplace, conquering an open prairie, leading a religious sect, or cavorting in a bar—in public settings rather than private homes. With few exceptions, such as the Puritan episode in *American Document,* which portended Graham's growing interest in male-female relationships that would dominate her grand works of the 1940s and 1950s, white women were the representative Americans. They were individuals who made up society, without reference to men or designated female roles such as mother or wife.

American Document went on from Bennington to great success in New York and then on a tour around the country. The piece brought together many familiar American topics—Native Americans, Puritans, slavery—under the call to social justice and political commentary that pervaded the Popular Front era. Though it made no specific enunciation on class struggles, leftist papers embraced the work, and Graham's company premiered *American Document* in New York at a benefit for *New Masses* at Carnegie Hall on 9 October 1938. That week the magazine featured a caricature of Graham by Al Hirschfeld on its cover, and Owen Burke, the dance critic, applauded Graham's efforts, particularly in "bringing modern dance to the people." Burke emphasized Graham's demand "that the American people remember its tradition, collect its strength, remember that their country was conceived and molded in the struggle for democracy, that it carry forward."[52] Overt address to the audience by the Interlocutor enhanced the sense of urgent summons; audience members contributed to the hope of democracy in their necessary role as witnesses and in answering the call to action. It was the active, participatory theatrical experience that Graham envisioned modern dance to be.

Lincoln Kirstein, the philanthropist who fostered an American ballet tradition and also a critic of modern dance, declared *American Document* a resounding success. He praised its sincerity of purpose, stating that "its surface finish resembled some useful Shaker wood-turning." With simple grace and functional style, Graham "seemed an incarnate question of everything we fear and hope for in our daily lives."[53] Kirstein prodded ballet choreographers to achieve similar relevance, also by using American subjects. Leonide Massine, once a choreographer for Diaghilev's Ballets Russes, had created one of the first Americana ballets, *Union Pacific,* in 1934. The ballet told of the linking up of the eastern and western railroad tracks at Promontory Point, Utah. Even with a libretto by Archibald MacLeish, it fared badly, being criticized as an overly Russian, and therefore an inauthentic and superficial, view of America.[54] American ballet choreographers proved more convincing. In Chicago, Ruth Page created *An American Pattern* (1938) and *Frankie and Johnnie* (1938); in Philadelphia, Catherine Littlefield choreographed *Barn Dance* (1937); in New York, Lew Christensen made *Pocahantas* (1936) and *Filling Station* (1938), and Eugene Loring followed his popular *Billy the Kid* (1938) with *The Great American Goof* (1940) and *Prairie* (1942).[55]

Beginning with Massine's *Union Pacific* in 1934, the iconography of the West inspired choreographers concerned with creating an American ballet style. The music of Aaron Copland contributed a great deal of Americana character to these ballet works. Copland flavored his orchestral music with embellished folk tunes and syncopated rhythms reminiscent of jazz. Sparse harmonies, simple orchestration, and lyrical melodies mythologized the honest practicality and freedom of space in the countryside and the West. To music by Copland, Eugene Loring's *Billy the Kid,* the story of capturing the legendary western outlaw, garnered critical acclaim as the first broadly successful American ballet. Dancing in cowboy boots, Loring created stylized, utilitarian moves, such as a hopping step to evoke horseback riding; a country swing between men and women conveyed the flavor of living in a southwestern town.

Loring used traditional ballet technique sparsely. Instead, he borrowed modern dance elements, such as the parallel orientation of feet and hips, on which he fused the cowboy actions of getting on and off a horse. Loring, in fact, performed with Kirstein's company, Ballet Caravan, at the Bennington Summer School of the Dance in 1937 and was at least exposed to modern dance then. In *Billy the Kid* he incorporated modern dance movement elements and structure, beginning and ending the ballet with a "parade of people" coming across the stage in a diagonal line in slow poses to the dramatic Copland score. The framing of the piece by this fugue-like procession resembled the walk-around of *American Document. Billy the Kid* debuted in Chicago on 16 October 1938, a couple of months after the premiere of *American Document* at Bennington, and Kirstein may have informed Loring of Graham's dance. Loring later admitted that *Billy the Kid* owed a great debt to modern dance.[56]

Agnes de Mille's *Rodeo* (1942) continued ballet choreographers' western imaginations. *Rodeo* featured Copland's music, was set in a cow town, depicted a clear story, and celebrated the taming of the individual—all told from a woman's viewpoint. The woman wanted to be a cowboy but also wanted to lasso a man. In the end she gave up the former goal for the latter by putting on a dress and becoming a more traditional girl. Although de Mille's cowgirl retained her spunkiness throughout the story and did not give up her quirkiness for marriage, the dance still evolved around romantic pursuit. Graham's *Frontier* pioneer became de Mille's domesticated girlfriend. More rousing and funnier than *Billy the Kid, Rodeo* mainly used gestural movement, more common in acting, rather than a modified—or Americanized—ballet technique.[57]

Billy the Kid and *Rodeo* offered appealing narratives in the storytelling tradition of such classic ballet works as *Swan Lake* and *Giselle* and portrayed a heroism different from that of modern dance productions. In *Billy the Kid* the individual fell as "a casualty in the establishment of order."[58] "Billy represented the basic anarchy inherent in individualism in its most rampant form," Kirstein wrote.[59] This view of the individual and society—the threat of the anarchic individual and society's subduing of him or her— was not the rendition of this theme that modern dancers imagined. In other views of the West, Sophie Maslow, a prominent member of Graham's company also involved in political issues, explored American folk traditions in *Dust Bowl Ballads* (1941) and *Folksay* (1942). To music by the folksinger Woody

Guthrie, Maslow depicted herself as an Oklahoma farmer in *Dust Bowl Ballads,* forced to endure poverty on the plains and migration to an unknown place and future. *Folksay* concerned rural life, too, but celebrated folk traditions that unified the poor and struggling. Maslow's accounts of the difficulties and contained joy of poverty in rural life contrasted sharply with ballet choreographers' western works. Critical views of America, its past and present, and choreographic visions of democracy fell away in the new ballet works that offered humor, reinforcement of conventional gender roles, and regulated order.

The American subjects of ballet pieces and ballet choreographers' free use of modern dance movements signified the beginnings of an American style of ballet. In the late 1930s and early 1940s the boundaries between ballet and modern dance began to blur, even though distinctions in approach remained (as between Maslow and de Mille, for instance). In technique the new ballets rarely focused on delicate pointe work or traditional pas-de-deux partnering. Instead, they featured stylized folk dances and everyday motions to convey character and narrative. Modern dance loosened ballet technique, and both forms shared nationalist themes. Ballet Caravan toured the gymnasium circuit developed amongst modern dancers at Bennington, and modern and ballet choreographers utilized the talents of the same designers and composers, such as Aaron Copland.[60]

Another view of the West accompanied by Copland's music demonstrated the influence of ballet on modern dance. Graham's *Appalachian Spring* (1944) borrowed movement and a more genial spirit from ballet. The dance celebrated a newly wedded couple forging a life together in a pioneer setting, although some elements of tension arose with the return of the specter of Puritan fanaticism and repression in the role of the Revivalist, originally performed by Merce Cunningham. The work, however, presented a harmonic resolution of those tensions with the solidity of the motherlike Pioneer Woman and the promise of the Bride and Husband. The movement was less aggressive than in other works.[61] Instead of the angles that dominated *How Long Brethren?,* for example, circles reigned in *Appalachian Spring.* Large long skirts of the Pioneer Woman and the Bride greatly widened the arcs of turning movements. Dancers moved around a circle and traded partners in folk dance patterns. The whole cast remained on stage for the entire piece, creating an aura of insularity unbroken by entrances and exits or direct appeals to the audience. *Appalachian Spring* ended with a final portrait of the Husband standing behind the Bride, who sat in a rocking chair; the Revivalist and his followers knelt in prayer with their backs to the couple and the audience. The Bride motioned out to the horizon, and gazes from the Pioneer Woman and Husband followed her vision. The security of the home had replaced the risk of the open land of *Frontier* and *American Document*. The piece expressed a sense of domestic bliss and personal happiness rather than the communal view of unity that ended *American Document*.

Appalachian Spring represented an anomaly in Graham's oeuvre because of its pervasive gentleness. May O'Donnell, the original Pioneer Woman, attributed it to the peak of the romantic relationship between Graham and Erick Hawkins, who played the Husband.[62] Graham transferred the happiness and security found in her personal life onto the stage to counter the tumultuous times of war with a reminder of the survivability and warmth of the American hearth. The essence of the work, Graham wrote in a script to Copland, should be the soul of America: "This is a legend of American living. It is like the bone structure, the inner frame that holds together a people."[63]

Graham moved from a historical narrative of conflict in *American Document* to an evocation of America's domestic soul in *Appalachian Spring,* and this conciliatory picture with its emphasis on domesticity contrasted sharply with modern dancers' earlier Americana works. In *Appalachian Spring* the Pioneer had become the Pioneer Woman, and the dance was centered on the Bride. Native Americans and African Americans were absent in theme as well as on stage. Except for the sanctimony of Puritanism, the pastoral scene was untroubled. Graham shifted her view of the American past from a sweeping historical narrative and political statement to a portrait of a pleasing home in which traditional gender roles reigned. In the midst of the Depression *American Document* had challenged Americans to revive and better implement the country's founding principles; in the midst of a world war *Appalachian Spring* comforted audiences by presenting a hermetic picture of the past, removed and safe from the confusing and tumultuous problems of the present.

By the early 1940s the call to patriotism in the midst of World War II reflected larger societal changes, and modern dancers found fewer opportunities to broadcast their challenging views of America's past and present.

Although the shift from *American Document* to *Appalachian Spring* exhibited the changes in modern dance and society at large in terms more stark than the subtle, rambling way in which they actually occurred, the two dances point to important differences between the 1930s and the 1940s. The acknowledgment and staging of religious, racial, and gender differences in *The Shakers, Ponca Indian Dance, How Long Brethren?, Barrelhouse Blues,* and *American Document* sowed the seeds of the disassembling of modern dance. Even in the flawed enactment of democracy in these dances — particularly regarding racial issues — the call to action, led by women and rhetorically including a diverse group of Americans, proved too radical to survive as a coherent movement beyond the Popular Front era of the 1930s. The attempt at balancing individual expression with collective action that included a recognition of American pluralism was a fragile, if significant, achievement. In the midst of a world war the diverse factions that choreographic pictures of America attempted to unify could no longer be so easily reconciled.

7 : dance in war

In 1944, the same year as the premiere of Graham's *Appalachian Spring,* the young American ballet company Ballet Theatre performed Jerome Robbins's *Fancy Free*. Robbins extended the theme of adventure and possibilities prevalent in the western ballets to an entertaining tale of three seamen on a short leave in a big city. (This dance was the basis for the 1945 Broadway show and 1949 movie *On the Town.*) *Fancy Free* fused movement elements from a variety of dance styles, including modern dance and jazz dance, to music by Leonard Bernstein. Organized around a dance contest in a bar between three sailors vying for womanly affection, *Fancy Free* evoked the tap competitions in Harlem bars and the swing rivalry of the dance halls (see figure 7.1). The movement was flashier, with an emphasis on bravura jumps and turns, than traditional ballet. Bernstein's music added to the vernacular spirit with its jazz riffs and syncopated rhythms. If in movement style *Fancy Free* continued and built upon modern dance—thereby expanding the category of ballet—in theme and subject matter it differed drastically. The celebration of American military and leisure exploits in *Fancy Free* allowed for no impassioned explorations of the democratic tradition in America. In the new balletic documents of America, frivolity replaced seriousness and documentation itself seemed less important than a capricious, playful sketch.

The new American ballet garnered praise from unexpected places. John Martin, the early promoter of modern dance, wrote in 1943 that dance had completed "a cycle" and that the fervor that had energized modern dance was now transferring to ballet.[1] Even more unexpectedly, in 1945 the leftist periodical *New Masses* trumpeted the arrival of an American ballet, claiming that new ballets like *Fancy Free* were "modern and American because Ameri-

FIGURE 7.1. *Harold Lang, John Kriza, Jerome Robbins, and Shirley Eckles in* Fancy Free *by Jerome Robbins. (Jerome Robbins Dance Division, The New York Public Library for the Performing Arts, Astor, Lenox and Tilden Foundations)*

can concepts of tempo and humor, of uninhibited rhythms and color, pervade the patterns of movement they create, and each work sparkles, in its own way, with the authentic gleam of our unique national brand of youth, sprightliness and wit."[2] The embrace of ballet by *New Masses* reflected a changed political environment in which ballet choreographers' whimsical Americana dance works ultimately triumphed over modern dance choreographers' more critical visions. As modernism moved into the war years, ballet took over the concert dance scene by using the freedom of movement opened up by modern dance and drawing on popular stories and themes of the American past. *Fancy Free* cemented the end of the Americana era of modern dance and heralded its ascendancy in ballet and musical theater.

Despite the rise of ballet, there was also recognition that modern dance had established itself. Acknowledged leaders gave regular performances, and training flourished in colleges, universities, and dance schools. Initial histories appeared—John Martin's *America Dancing* in 1936 and *John Martin's Introduction to the Dance* in 1939, Walter Terry's *Invitation to Dance* in 1942, followed by Margaret Lloyd's more definitive *The Borzoi Book of Modern Dance* in 1949—and in 1940 the Museum of Modern Art established a dance archives. The art form still inspired controversy, however, such as the occasional denunciations by dance critics Walter Terry and Edwin Denby.[3] Dancers settled, too, most practically in the move by Doris Humphrey and Charles Weidman into a new studio in November 1940. The studio converted into a performing space, what Humphrey called a "home of our own with room to play in." "We have liked to think of ourselves as pioneers and the road as the old trail into new lands. We hope for a new road. For a while we are content to stay at home," she explained.[4] The next summer at Bennington, Humphrey created *Decade* (1941), a re-visiting of the first ten years of the Humphrey-Weidman company. Not a particularly innovative work, *Decade* represented a sliding into a new phase in the development of modern dance. No longer battling for legitimacy or shocking audiences, modern dancers struggled to maintain momentum and growth.

The rise of American ballet made sustained growth more difficult, and the critic George Beiswanger, an advocate of modern dance, articulated the greatest fear: "[I]t is quite possible that the final and only lasting service of the modern dance will be the rejuvenation of ballet." Although Beiswanger condemned ballet's "cannibalization" of all "fresh and exciting . . . impulses," he recognized that ballet had better funding, more solid organizations, and bigger audiences.[5] War and the changing political atmosphere only exacerbated the dilemma. Modern dancers had to fight to procure enough of the scarce funds during the war to put on productions. The Bennington Summer School of the Arts stopped after 1942 because oil shortages forced the college to close during the harsh months of the winter and hold courses through the summer. And if a dearth of men had always been a problem in the dance profession, the war only heightened the shortage as male dancers were called to serve in the armed forces. Defending the value of modern dance took on an intensified tone with a 1942 editorial in *Dance Observer* declaring modern dance to be "a morale builder, a social tie, a thousand things in addition to its essence as an art."[6]

Modern dancers now had to figure out the role of art in wartime, specifically that of World War II. Propelled out of a focus on the internal struggles of the country prompted by the Great Depression, Americans entered a worldwide conflict that was consuming and alarming. In this atmosphere, nationalism took on a different tenor, moving from a prod to realize America's founding ideals to an embrace of America as a triumphant model of democracy. Modern dance did not have a clear role in this wave of celebratory patriotism, nor did modern dancers have many opportunities to reconfigure their ideals to new demands. Moving from independent productions sponsored by the government in the WPA projects, dancers either worked directly for war departments or as part of the government's entertainment efforts. Mary Jo Shelly, one of the administrators of the Bennington program, left the college in the fall of 1942 for a position as lieutenant in charge of physical training in the women's naval reserves, or WAVES. Ruth St. Denis worked the graveyard shift at the Douglas Aircraft Factory in Santa Monica. Jane Dudley, Sophie Maslow, and William Bales performed at Camp Dix in New Jersey, prompting a soldier to remark that he "never knew [he] could be moved by girls dancing in bare feet."[7] The Humphrey-Weidman Group performed as USO entertainers at Fort Monmouth in New Jersey in 1942; Katherine Dunham appeared in the Hollywood short film "Star-Spangled Rhythm," designed to boost the country's morale during wartime; and Helen Tamiris choreographed works for the U.S. Department of Agriculture ("It's Up to You" [1943]) and then for Franklin D. Roosevelt's 1944 election campaign, with "The People's Bandwagon." Doris Humphrey, Charles Weidman, Martha Graham, and Ted Shawn were also named in ideas for a theatrical project, *This Is the Civilian*. Conceived as the homefront equivalent to the popular Irving Berlin production *This Is the Army* that was making its way around military bases worldwide, the project was apparently never realized. The script began with poems of Walt Whitman in a paean to freedom of expression, celebrated America's physical prowess, and ended with original songs and dances of America. One section, "The Champions," stressed the good aspects of the "American sense of competition," a sharp contrast to Humphrey's earlier *Theatre Piece* (1936), which she had described as a "grim" picture of "survival by competition."[8] The war demanded a reconsideration of principles.

Ted Shawn's more conservative brand of nationalism and Americana dances moved most easily from theater buildings to theaters of war. Shawn's increasing age, the exhaustion of constant touring, dancers' desires to go on to something else, and the impending possibility of war all contributed to the demise of Shawn and His Men Dancers in 1940 after seven years of performing. By 1942 almost all of the dancers from Shawn's company, the accompanist and composer Jess Meeker, the dance critic Walter Terry, and many other male modern dancers were serving in the armed forces (Shawn, then fifty-one, escaped service because of his age). Once there, they found ways to dance. José Limón performed throughout his service in 1943–44 at Camp Lee, Virginia, and Camp Dix, New Jersey. Paul Magriel, an author of books and articles on dance, was the base librarian at Kessler Field in Biloxi, Mississippi, and put together a book of paintings done by soldiers in their spare time.[9] Barton Mumaw, Shawn's lover, was assigned to the technical school of the air corps at Kessler Field in 1942, and Shawn lived at the Hotel Biloxi to be near him. Within a few months Shawn and Mumaw performed in nearby Gulfport and gave performances and lecture-demonstrations at the base that were benefits to raise money for a "Reception Cottage," which Shawn described as "a charming home-like place dedicated to the purpose of providing privacy for boys to say goodbye to their womenfolk when they are shipped away."[10] Shawn and Mumaw both received commendations from Colonel Robert E. M. Goolrick, the commanding officer, for their efforts to raise money for the cottage.

Shawn did not comment on the irony of two gay lovers raising money for a building devoted to privacy with womenfolk, nor did Shawn's close relationship with Mumaw seem to cause consternation for military officers at a time when homosexuality was deemed a mental illness by the U.S. military and grounds for a dishonorable discharge. In fact, the 1943 Cornell Selectee Index, created by a group of doctors to simplify the initial psychiatric exams of inductees, included a category of occupational choice: interior decorators, window dressers, and dancers were suspected of homosexual inclinations. Allan Bérubé argues that gay men and women not only populated the wartime military but even developed a stronger sense of individual and group identity through the forced same-sex living circumstances and the military's attempts to define homosexual characteristics and behavior. While definitions tightened and prohibited some men from being admitted to the armed services, once there, inductees found regulation of sexual behavior and rigid gender roles loosened. Within this intense and unusual situation, female impersonators (many of them mimicking ballerinas) flourished as entertainment on bases in well-known shows such as *This Is the Army*. Military and popular press reviews downplayed the association of female impersonation with homosexuality, which was more common to writings both before and after the war. In the exigencies of war the threat of homosexuality somewhat diminished.[11]

In this atmosphere, Shawn and Mumaw's relationship received little notice, and their performances roused only cheers. "They behaved like a dance fan audience at Carnegie Hall, even to bravos," Shawn noted of the 2,300 men at Kessler Field who had bought tickets to see their performance.[12] Mumaw performed solos to continued acclaim when he transferred to a base in England, and male members from the Littlefield Ballet, Ballet Theatre, Ballet Caravan, and Shawn and His Men Dancers performed in a rendition of *This Is the Army* in 1944 at an unspecified base. The reviewer noted that "Ted Shawn would probably have apoplexy if he could see one of his former dancers, trained in the uncompromising virility of the Shawn technique, swish his skirts as Betty Grable; yet on second glance he would undoubtedly take pride in the dancing of Charles Tate, for Pfc. Tate is excellent as Betty Grable and, in matters of dancing infinitely more accomplished."[13]

The enthusiastic reaction to dance—even modern dance—in the armed forces probably had more to do with the boredom and stress of military life than with a new passion for dance. But some men may have also been interested in dance because of a sexual attraction to men, whether because of the absence of women on the bases or not. Walter Terry, stationed in Egypt, wrote to Shawn that Shawn and His Men Dancers were well known among "the boys" there. The soldiers were reading Terry's recently published book, *Invitation to Dance*, that heralded Shawn's *O, Libertad!* as "the story of America with its cruelties, its greatness, its success and its failures told in terms of dance, told through the bodies of American men." And a picture Shawn sent of himself "has wound up over my bed (if you don't mind being a pin-up boy!)."[14] When Terry himself performed a Native American dance in the manner of Shawn at the Royal Opera House in Cairo, he claimed that his picture in *Stars and Stripes* "grac[ed] the walls of several of my buddies: one, Bill Joyce, an ex-Boston-cop has my photo sharing honors with his fiancee, and in another barracks I am flanked by Betty Grable and Ann Corio."[15]

The positive reaction to modern dance and female impersonation in the

FIGURE 7.2. *Walter Terry and Charles Tate, dancing in the army. (Ted Shawn Collection, Jerome Robbins Dance Division, The New York Public Library for the Performing Arts, Astor, Lenox and Tilden Foundations)*

military demonstrated the fluidity of sexual identity and behavior during wartime service. Certainly homosexual contact flourished, from tight sleeping quarters to "Find-Your-Buddy-Week," which encouraged close friendships among men.[16] For gay male dancers, the war provided a way to prove their patriotism and their virility. But at least Terry recognized that Shawn had epitomized that ideal long before the war. In a letter to Mumaw in 1944 Terry upheld the vision of Shawn as reason enough to fight the war: "[T]he dance contribution [of Shawn] has stood for the very best in America, has revealed our physical prowess, our spiritual heritage, our vision and something that I can describe only as the clean freshness of the New World. Such dances being as they are distillations of America, are worth living and fighting for."[17]

When Terry wrote of the "clean freshness of the New World" that Shawn's Americanism reflected, he was stationed in northern Africa and did not comment on the African elements in the New World nor on the overt denigration of African American contributions that Shawn's vision of American dance represented. Racism persisted throughout the war—most evident in the continued segregation of troops—and African American artists thrust into the spotlight the hypocrisy of maintaining American racial segregation while fighting against fascism abroad. Calling for a "double victory" against racial discrimination overseas and at home, African Americans inflamed the civil rights movement with new momentum; in the middle of this maelstrom Pearl Primus began her dance career.

Born in Trinidad in 1919, Primus moved with her family to the United States when she was two. Primus's father held various jobs in New York City, ranging from building superintendent to war plant employee, seaman, and carpenter. Like Katherine Dunham, Primus excelled at school; she received a B.A. in biology from Hunter College in 1940 and prepared to go to medical school at Howard University. To obtain money she sought jobs as a laboratory technician but did not get any because of racist hiring practices. As with many others during the Depression, Primus found a job with the federal government, working in the wardrobe department of the National Youth Administration. She soon found herself on stage in a production of *America Dances,* replacing a dancer who had not shown up, and relying on her background as a field and track athlete in high school and college to make up for her lack of dance training. Rather inadvertently, her dancing career began.[18]

After staying with the production until its demise when the United States entered World War II, Primus received a scholarship from the New Dance Group, a school that retained a leftist political focus after many others had abandoned those goals in the early 1940s. The New Dance Group trained African American dancers as part of its advocacy of a social purpose for dance, with widening the opportunities for black dancers being one way to implement that goal. Primus took classes in a variety of techniques, from Martha Graham and Hanya Holm to the dances of her home-land taught by fellow Trinidadian Beryl McBurnie. Her performing career began quickly with a series of solos at the 92nd Street Y on 14 February 1943. Like Dunham, Primus offered a range of dance styles in one perfor-mance. Her second concert, at the 92nd Street Y in April 1944, began with four dances that a critic grouped together as "Primitives" and then went "through studies in the traditional American Negro forms to the dances of protest and exaltation which [she] has made out of the idioms of her racial heritage in organic union with those of the modern dance."[19] Primus started with Africa, moved to Harlem dance halls, and ended with modern dance evocations: she followed the pattern established by Dunham and the 1937 Negro Dance Evening that created a continuity between Africa and America, dance halls and concert stages. Acclaimed for flying leaps, Primus crossed continents and artistic barriers with ease.

Primus's interest in African dances gleaned from books eventually prompted her to switch her studies from medicine to psychology and, finally, to anthropology. When she began graduate work at Columbia University in the mid-1940s, her anthropological curiosity first took her to Georgia, Alabama, and South Carolina, where she posed as a migrant worker and picked cotton in an effort "to know her own people where they are suffering most."[20] Primus utilized her field experience to add authenticity to her choreography about sharecropping, lynching, and evocations of African American spirituals. Except for this excursion, however, Primus focused on Africa. For its last grant, the Rosenwald Foundation (which had earlier supported Dunham) funded Primus's first trip to Africa in 1948. Just as Dunham was able to enter deeply into Haitian society, Primus found acceptance, induced by her dancing ability, by Africans. The Watusi dancers of the Belgian Congo renamed her "Omowale" — "child returned home" — on her first journey there.[21] The way Primus learned dances reflected the very different place she secured in these societies. If she could not pick up a move exactly through watching and imitating, "a native dancer would hold her body against his or her own so she could literally absorb the movement."[22] It is hard to imagine a white anthropologist, even a dancer, achieving this closeness.

Primus's anthropological excursions shaped her dances, beginning with her trip to the South. In *Hard Time Blues* (1943) she depicted the struggles

FIGURE 7.3. *Pearl Primus in Africa.* *(Jerome Robbins Dance Division, The New York Public Library for the Performing Arts, Astor, Lenox and Tilden Foundations)*

of slaves in the American South, leaping throughout the solo and using jumps—defying gravity—as signs of protest against sharecropping. *Strange Fruit* (1943), another dance of defiance, was a solo inspired by Abel Meeropol's song (made famous by Billie Holiday) about a lynched body hanging from a tree.[23] Dancing only to the narration of the lyrics, Primus identified the character as a white woman of the lynch mob, not a friend or relative of the victim, and began the dance with the terror of the aftermath. Structured along an angle from the back to the front of the stage, where the horrific awning of the sacrificial tree governed the woman's misery, Primus hurled herself to the ground, writhing, only to pull herself upright and run beseechingly down toward the audience. Back to the ground again, Primus clasped her hands, with arms straight above her head as if her wrists were held in manacles, twisted her arms above and around her head, and hollowed out her torso in contortions of pain. The piece ended with a resigned walk, an arm thrust upward with eyes angled toward the floor, that became a defiant march, gaze up and unchecked.[24]

Primus worried about the applause *Strange Fruit* received, asking, "Do people really get the message, and do they transfer it to the poor, socially upset, frustrated man in the street? Do they simply accept me as a different type of colored person and let it go at that? I want my dance to be a part of the conscience of America."[25] Primus carried forward the concerns of modern dancers of the 1930s in wanting to reach a broad audience; a good dance was one that coal miners and sharecroppers could understand, she proclaimed.[26] Aiming for popular appeal—but including a social message—her dances often addressed the effect of racial discrimination on the whole country, not just on African Americans themselves. By portraying a white woman in *Strange Fruit,* Primus extended the horror and incomprehensibility of racism to white people. She also made the representation of black and white bodies on stage a two-way street, instead of the one-way pattern of white women standing in as African American men and women that was established in the 1930s, most overtly by Helen Tamiris in *How Long Brethren?* Primus's portrayal of a white woman in *Strange Fruit* was the exception, however, and probably succeeded because the subject of the dance concerned racial discrimination in the United States. But in her joining of attention to audiences and to social change that coalesced in dances on American themes, she kept alive modern dancers' commitment to affect "the conscience of America."

Primus did so by deliberately infusing her artistry with politics. She linked *Strange Fruit* with *Hard Time Blues* by highlighting the discrimination African Americans consistently confronted. "The hurt and anger that hurled me to the ground in that solo [in *Strange Fruit*] were translated into an anger that took me into the air in *Hard Time Blues.*"[27] In the 1940s she found good company with other African American artists with similar concerns. In April 1943, very early in her career, Primus found a home at Café Society in downtown Manhattan, a rather "earnest club" with radical political leanings. On a small stage cramped by a low ceiling, she performed her variety of dances before integrated audiences, with blues pieces often accompanied by Josh White, the African American political folksinger.[28] Besides offering an atmosphere where white liberals expressed "their strong color sympathy," Café Society provided Primus with an entry into and support from a community of politically active African American singers and entertainers that included Teddy Wilson, Hazel Scott, Lena Horne, Billie Holiday, and Paul Robeson.[29] These connections led to Primus's participation in the Negro Freedom Rallies during the war years, which promoted the fulfillment of democracy at home as well as around the world. For the June 1944 program at Madison Square Garden, Owen Dodson and Langston Hughes wrote and directed a pageant entitled "New World A-Coming," in which Primus appeared.[30] Similarly, Katherine Dunham took more vociferous stands against discrimination in the 1940s, in hotels on tour and even from the stage. "I must protest because I have discovered that your management will not allow people like you to sit next to people like us. I hope that time and the unhappiness of this war for tolerance and democracy, which I am sure we will win, will change some of these things—perhaps then we can return," she proclaimed to an audience after a performance in Louisville in October 1944.[31]

In their overt attention to politics in the war years, African American modern dancers took a radical stance: not in advocating the overthrow of capitalism but in seeking to change society by demanding full inclusion within American democracy. Their more confrontational tone attested to the changes that had occurred in the dance field and beyond. Primus's quick rise was testament to her ability but also to an opening up of possibilities, particularly in contrast to the harsh discrimination Edna Guy confronted when she looked for classes and performance opportunities in the 1920s. Primus trained with white dancers, performed with them, and appeared in the same institutions where most white modern dancers produced their shows. Primus and Dunham commanded attention in a new way, not just as informers sharing insights about the Caribbean and Africa, but as artists and political activists fighting for their rightful place in American society. Having achieved recognition, African American dancers began protesting more vocally against the limitations they continued to face.[32]

In 1945 Juana de Laban, a dancer writing in *Dance Observer,* noted the success of African American modern dancers and exalted their rise "to a place of distinction in the arts" as "one of the most gratifying signs of the real meaning of the democratic way of life." The dynamic success of African American dancers was the exception, however, according to de Laban. Using Martha Graham's article "Seeking an American Art of the Dance" in Oliver Sayler's 1930 *Revolt in the Arts* as a benchmark, de Laban lamented the state of the profession, seeing change but not progress. Modern dance affected theatrical works, particularly on Broadway in *Oklahoma* (1943) and *On the Town* (1945), and ballet, particularly in its use of American themes. But modern dance itself suffered from a "preoccupation with the intellectual and the abstract" and was losing its audience because of this concern. De Laban called for rejuvenation of American material, such as that of Native Americans and African Americans, "for a better understanding of our polyglot culture and a vigorous attempt to interpret it in terms which satisfy the American audience."[33]

De Laban pressed for the continued effort to combine dance with social concerns that had shaped the art form in the 1930s, but in 1945 her declaration prompted a vigorous attack by Joseph Gifford in the following issue of *Dance Observer*. As a dancer just coming of age professionally, Gifford promoted the interests of a new generation of modern dancers. He denounced the "artificial nationalism" that permeated the field and called for greater devotion to art. Celebrating personal expression, Gifford accused de Laban of "that almost frightening emphasis on such things as audience acceptance" and declared that "we must forget the audience when we create."[34] Speaking to the need to go beyond modern dance's origins and continue to develop it as an art form, Gifford condemned many of the principal elements—the importance of the audience, the value of nationalist and political motives, and the relationship of the individual to the group—that had shaped modern dance in the 1930s.

The debate revealed the growing separation between generations of modern dancers as well as the contentious issues at play in the 1940s. The changes affected the aging generation too. The postwar world pushed this generation of modern dancers down different paths: to more psychologically informed choreography, teaching and administrative duties, musical theater, or fame abroad.[35] After the affectionate *Appalachian Spring,* Graham resolutely delved into Greek mythology, the unconscious, and tortured relations between men and women. *Cave of the Heart* (1946), to music by Samuel Barber and set design by Isamu Noguchi, dramatized the myth of Medea and was a study in jealousy. In these dances Graham achieved the height of her fame in the 1940s and 1950s. Humphrey remained on course as the most conceptual of modern dance choreographers and began turning her attention to teaching choreography. She stopped performing in 1944, separated from her dance partner Charles Weidman, and bolstered the new company and choreographic pursuits of José Limón. Helen Tamiris and Hanya Holm turned to musical theater choreography almost exclusively after the war, where the continued effort to define an American dance had more support. Holm's first big success was *Kiss Me, Kate* (1948), and Tamiris gained praise for her choreography for *Annie Get Your Gun* (1946), *Inside U.S.A.* (1948), which featured an integrated cast, and *Touch and Go* (1949). Tamiris also chose Pearl Primus to star in a revival of *Showboat* that toured the country in 1946. By the late 1940s Primus and Dunham spent most of their time outside the United States, touring and researching in Africa, Europe, and South America.

Some dancers bridged the older and newer generations. Anna Sokolow worked in Mexico and then returned to the United States to choreograph some of her most powerful works, including *Lyric Suite* (1954) and *Rooms* (1955). Donald McKayle drew on the technique of Graham to choreograph powerful statements on African American experience, beginning with *Games* in 1951. Talley Beatty left Katherine Dunham's company in the early 1940s, created an innovative film with Maya Deren called *Study in Choreography for Camera* (1945), and worked in Broadway shows, dancing with Pearl Primus in *Showboat* (1946). Like Primus and McKayle, Beatty also choreographed powerful dances of social commentary during this time, especially *Southern Landscape* (1947). A solo section of that piece, "Mourner's Bench," can be seen as a provocative reformulation of Graham's *Lamentation* (1930). Both dances expressed grief and constructed movement around a long, simple bench stretching horizontally across the stage. But for Beatty grief arose because of another death of an African American and prompted a beseeching of God to explain the horror; he situated emotion in the context of African American lives rather than in abstraction. José Limón also left the company of his mentor and formed his own group in 1946. He still sought Humphrey's tutelage, however, and named her artistic director. Under her guidance his choreography highlighted the emotional drama of modern dance, often in stories from his Mexican heritage. *La Malinche* (1949) drew on fables and folktales to tell the story of the Spanish invasion of Mexico.

Other new dancers contributed to the debate in the mid-1940s, declaring their lack of concern with social and political problems. "I am a dancer, and I think that means I ought just to dance," an anonymous young dancer proclaimed in *Dance Observer*.[36] Gertrude Lippincott, a choreographer and educator, went further, announcing that for the artistic revolt to continue, a modern dancer must create alone, not just divorced from the political and social scene but in isolation with "his conscience alone." This pronouncement drew criticism, as might be expected, from stalwart believers in the importance of group efforts and the tie of "good art and good politics." But the young dancers' new manifestos resonated. Challenging Graham's plea to recognize how the "headlines that make daily history affect the muscles of the human body," these dancers called for art that went "deeper than the level of newspaper headlines," as Lippincott described it.[37] Instead of using dance to amplify the meaning of headlines, the next generation moved away from headlines altogether.

Merce Cunningham led this group of modern dancers who defined themselves against the earlier generation by eschewing the nationalist goal of creating an identifiable American art form, deepening abstraction and intellection, and divorcing tenets of art from social and political concerns. Susan Leigh Foster argues that Cunningham focused on the "physical facts" of the body rather than on the body as a vehicle for conveying emotion: "[T]he body's intrinsic interest, then, resides not in its ability to display or to make manifest but rather in its own consummate physicality."[38] The composer John Cage, Cunningham's collaborator and lover, argued in 1944 that "where any strength now exists in the modern dance, it is, as before, in isolated personalities and physiques."[39] Building on these ideas, Cunningham began experimenting with chance, a choreographic method that divided steps and then rearranged them according to a draw directly before a performance. This method subjected the dancers and the movements to a variable intellectual process. The compositional procedure became the focus of the performance rather than the display of each dancer's expressiveness or dramatization of a particular subject. Instead of using art to reveal cultural and national identity, Cunningham led new modern dancers to insist on the autonomy and purity of physicality and art—and the iconoclasm of the individual artist.

The commitment to iconoclasm prompted a move away from group concerns both on stage and off that reflected a belief in a more austere notion of the artist. In 1930 Doris Humphrey defined herself against her teacher, Mary Wood Hinman, claiming that Hinman was a humanist and she an artist. Hinman wanted dance to reach as many people as possible; Humphrey wanted to make beautiful work, with less concern for reaching the widest possible audience.[40] In reality, the distinction between humanist and artist was not so stark in the 1930s because radical politics provided a bridge between populist concerns and artistic ingenuity. Modern dancers believed that their art form derived from the social scene and that their artistic statements had social impact. But if women like Mary Wood Hinman found the most satisfaction in teaching dance in settlement homes in the 1910s and 1920s, the pull toward artistry that Humphrey described set modern dance on an upward course toward the highbrow realm of modernism. After World War II, modern dancers sharpened the distinction between humanist and artist more clearly, eschewed politics, and defined themselves strictly as artists. Instead of seeking to engage as many people as possible either in audiences or by representing various groups on stage, Cunningham primarily collaborated with musicians and visual artists in the late 1940s and early 1950s and performed to small audiences made up of more artists. In the summer of 1952 at Black Mountain College in North Carolina, Cunningham, Cage, and visual artist Robert Rauschenberg performed concurrently, a harbinger of avant-garde collusions. Unlike planned compositions, these kinds of collaborations created union among genres in simultaneous performances of different artistic visions that required informed audiences.[41]

These wholly unique and transitory events were meant to remove art from social forces so as to reveal aesthetic principles in their purity. But the dominance of gay men in these events and in the next generation of modern dancers betray the continuing force of social dynamics in shaping the arts. Finding ways to dance in the army, gay men took over a significant portion of the leadership of modern dance in the postwar years even though women still far outnumbered men in the profession. The close concern of the individual artist with his or her idea, so resonant in Abstract

Expressionist painting at this time, also suited gay men dancers, content in their homosexuality and choice of profession. They neither defended nor promoted the role of men in dance as vociferously as Ted Shawn had done. What they took from Shawn was a commitment to high art and to a cadre of gay men at the helm. Even if devoted to individual visions of art, the collaborations of Cunningham, Cage, and Rauschenberg exemplified the reinforcement, connections, and inspiration that gay men found together. Mainly a group of white men, they moved easily in society, able to devote their attention to intellectual and abstract ideas without the hindrances and battles that white women and African American men and women still faced. The dominance of men in the next generation of modern dancers also suggests that modern dance followed a pattern similar to that found in other professions, such as elementary education or nursing: in a female-dominated profession, the few men usurped leadership roles (a phenomenon termed the "glass escalator," in contrast to the "glass ceiling" women confront in male-dominated professions).[42] Women continued to excel in modern dance, but the few men in the profession succeeded more easily.

The shift in gender roles in the dance world paralleled a larger societal return to more traditional roles for men and women in the wake of World War II. This social conservatism mirrored a growing political conservatism.[43] In contrast to the growing activism of African American modern dancers, few white modern dancers remained politically active in the 1940s, with the exception of those involved in the New Dance Group, the school that had nurtured Primus. During World War II Helen Tamiris had beseeched other dancers to join her on the Artists' Front to Win the War Committee, headed by Charlie Chaplin and the actor Sam Jaffe, but few did.[44] In fact, by the late 1940s, and especially in the 1950s, Tamiris's political alliances began to haunt her. The politically active dancer and choreographer Jane Dudley remembered that Tamiris "got clobbered later" for having involved herself with Communist affairs.[45] During the late 1940s and early 1950s the House Committee on Un-American Activities identified Tamiris's participation in many suspected Communist activities and Communist-front organizations. Tamiris was the most often cited dancer even though others—such as Edna Ocko and Edith Segal—had played much larger roles in the Communist Party. Tamiris herself referred to the "cruel McCarthy period" in a letter, although there is little evidence to indicate specifically how it was cruel to her. Although Tamiris continued to fight for modern dance, she received little attention and died in 1966, lonely and poor.[46]

Modern dance ended up in the HUAC hearings not only in the many mentions of Tamiris but also in the proceedings of the only dancer who testified, Jerome Robbins. By May 1953, when he spoke before HUAC, Robbins had achieved fame as a choreographer of some repute. In his testimony, Robbins admitted to being a Communist Party member from 1943 to 1947. He had joined because of the Party's fight against anti-Semitism, having himself experienced moments of "minority prejudice" (he had changed his name from Jerome Rabinowitz). Never very involved, he became disenchanted with policy shifts, the petty bickering that seemed to occupy the meetings, and the pressures to justify and explain his art. He remembered being asked by someone how dialectical materialism had helped him choreograph *Fancy Free*—a question he said he found patently absurd then (as did the committee members during his testimony). Robbins offered names of others who had attended meetings, although the only person he named from the dance world was the dance critic of *New Theatre,* Edna Ocko. He completely refuted his earlier beliefs and even expressed his disappointment with the Party's lack of attention to minorities. To Representative Scherer's opinion "that the Communist Party is as anti-Semitic as the Nazi Party ever was," Robbins replied, "[I]t appears to be that way." Robbins won high praise from committee members for his honesty, and *Fancy Free* drew considerable praise for its Americanness. "It's always been identified everywhere it's played as a particularly American piece, indigenous to America, and that its theme has great heart and warmth," Robbins explained to the committee.[47] The committee's embrace of *Fancy Free* demonstrated the extent to which ballet had become the most celebrated American dance form. As Tamiris "got clobbered," Robbins gathered accolades. Those dancers who went from Popular Front action to American patriotism flourished, while those who remained dedicated to political radicalism floundered.

This political change affected the institutionalization of modern dance as well. After a six-year break during the war, the influential Bennington College Summer School of the Dance moved to Connecticut College in 1948. In the early 1950s the program sought money from the Rockefeller Foundation, which prompted a search by the foundation into the participants' political activities. They found a number of modern dancers in what HUAC had identified as Communist-front organizations, such as the New Dance League and *New Masses*. The program eventually received some money from the foundation in 1954 because "the group on whom there were the most questions [William Bales and Sophie Maslow] has been dropped by Connecticut College on artistic grounds."[48] Political concerns shaped aesthetic judgments in the anti-Communist fervor of the early 1950s, and modern dance suffered from its roots in political radicalism.

Foundations in general gave little attention to the arts, especially dance, because foundation officers wanted long-range results, but not sustained commitments to continual funding. The performing arts, in particular, did not fit that strategy. In the postwar years the Rockefeller Foundation began reassessing its policy on giving to the arts, starting by gathering definitions of the fields and identifying their leading practitioners and audiences. The foundation funded the development of Labanotation to record dance, general books on dance, and a 1956 survey on the status of dance across the country by Anatole Chujoy, a dance critic. But most of the officers' curiosity was about ballet. By the mid-1950s Rockefeller Foundation program officers, Chujoy, and even the modern dance cheerleader John Martin agreed that modern dance had lost its distinctiveness and now mostly resembled ballet.[49] When plans for Lincoln Center on the Upper West Side of Manhattan began in the 1950s, the prominent role of Lincoln Kirstein in the venture assured that the new venue would host only ballet and furnish the permanent home for his and George Balanchine's company, the New York City Ballet. And when the Ford Foundation decided to underwrite dance in the early 1960s, it gave an almost $8 million grant—the single largest contribution by a foundation to one art form—exclusively to ballet companies.[50]

Other considerations affected the place of modern dance at the 92nd Street Y in New York City, which had provided a needed home for the nascent art form in the 1930s. Attention to specifically Jewish concerns grew in the wake of the Holocaust and caused Jewish dancers and institutions to reconsider what kind of dance was most important. In 1944 Dvora Lapson, an educator and expert on Jewish dance, advocated the use of dance in synagogues and religious schools and berated Jewish centers and Y's for their support of concert dance and their neglect of "Jewish dance."[51] Even as

Doris Humphrey assumed the directorship of the modern dance division at the 92nd Street Y in 1944, William Kolodney, still in charge of cultural programming, instituted a change in the dance offerings when he engaged Fred Berk, an Austrian-born Jew who fled to the United States via England and Cuba, to develop a "Jewish dance division" at the Y in 1947. Although modern dance classes and performances still occurred at the Y, Israeli folk dancing grew under Berk's inspiration and energy, burgeoning into annual Israeli Folk Dance Festivals beginning in 1952. The cultural pluralism that the Y fostered in the 1930s narrowed in the postwar years to accommodate a bolstering of Jewish identity and heritage. More removed from changing priorities of performing venues, colleges and universities provided the most constant institutional home for modern dance at this time, where it continued to dominate dance offerings.

The rumbling debates that occurred throughout the 1940s over various aspects of modern dance reflected the maturation of an art form that could be considered quite typical. By the end of the 1930s modern dance reached an accepted stature through artistic innovation and effect, the interest of audiences and critics, training schools and programs, established repertoire, and government recognition. As leading dancers and choreographers aged, new hurdles appeared. How does an art form expressly based on individual vision institutionalize itself? How does it transmit itself to new practitioners? And do such processes alter the fundamental principles upon which it began? These questions came to a head in the aftermath of a world war that dramatically changed the conditions in which modern dance first flourished. With the United States no longer in the depths of an economic depression or the exigencies of war, American strength and resilience appeared plentiful and sound, even though the fears of drastic conditions returning undergirded the tenor of those years. Modern dancers had defined their art form in desperate times and believed in the inextricability of art's meaning from contemporary social and political concerns. As prosperity gained hold in the postwar years and modern dance had a past on which to draw, the debate about meaning focused more directly on aesthetic principles themselves. The art form became more concerned with art to the exclusion of its place in the social scene, as the first generation of modern dancers had defined it. Although modern dancers in the 1930s maintained the distinction between high and low cultural forms, their ideas about audience appeal, the utilization of folk and ethnic traditions, and the political import of art flowed between those extremes. After World War II modern dance ascended even further into the highbrow realm, rigidifying those modernist distinctions.

Modern dance gathered momentum in the 1930s because a focus on bodies coalesced with the search to find an American way in the arts that favored an experiential approach, attention to the polyglot nature of the country's population, and revivification of the democratic tradition in the midst of an economic depression and an impending crisis in Europe. This desperate time promoted fluidity in social roles as people struggled to find ways to survive. In modernism that fluidity allowed for the emergence of an art form filled with women striving to compose serious and meaningful statements with their bodies. Modern dancers figured out ways to combine their ardent embrace of individualism with group movement and communal ventures—primarily in dances of America. For white modern dancers, ideas of America successfully captured both social and political demands and ideals. White women rejecting stereotypes of femininity and white gay men countering notions of effeminacy molded an American modern dance to allow for new models of gender and sexuality. For African American dancers, culture and nation overlapped but did not necessarily coincide in their dances. While they fought for and pushed Americans to realize ideals of equality of opportunity and open democracy, they embraced the culture of Africa and the Caribbean to which they felt they more truly belonged. The growing attention to African American dancers in the postwar world—Pearl Primus, Talley Beatty, Donald McKayle, and, eventually, Alvin Ailey—occurred alongside their continued political activism and the increasing fervor of the civil rights movement.

The success of gay men in modern dance in the 1940s demonstrated the continuing impact of social forces in the evolution of modernism in the United States. Despite communal successes in the 1930s, belief in individual creativity and expression reigned in the 1940s, and the more patriotic unity necessary in wartime pressed modern dancers to recognize the limits of their political and ideological beliefs. White gay men took over leadership roles and secured increasingly substantial roles in the avant-garde. Whereas confrontational notions of art infiltrated the mainstream in the 1930s, experimental artworks were pushed to the borders of the art world in the 1940s and 1950s; the intellectual thrust of Merce Cunningham strengthened the common belief that modern dance was an exclusive and esoteric activity. It is not surprising, then, that modern dance ascended in universities and colleges. Modern dance began with a vital intellectual foundation, and while modern dancers of the 1930s maintained hope for populist appeal and social relevance, these elements largely fell victim to more strict aesthetic and philosophical goals among the next generation of modern dancers.

The diffusion of modern dance after World War II—into Broadway show dancing, ballet, and other artistic genres, and throughout universities and colleges—revealed its strength as a malleable technique able to be used in a variety of ways. That diffusion, however, also contributed to its inability to gain institutional support or financial stability, or to retain and market its beginnings as an original American art form (something jazz music has been able to do more successfully). These modern bodies proved too confrontational. As modernism marched on in the postwar world, drawing more institutional force and popular credence, modern dance sloped to the high end of the cultural spectrum. On the edges of society, modern dancers found what power they could on the edges of the arts.

coda THE REVELATIONS OF ALVIN AILEY

In January 1958 the New York City Ballet premiered George Balanchine's *Stars and Stripes*. To music by John Philip Sousa, ballet dancers displayed military precision in straight lines and unison movements of the corps. In Cold War America, the Russian émigré Balanchine celebrated America's military prowess and apparently unified (and uniform) populace. The New York City Ballet reigned supreme in the dance world, suited to the times by waging a dance battle on the European turf of ballet—and winning with an aggressive and speedy American style. After World War II, the American takeover of ballet was a powerful cultural weapon. The success of American ballet, wresting dominance from the Soviet Union, was a more important artistic battle than upholding the disparate, experimental, and confrontational style of modern dance.

Despite ballet's winning the dominant place in American concert dance in a changed political environment, the concurrent emergence and success of Alvin Ailey points to changing social dynamics in modern dance as well. The same year *Stars and Stripes* premiered, Ailey made his choreographic debut in New York City at the 92nd Street Y. The Alvin Ailey American Dance Theater, formed in 1958, fused in movement and theme the nationalist political focus of the 1930s with the racial heritage of America—thus embracing and altering American modern dance.

Alvin Ailey was born in Texas in 1931 just as Martha Graham, Doris Humphrey, Ted Shawn, Katherine Dunham, Helen Tamiris, and others were solidifying the new modern dance. Ailey grew up amid fierce racial segregation; when he was five, his mother was raped by a white man. Ailey moved to Los Angeles as a teenager and there became fascinated with Bill Robinson, Fred Astaire, and the Nicholas Brothers. He took gymnastics in school and went to a performance of the Katherine Dunham company, at which time, he recalled, he became "completely hooked" on dance.[1]

Soon after, Ailey sought out dance lessons at the school of Lester Horton, the progenitor of modern dance in Los Angeles. By the 1940s exclusion of African American students from dance classes had diminished, with the New Dance Group in New York City and Lester Horton in Los Angeles leading the way in active integration of African Americans. Some of the most famous African American dancers, including Ailey, Carmen de Lavallade, and Janet Collins, received training from Horton. Ailey had to travel an hour and a half on the bus each way to Horton's studio, but once there, he received vital support and opportunities. After Horton's death in 1953 Ailey became the company choreographer.

The year 1954 marked a transition for Ailey. From an appearance in the movie *Carmen Jones,* Ailey caught the attention of its choreographer, Herbert Ross. He took up Ross's invitation to appear in his next Broadway production, *House of Flowers,* a rendering of love and life on a Caribbean island with a story by Truman Capote. In New York Ailey trained with Martha Graham, Hanya Holm, Doris Humphrey, Anna Sokolow, and the ballet teacher Karel Shook. As was quite common for modern dancers at the time, he performed primarily in Broadway shows. Concerned that African American dancers lacked concert opportunities, Ailey pulled together dancers for a concert appearance at the 92nd Street Y in 1958 and debuted *Blues Suite.*

Two signature Ailey dances, *Blues Suite* (1958) and *Revelations* (1960), focused on the experience of African Americans. Ailey felt that *Blues Suite* was "a somewhat angry statement about the racial conditions [of the United States], and that *Revelations* was a very positive, very spiritual expression of our creating an environment in which we could survive" (a combination that paralleled Primus's expression of a fuller vision of the United States in *Strange Fruit* and *Hard Time Blues*).[2] In movement terms *Revelations,* first choreographed in 1960 and edited substantially during the 1960s (primarily in cutting the length and changing from simple voice and guitar accompaniment to that of chorus and orchestra), combined the dance technique contributions of Martha Graham, Doris Humphrey, and Lester Horton with those of Asadata Dafora, Katherine Dunham, and Pearl Primus. *Revelations* began with a solid group center stage on wide, deep-bended legs, arms spread sideways, arcing at the elbows, and heads focused on the floor (see

FIGURE C.I. *Alvin Ailey American Dance Theater in* Revelations. *(Jerome Robbins Dance Division, The New York Public Library for the Performing Arts, Astor, Lenox and Tilden Foundations)*

figure C.1). The winged image subtly shifted as the spiritual "I Been 'Buked" played on. Stretched arms and heads that angled downward slowly lifted upward, swaying, to the sky. From this gentle transformation the piece grew in intensity and excitement through solos and duets and ended in a rollicking church scene to "Rocka My Soul." Ailey used the sunken torso contractions of Graham throughout *Revelations,* but placed them on the musical beat and in rhythmic succession. Agonizing backward falls to the ground appeared in the duet "Fix Me Jesus," where the man caught the falling woman, but they were repeated in a quick series that emphasized the upswing of the movement rather than the gravity-laden force of the fall. The section "Wading in the Water" featured colorful costumes, shoulder isolations, and full body contractions reminiscent of Dunham and Primus. Even more, the joy and hope of survival of the piece aligned Ailey with Dunham and Primus. Invariably, *Revelations* roused the audience to their feet in the final section, clapping and swaying along with the dancers on stage.

Ailey focused on the theme of African Americans' struggle for freedom and opportunity in his choreography, employed African American, Asian, white, and Latino/a dancers in one company, and fused African and Caribbean movements with modern dance technique—all under an American banner. His company cemented the small triumphs in the changing social composition of dance that had occurred since Edna Guy's difficulties in the 1920s. In 1944 Martha Graham had employed Yuriko, a Japanese American who came to the Graham school from a California internment camp; in 1951 Mary Hinkson and Matt Turney, African American women trained at the University of Wisconsin, joined the Graham company. Janet Collins and Arthur Mitchell broke color barriers in ballet: Collins performed with the Metropolitan Opera Ballet from 1951 to 1954, and Mitchell debuted as a soloist in the New York City Ballet in 1955. Ailey, on the other hand, deliberately placed the experience of African Americans and African American dancers themselves at the core of his American dance.

Ailey's work, though, contrasted with that of other modern dancers in the 1960s. Modern dance burgeoned again in the early 1960s, led by the small but influential group of innovators associated with the Judson Church, including Robert Dunn, Yvonne Rainer, Steve Paxton, and Trisha Brown. Influenced by the collaboration of Merce Cunningham and John Cage, the Judson Church choreographers forsook the technical precision and nationalist concern of the 1930s moderns and, instead, celebrated pedestrian motions, challenged the strictures of choreography with the use of improvisation and chance, questioned the dependency of dance on music, and eschewed narrative and theatrical elements of performance. The development of postmodern dance paralleled the rebellion of Pop Art to Abstract Expression, and the continued experimentation contributed to the rise and definition of postmodernism in the arts within the avant-garde of New York City.[3] Ailey, however, retained the attention to narrative and theatricality and to a harmonic dependency between music and dance; consciously evolving an American style of modern dance, he drew audiences outside New York City and the avant-garde. From the segregation of African American dancers and choreographers in the 1930s, Ailey successfully secured a place for African Americans within self-consciously American works in the 1960s. If many postmodern dancers and choreographers used the modern dancers of the 1930s as a springboard against which to rebel, Ailey incorporated and carried on the political orientation and broad appeal of the earlier dancers.

What the prominence of Ailey shared with postmodernists was the continued leading role of gay men in modern dance begun in the late 1940s. While women, both white and African American, had led the movement in the 1930s, by the 1960s men, both white and African American, led the art form, even though it continued to attract far more women than men. In 1973 the Alvin Ailey company revived Ted Shawn's *Kinetic Molpai* and merged the tradition of white gay men with that of African American men. The achievement and influence of choreographers such as Trisha Brown and Twyla Tharp demonstrate that modern dance offered a welcoming place for women leaders, and still more so than ballet. But the continued prominence of men in modern dance, particularly relative to their small numbers, suggests that men still retain an advantage in this female-dominated profession.

The emergence of Ailey in the trajectory of modern dance illuminates how social dimensions of our bodies shaped artistic movements in the United States in the twentieth century. In the 1930s dancing pictures of America remained white; the depictions of Africa and the Caribbean by African American dancers only reinforced the whiteness of physical portraits of America. Racial integration in the dance world occurred slowly and correlated to increasing political activism for civil rights. But the rise of Ailey was definitive. His success occurred at a time of political liberalism and redefinition of the United States as fundamentally ethnically diverse. He formed his own company, called it American, and proceeded to choreograph America. The U.S. government's choice of Ailey to represent America's concert dancing prowess abroad as cultural envoy in the John F. Kennedy International Exchange Program in 1962 finally sanctioned African Americans' rightful place as practitioners in, and creators of, modern dance.

Ailey's success in the 1960s rests on the foundation established by Dafora, Dunham, Primus, and other African American dancers in the 1930s and

1940s. If the debate between the freedom and distinctiveness of the individual and the need for and belief in collective harmony formed the creative tension of modern dance, Dunham's and Primus's position as dancers and anthropologists highlighted what was at stake. In bringing insights on this question from the Caribbean and Africa, they shed light on the social dimensions that structured the concert stages and neighborhoods of the United States. They insisted upon a broadened definition of art and culture and a loosening of rigid social categories of race, gender, sexuality, and class. The history of modern dance reveals the limitations that remained despite their push: divisions of art into high and low went largely unchallenged and perpetuated class and racial prejudices. But the revelations of Alvin Ailey show that these bodies could indeed rearrange the "headlines that make daily history" and move the world.

notes

ABBREVIATIONS

CUOHROC
  Oral History Research Office Collection, Columbia University, New York,
  New York
DC/NYPL
  Dance Collection, Jerome Robbins Dance Division, The New York Public
  Library for the Performing Arts, Astor, Lenox and Tilden Foundations, New
  York, New York
DH
  Doris Humphrey Collection, DC/NYPL
FTP-GMU
  Federal Theatre Project Oral History Collection, Special Collection and
  Archives, George Mason University Libraries, Fairfax, Virginia
RSD
  Ruth St. Denis Collection, DC/NYPL
TS
  Ted Shawn Collection, DC/NYPL

INTRODUCTION

1. *New York Times,* 5 January 1930.

2. *New Yorker,* 18 January 1930, 57–59.

3. Margaret Gage, "A Study in American Modernism," *Theatre Arts Monthly* 14
(March 1930): 229–32.

4. Humphrey quoted in Humphrey and Cohen, *Doris Humphrey,* 89.

5. Sayler, *Revolt in the Arts,* 12, 13.

6. Reminiscences of Jane Dudley, 20 December 1978, CUOHROC, 21.

7. Modernism has attracted immense interest among scholars, particularly in the fields of art history and literature. While I have drawn on recent studies such as Miller, *Late Modernism,* and Albright, *Untwisting the Serpent,* I have benefited most from historians and American studies scholars seeking to understand the social impact of these transformations in the arts. See Singal, "Towards a Definition of American Modernism"; Lears, *No Place of Grace;* Kern, *Culture of Time and Space;* Huyssen, *After the Great Divide;* Lawrence Levine, *Highbrow/Lowbrow;* Denning, *Cultural Front;* Scott and Rutkoff, *New York Modern;* Crunden, *Body and Soul;* Stansell, *American Moderns;* and classic works by Henry May, *End of American Innocence,* and Kazin, *On Native Grounds.*

Few cultural historians of the 1930s, however, have included modern dance in their analysis, and when they have done so they have usually used particular works by Martha Graham as examples of their broader claims. For example, see Stott, *Documentary Expression,* 123–28, and Susman, "Culture and Commitment," in *Culture as History,* 206–7. These mentions of Graham's *American Document* and *Appalachian Spring,* respectively, serve as good examples of these historians' larger claims, but neither traces the particular development of modern dance. Thus they miss the difference between *American Document* and *Appalachian Spring,* for example, that I will draw out in Chapter 6.

8. Within general studies of modernism, dance has received little attention. Dance scholars have sought to address that gap, particularly Lynn Garafola in *Diaghilev's Ballets Russes,* which places dance innovations in the first part of the twentieth century in Europe within the realm of other arts and ongoing social and political transformations. Mark Franko has offered the most trenchant theoretical account of dance modernism in the United States in *Dancing Modernism/Performing Politics.* See also Burt, *Alien Bodies;* Manning, *Ecstasy and the Demon;* Thomas, *Dance, Modernity, and Culture;* and Francis, "From Event to Monument." My intention is to integrate studies on modernism with important new work in dance studies, in particular, that on gender and race. There are several anthologies that demonstrate the insights emerging from dance scholarship; see Foster, *Choreographing History* and *Corporealities;* Morris, *Moving Words;* Desmond, *Meaning in Motion* and *Dancing Desires;* Doolittle and Flynn, *Dancing Bodies.*

9. Baldwin, *Tell Me How Long the Train's Been Gone,* 332.

10. Humphrey, *Art of Making Dances,* 106.

1. *New York Times,* 26 April 1922.

2. For a general overview of American ballet in the nineteenth and early twentieth centuries, see Barker, *Ballet or Ballyhoo,* and Horowitz, *Michel Fokine.* For its place in vaudeville and burlesque, see Allen, *Horrible Prettiness;* Cohen-Stratyner, "Ned Wayburn and the Dance Routine"; Cohen, "Borrowed Art of Gertrude Hoffman."

3. On Duncan, see her autobiography, *My Life,* and Daly, *Done into Dance.* On Fuller, see Sommer, "Loïe Fuller." For a general overview of dance innovations during this period, see Kendall, *Where She Danced;* Ruyter, *Reformers and Visionaries;* Jowitt, *Time and the Dancing Image;* Tomko, *Dancing Class.*

4. St. Denis, *Ruth St. Denis;* Shelton, *Divine Dancer.* For an analysis of St. Denis's use of Asian sources, see Desmond, "Dancing Out the Difference." For an analysis of the influence of religion on her dances, see LaMothe, "Passionate Madonna."

5. Tomko, *Dancing Class,* chap. 2; Blair, *Torchbearers;* McCarthy, *Women's Culture.*

6. Julia Ward Humphrey to Doris Humphrey, 29 August 1917, Folder C243.12, DH.

7. For the fullest treatment of this idea in dance, see Kendall, *Where She Danced.* On changing images of women at the turn of the century, see Banner, *American Beauty;* Banta, *Imaging American Women;* Cott, *Grounding of Modern Feminism.*

8. Tomko, *Dancing Class;* Peiss, *Cheap Amusements;* Erenberg, *Stepping Out.*

9. Tomko, *Dancing Class,* chaps. 3, 5.

10. The Jewish population in New York, mostly settled in the Lower East Side, grew from approximately 510,000 in 1900 to 1,713,000 in 1925 — from 6.7 percent to 28 percent of the population of the city as a whole. Rosenwaike, *Population History of New York City,* 111; Tomko, *Dancing Class,* chaps. 3–4 (on the influence of Ruskin and Morris, 86–88); Kuzmack, *Woman's Cause,* chap. 4, on settlement reformers (on Wald, 99–105).

11. Crowley, *Neighborhood Playhouse,* 41. See also biographical material on the Lewisohn family, mainly photocopies of newspaper articles collected by Florence Lewisohn, American Jewish Archives, Cincinnati, Ohio.

12. The best sources on Tamiris are a draft of her autobiography, a published chronology of her career, and primary sources in DC/NYPL: see Tamiris, "Tamiris in Her Own Voice"; Schlundt, *Tamiris;* correspondence, clipping files, papers, film clips, photographs in Helen Tamiris Collection, DC/NYPL.

13. Tamiris, "Tamiris in Her Own Voice," 12.

14. It is unclear exactly what years Tamiris spent at the Metropolitan and when

she went on the South American tour. Daniel Nagrin suggests that her first season with the Metropolitan may have been 1917–18 and that she went on a tour of South America in 1920. Ibid., 53–54 n. 21, 54 n. 27.

15. Ibid., 17–22.

16. Tamiris, "Manifest[o]," [1927], included in ibid., 66.

17. Reminiscences of Faith Reyher Jackson, 21 April 1979, CUOHROC, 93. The connections between modern dance and the political left will be developed further in Chapter 5. See also Graff, *Stepping Left,* and Franko, *Dancing Modernism/Performing Politics.*

18. Tamiris, "Tamiris in Her Own Voice," 32.

19. Ibid., 37.

20. Ibid., 51–52.

21. Sayler, *Revolt in the Arts,* 4, 11.

22. Reminiscences of Otto Luening, 23 January 1979, CUOHROC, 72.

23. Doris Humphrey to her parents, 13 February 1928 postmark, Folder C269.6, DH. On the relationship between the arts in modernism, see Albright, *Untwisting the Serpent.*

24. Humphrey, *Art of Making Dances,* 106; Doris Humphrey, "I was . . . trained in all forms of the dance," n.d. [1930s?], Folder M43.1, DH.

25. Tamiris, "Tamiris in Her Own Voice," 40.

26. Gertrude Stein, "Tender Buttons," in Van Vechten, *Selected Writings,* 483.

27. Graham quoted in Armitage, *Martha Graham,* 97.

28. John Martin, "The Modern Dance: The Fourth of a Series," *American Dancer* 10, no. 5 (March 1937): 15, 42; see other articles in the series in December 1936, January 1937, and February 1937 issues. See also Martin, *Modern Dance,* a compilation of his lectures at the New School for Social Research, and *America Dancing.* Mark Franko discusses the role of emotion in modernism in the case of Graham in *Dancing Modernism/Performing Politics,* chap. 3, and the criticism of John Martin and Lincoln Kirstein in "Abstraction Has Many Faces."

29. Martha Graham, "Seeking an American Art of the Dance," in Sayler, *Revolt in the Arts,* 250.

30. For treatment of this interest amongst anthropologists and writers, see Torgovnick, *Gone Primitive,* and Clifford, *Predicament of Culture.*

31. Martha Graham, "The Dance in America," *Trend* 1, no. 1 (March 1932): 6. It is clear that in naming African American dance as "indigenous" to America, Graham did not take into account African Americans' forced transplantation into this country.

32. For another view from the time period of the holistic power of Native American dancing, see Dane Rudhyar, "The Indian Dances for Power," *Dance Observer* 1, no. 6 (August–September 1934): 64. The work of Jacqueline Shea Murphy explores the relationship between Native American dance and modern dance; see "Lessons in Dance (as) History: Aboriginal Land Claims and Aboriginal Dance, circa 1999," in Doolittle and Flynn, *Dancing Bodies*, 130–67.

33. In *Digging the Africanist Presence in American Performance,* Brenda Dixon Gottschild explores the appropriation of African and African American dance traits by white concert dance choreographers, including the ballet choreographer George Balanchine.

34. Austin, *American Rhythm,* 66.

35. For an extended treatment of the connection between dance and modernist poetry, see Rodgers, *Universal Drum.*

36. Humphrey, *Art of Making Dances,* 104. See also Doris Humphrey to Charles Woodford, July 1931, Folder C287.1, DH. On the inherent rhythmic talent of African Americans, see Humphrey to her parents, 2 August 1927 postmark, Folder C267.7, ibid.

37. Humphrey quoted in Siegel, *Days on Earth,* 55.

38. Ibid., 69.

39. Ruth St. Denis, "The Color Dancer," *Denishawn Magazine* 1, no. 2 [1924]: 1–4; Edna Guy to Ruth St. Denis, 15 November [1924?], Folder 749, RSD.

40. Edna Guy to Ruth St. Denis, n.d. [1930?], Folder 747, ibid.

41. Pauline Lawrence, Humphrey's friend and accompanist, describes going up to Harlem with Betty Horst, the wife of Martha Graham's accompanist, Louis Horst, in a letter to Humphrey dated 13 July 1932, in Folder C319.2, DH.

42. Scholarly work on the artistic activities of African Americans in the first half of the twentieth century has generally focused on writers and painters. Appraisals of the male writers of the Harlem Renaissance, in particular, rule most interpretations. See Huggins, *Harlem Renaissance.* Lewis, in *When Harlem Was in Vogue,* presents a detailed view of the leaders of the Harlem Renaissance, their place in the African American community, and the relatively short life of the focused artistic outpouring. More recently, attention has been given to the women of the Harlem Renaissance; see Hull, *Color, Sex and Poetry,* and Dearborn, *Pocahontas's Daughters,* chap. 3. For a detailed view of an African American painter, see Kirschke, *Aaron Douglas.* For views of the interaction between white and black New Yorkers during this period, see Douglas, *Terrible Honesty,* and Hutchinson, *Harlem Renaissance in Black and White.*

43. Johnson, *Black Manhattan,* 260.

44. Edna Guy to Ruth St. Denis, 11 August [1930?], Folder 746, RSD.

45. The best overview of African American dancers in the 1920s and 1930s is Perpener, *African-American Concert Dance.* For a review of the Negro Art Theatre Dance Group concert that highlights many of the issues confronting African American dancers, see John Martin, "Dance Recital Given by Negro Artists," *New York Times,* 30 April 1931.

46. Edna Guy to Ruth St. Denis, 15 November [1924?], Folder 749, RSD.

47. Humphrey quoted in Humphrey and Cohen, *Doris Humphrey,* 75. On Humphrey's view of entertainment, see Doris Humphrey to her parents, 31 August 1930 postmark, Folder C278.12, DH.

48. Sayler, *Revolt in the Arts,* 16.

49. Doris Humphrey, "This Modern Dance," *Dancing Times,* no. 339 (December 1938): 272. See also Doris Humphrey, "Purpose of my dance . . . in the social scene," n.d. [early 1930s?], notes for a lecture-demonstration, Folder M60.1, DH.

CHAPTER TWO

1. *Vanity Fair* 43, no. 4 (December 1934): 40. For a discussion of the inclusion of cooch dancing in burlesque, see Allen, *Horrible Prettiness,* 227–36.

2. Doris Humphrey to her mother, 15 November 1937 postmark, Folder C397.10, DH. Sally Rand to Doris Humphrey and Charles Weidman, 30 March 1942, Folder C523.8, ibid.: "I have always had such tremendous admiration for your work, not only for its sheer beauty but because of the intellectuality that is so obvious in it."

3. Within the past decade dance scholars have begun to untangle the gendering of the art form. See Hanna, *Dance, Sex, and Gender;* Adair, *Women and Dance;* Manning, *Ecstasy and the Demon;* Daly, *Done into Dance;* Carol Martin, *Dance Marathons;* Banes, *Dancing Women;* Tomko, *Dancing Class.*

4. Doris Humphrey, "Purpose of my dance . . . in the social scene," n.d. [early 1930s?], notes for a lecture-demonstration, Folder M60.1, DH.

5. The best overview of women in the 1930s is Ware, *Holding Their Own.* Her chapter on women in literature and the fine arts, however, includes no discussion of women in dance. Dance continues to be overlooked in general discussions of the arts or performing arts. As the rare artistic realm where women dominated, it deserves increased attention for the perspective it can bring to other areas where there were few women. For the plight of women in the field of music, see Ammer, *Unsung.* Huyssen suggests that in women's exclusion from high art in modernism, mass culture ("modernism's other") becomes gendered as feminine; see *After the Great Divide,*

chap. 3. Because modern dance was dominated by women, however, its development as a realm of high art offers a more complicated picture of the gendering of modernism. For a beginning analysis based on Isadora Duncan, see Francis, "From Event to Monument."

Also, the most prevalent question about women in the 1930s among historians of women is how and if the fight for women's rights continued after the passage of suffrage. Nancy Cott's *Grounding of Modern Feminism* ends with women's "resort to individualism" in the late 1920s (281), as does Mari Jo Buhle's *Women and American Socialism*. Both accounts suggest that the embrace of individualism resulted in a turn away from collective feminist goals. For a different view, see Pamela Haag's discussion of the "bifurcated female self" of women in relation to sexuality during this same time period, "In Search of 'The Real Thing.'" The development of modern dance challenges Barbara Melosh's finding, in *Engendering Culture*, of the "containment of feminism" in other New Deal artistic activities.

6. Dr. George Graham, quoted in Terry, *Frontiers of Dance*, 1. For Graham's own description of these early years, see her autobiography, *Blood Memory*, 18–27. Other biographical sources on Graham include McDonagh, *Martha Graham*, and de Mille, *Martha*. See Bird and Greenberg, *Bird's Eye View*, for a good perspective on working with Graham.

7. Graham, *Blood Memory*, 61–65.

8. Biographical sources on Humphrey include her autobiography, *Doris Humphrey*, edited and completed by Selma Jeanne Cohen, and Siegel, *Days on Earth*. For more on the relationship between Mary Wood Hinman and Humphrey, see Tomko, *Dancing Class*, 160–65.

9. Humphrey and Cohen, *Doris Humphrey*, 62; Doris Humphrey to her parents, 2 July 1928 postmark, Folder C270.10, DH. For more on the place of Jews in the art form, see Chapter 6.

10. Dorothy Dunbar Bromley, "Feminist—New Style," *Harper's*, no. 929 (October 1927): 552–60. For a treatment of youth culture in the 1920s, see Fass, *The Damned and the Beautiful*.

11. Doris Humphrey, "What Shall We Dance About?," *Trend* 1 (June–July–August 1932): 46.

12. Dewey, *Experience and Nature*, 393.

13. The gendered dimensions of individualism have garnered attention from women's historians in particular. Linda Kerber and Elizabeth Fox-Genovese tackle the issue directly. In "Can a Woman Be an Individual?: The Discourse of Self-Reliance," in Curry and Goodheart, *American Chameleon*, 151–66, a discussion pri-

marily based on evidence from the eighteenth to the mid-nineteenth century, Kerber concludes that women did not fit into male conceptions of individualism as a "trope whose major theme was the denial of dependence" (160–61), but she does not sufficiently probe those women who insisted on using the label and what they meant by it. In *Feminism without Illusions* Fox-Genovese primarily examines the use of individualism in the contemporary feminist movement; while calling for a historical approach to the concept, she concentrates mainly on the nineteenth century and then jumps to the feminist movement beginning in the 1960s. For an overview of individualism in American intellectual history, see McClay, *The Masterless*. McClay discusses only the debates over individualism within the feminist movement and scholarship on women since the 1960s (283–87), neglecting women's thoughts on the matter throughout American history.

14. Humphrey, "What Shall We Dance About?," 48.

15. Katherine Dunham, "Notes on the Dance," in Clark and Wilkerson, *Kaiso!*, 211–16.

16. Graham quoted in Armitage, *Martha Graham*, 88.

17. Cheney, *The Theatre*, 12.

18. See the reminiscences of Martha Voice Bartos, 4 April 1979, CUOHROC, 48; Kathleen Slagle Partlon, 15 August 1979, ibid., 77; and Natalie Harris Wheatley, 23 August 1979, ibid., 63. Doris Humphrey mentioned to her parents in 1928 that only two dancers had not returned to her company that fall, one because of a recent marriage; see Humphrey to her parents, 24 September 1928 postmark, Folder C271.9, DH.

19. Charles Woodford to Doris Humphrey, August 1931 postmark, Folder C290.16, ibid.; Doris Humphrey to her parents, 12 June 1932, Folder C302.4, ibid.

20. George Crane to Doris Humphrey, 16 October 1942, Folder C524.11, ibid. Hanya Holm had a son during a marriage in Germany, and after her divorce and move to America in 1931, he eventually joined her in New York. Holm raised the child while teaching and choreographing, but her greatest period of activity started later in the 1930s, by which time her son had become an adolescent; see Sorell, *Hanya Holm*, 13–14.

21. Doris Humphrey to her parents, January 1930 postmark, Folder C276.2, DH.

22. Powys, *In Defence of Sensuality*, 149; Doris Humphrey to Charles Woodford, n.d. [May 1933?], Folder C336.6, DH.

23. Doris Humphrey to her parents, 24 November 1929 postmark, Folder C275.12, ibid.

24. See Doris Humphrey's interchangeable use of "pioneer" and "pioneer

woman" in "Purpose of my dance." Similarly, Graham was often referred to as both a pioneer and a pioneer woman because of her 1935 solo *Frontier.*

25. Doris Humphrey, "New Dance," [1936], reprinted in Kriegsman, *Modern Dance in America,* 284. See also Doris Humphrey to her parents, 24 September 1928 postmark, Folder C271.9, DH.

26. Tobias, "Conversation with Martha Graham," 62.

27. Doris Humphrey to her parents, 24 November 1929 postmark, Folder C275.12, DH; the same thought is expressed in another letter to her parents, 4 December 1928, Folder C271.16, ibid.

28. Doris Humphrey, "New Dance," [1936], reprinted in Humphrey and Cohen, *Doris Humphrey,* 240.

29. Film of a 1972 American Dance Festival performance, DC/NYPL.

30. Grant Hyde Code, "Contemporary American Dance," n.d. [1939/1940?], [draft for an article or book?], Grant Hyde Code Collection, DC/NYPL. Code often opened up the Brooklyn Museum for dance performances and housed a short-lived project there called the Young Choreographers Laboratory under the Federal Theatre Project. Code eventually lost his job in 1939, perhaps due to financial cutbacks, and attempted to get money by writing about dance. His articles appeared in dance periodicals and *Theatre Arts Monthly.* This manuscript seems to be a draft for a longer project that was never realized.

31. For a treatment of jazz in this period, see Erenberg, *Swingin' the Dream,* and Stowe, *Swing Changes.*

32. The phrase is most commonly associated with Du Bois, *Souls of Black Folk,* chap. 1.

33. Humphrey, "New Dance," [1936], in Humphrey and Cohen, *Doris Humphrey,* 241. See also Doris Humphrey to Letitia Ide, [1930], Folder 280.1, DH.

34. Doris Humphrey, "This Modern Dance," *Dancing Times,* no. 339 (December 1938): 272. See also Humphrey, "Purpose of my dance."

35. Recounted by Graham in "Martha Graham Reflects," *New York Times,* 31 March 1985.

36. Laura Mulvey developed the notion of a "male gaze" in "Visual Pleasure and the Narrative Cinema." Since then understanding spectatorship has been a concern for many scholars. More recent explorations include Hansen, *Babel and Babylon,* and Lizabeth Cohen, "Encountering Mass Culture at the Grassroots." One of the best explorations in dance is Susan Manning, "The Female Dancer and the Male Gaze: Feminist Critique of Early Modern Dance," in Desmond, *Meaning in Motion,* 153–66.

37. *New Dance,* January 1935.

38. King, *Transformations,* 84.

39. For an example of the use of sexlessness, see John Martin, *America Dancing,* 79.

40. *New York World Telegram,* 20 August 1936.

41. On "Humphrey type," see the reminiscences of Vivian Fine, 10 December 1978, CUOHROC, 39. Terry quoted in Sorell, *Hanya Holm,* 157, 159, 77.

42. Cahn, *Coming On Strong,* 164–77. This connotation would become even more pervasive in the 1950s and beyond; see ibid., chap. 7.

43. Vida Ginsberg Deming remarks on the seriousness toward art and dance that resulted in a "convent" quality at Bennington; see her reminiscences, 11 April 1979, CUOHROC, 40. Kathleen Slagle Partlon also likened touring to being in a "nunnery," where there was little time for social activities of any kind; see Partlon's reminiscences, 15 August 1979, ibid., 66.

44. Siegel calls Humphrey's and Lawrence's relationship undefined and concedes that it could have included sex, mainly because they had a "complete partnership" that ranged from professional cooperation to a communal living arrangement; see *Days on Earth,* 72. A former Humphrey-Weidman dancer reiterated this possibility and that of a liaison between Hill and Shelly. Miriam Raphael Cooper, interview by the author, New York City, 8 December 1994.

45. For an account of Graham expounding on "free love" before classes, see Soares, *Louis Horst,* 37–38. Claudia Moore Read remembers people from "the hinterlands" who were attending Bennington being upset by the affair between Erick Hawkins and Martha Graham: "Morally that's disgusting at that time." See Read's reminiscences, 29 September 1979, CUOHROC, 125–26.

46. Pauline Lawrence to Doris Humphrey, June 1931, Folder C293.2, DH.

47. Horst writing in *Denishawn Magazine* in 1925, quoted in Soares, *Louis Horst,* 46. Horst's own many flirtations with women modern dancers before, during, and after his affair with Graham, while he remained married the entire time, seemingly confirmed the truthfulness of this characterization for him.

48. Graham quoted in Armitage, *Martha Graham,* 97.

49. See Weber, *Patron Saints,* for an account of Kirstein's involvement in the recognition of modern painting and sculpture, both as a student at Harvard and later in New York City and Hartford, Connecticut. For an insightful commentary on the role that the critics Kirstein and John Martin had on defining dance modernism, see Franko, "Abstraction Has Many Faces."

50. Lincoln Kirstein, "Prejudice Purely," *New Republic* 78 (11 April 1934): 243–44.

51. Humphrey, "Purpose of my dance."

52. Telephone interview by the author with Connie Stein Sarason, 12 September 1995; reminiscences of Polly S. Hertz, 18 September 1979, CUOHROC, 40.

53. Graham in Sayler, *Revolt in the Arts,* 249, and Armitage, *Martha Graham,* 97.

CHAPTER THREE

1. Doris Humphrey, "Dance, Little Chillun!," *American Dancer* 6, no. 10 (July 1933): 8; see also Doris Humphrey to her parents, 30 January 1933 postmark, Folder C329.10, DH.

2. Carl Van Vechten, "The Lindy Hop" (1930), reprinted in *Dance Writings of Carl Van Vechten,* 40.

3. Houston Baker Jr., *Modernism and the Harlem Renaissance,* offers an insightful view of African American writers and critics. Gilroy, *Black Atlantic,* places the question of race and modernism in a diasporic context. Gates, "Trope of a New Negro," considers the negation of the "Old Negro" in the formation of the "New Negro." For more general accounts of African Americans in the arts, see Stuckey, *Slave Culture* and *Going through the Storm,* and Floyd, *The Power of Black Music.* See also Huyssen, *After the Great Divide,* for the division between high and low in modernism.

4. A variety of books in dance history are devoted to the topic of African Americans in dance but without the historical specificity I hope to lay out. The venerable *Jazz Dance* by the Stearnses still provides an entertaining introduction to the subject through interviews conducted with dancers of the period. Emery's *Black Dance* offers an overview that is exhaustive in tracing the occurrence of American black dance over time but cursory in its analysis. Two books give good pictorial narratives: Long, *Black Tradition in American Dance,* and Thorpe, *Black Dance.* Hazzard-Gordon, *Jookin',* addresses the varying sociological spaces in which black dance has occurred. John O. Perpener III offers the best overview of the period and provides biographical information on dancers who will not be discussed in depth here: Randolph Sawyer, Ollie Burgoyne, and Charles Williams. See Perpener, *African-American Concert Dance.* See also Creque-Harris, "Representation of African Dance," and Begho, "Black Dance Continuum."

Two recent books point to growing attention to dance in African American studies scholarship. *Digging the Africanist Presence in American Performance* by Dixon-Gottschild accents the application of theoretical concerns to dance. Malone, *Steppin' on the Blues,* skillfully examines the tradition of step dancing in African American communities. Two collections of short essays edited by Gerald Myers, *The Black Tradition in American Modern Dance* and *African American Genius in Modern Dance,* give a good overview of the issues that now concern dance scholars. Manning explores the relationship between white and African American dancers in various articles including "Cultural Theft—or Love?" and "Black Voices, White Bodies."

5. Richard Bone first suggested a Chicago renaissance in "Richard Wright and the Chicago Renaissance," and Floyd, *Power of Black Music,* elaborates on this idea (118–35). Apparently interest in dance occurred in the early 1930s in both Harlem and Chicago, whereas other art forms began rejuvenation in Harlem in the mid-1920s. The Chicago movement does seem to have taken off in the early 1930s (as opposed to Bone's date of 1935), and performance arts appear to have been more active than literature. Douglas, in *Terrible Honesty,* explores the different natures of the black and white communities in New York and Chicago, which may have contributed to less fluidity between black and white literary folk in Chicago.

6. W. E. B. Du Bois, "Kwigwa Players Little Negro Theatre," *Crisis* 32, no. 3 (July 1926): 134–36.

7. Alain Locke, "The Legacy of the Ancestral Arts," in *The New Negro,* 254–67.

8. Humphrey preferred *Porgy.* See Doris Humphrey to her parents, 11 April 1927, Folder C265.10, DH.

9. The questionnaire first appeared in *Crisis* 31, no. 4 (February 1926): 165. Answers by various writers, both white and African American, appeared in the following months.

10. Ibid.

11. George Schuyler, "The Negro-Art Hokum," *Nation* 122, no. 3180 (16 June 1926): 662–63; Langston Hughes, "The Negro Artist and the Racial Mountain," *Nation* 122, no. 3181 (23 June 1926): 692–94.

12. Erenberg, *Swingin' the Dream;* Stowe, *Swing Changes.*

13. Edna Guy to Ruth St. Denis, 27 May 1924, Folder 323, and 7 June 1924, Folder 324, RSD.

14. Katherine Dunham encountered problems in renting dance space in buildings in Chicago in the late 1920s and early 1930s; see Barzel, "Lost 10 Years," 94. On transportation problems and prohibitive costs, see the memoirs of Alvin Ailey and Judith Jamison: Ailey with Bailey, *Revelations,* and Jamison with Kaplan, *Dancing Spirit.*

15. Miriam Raphael Cooper, interview by the author, New York City, 8 December 1994.

16. For example, see Edna Guy to Ruth St. Denis, 27 May 1924, 7 June 1924, 7 November 1924, 8 January 1925, 27 October 1931, RSD. St. Denis and Guy shared a spiritual religiosity that fused a strong base of Christianity with the mysticism of

Eastern religious practices. St. Denis wrote in her autobiography, *Ruth St. Denis*, "I called her my little black prophetess as she called me her white prophetess" (348). Guy's letters to St. Denis are full of spiritual musings and poems.

17. Reminiscences of Faith Reyher Jackson, 21 April 1979, CUOHROC, 45.

18. Edna Guy to Ruth St. Denis, 27 May 1924, Folder 323, RSD.

19. *Dance Events* (3 December 1932), a short-lived weekly publication; clipping file, New Negro Art Theatre, DC/NYPL. The Writers Program of the WPA also gathered information about dance schools under "Negroes in New York: Dance." For a general overview of dance education amongst African Americans in New York and Chicago, see Sherrod, "Dance Griots."

20. See advertisements in *New York Amsterdam News*, 4 October 1933, and picture of young girl on pointe in ibid., 8 February 1933.

21. On segregation amongst the audience, see *Crisis* 37, no. 10 (October 1930): 339–40, 357–58. On Rand and Noma, see *New York Amsterdam News*, 1 November 1933.

22. Carmencita Romero talks about integrating all-white schools in Chicago during this same time; see Anne Haas, "More Than Samba," *Manhattan Plaza News*, November 1995, 1, 8, 11, Romero File, Ann Barzel Collection, Newberry Library, Chicago, Illinois.

23. Dorathi Bock Pierce, "A Talk with Katherine Dunham," *Educational Dance* (August–September 1941), reprinted in Clark and Wilkerson, *Kaiso!*, 75–77.

24. Mark Turbyfill, "Whispering in the Windy City: Memoirs of a Poet-Dancer," 164, Mark Turbyfill Collection, Newberry Library, Chicago, Illinois.

25. Frederick L. Orme, "The Negro in the Dance: As Katherine Dunham Sees Him," *American Dancer* 11, no. 5 (March 1938): 10, 46; Pierce, "A Talk with Katherine Dunham."

26. See letterhead of a letter from Katherine Dunham to Mark Turbyfill, 24 August 1933, Box 1, Folder 8, Mark Turbyfill Collection, Special Collections, Morris Library, Southern Illinois University, Carbondale, Illinois.

27. Naison, *Communists in Harlem*, 36. Miriam Raphael Cooper also remembers occasions when people of "different colors and different ages" performed the piece, due to the lack of African American modern dancers. As a Jewish woman with dark hair, she played the "Black" opposite a "very blond boy" as the "White" at another Communist function. Miriam Cooper Raphael, interview by the author, New York City, 8 December 1994.

28. Sherrod, "Dance Griots," 260.

29. Edna Guy to Ruth St. Denis, n.d. [1930?], Folder 747, RSD. In a telephone

interview by the author, 30 July 2001, the artist Mary Perry Stone confirmed that she told Guy that St. Denis was not treating her well.

30. See Edna Guy to Ruth St. Denis, 5 June 1933, Folder 431, RSD: "[Y]ou may count on me to maid you." Even later in life, Guy seems to have provided these kinds of services for St. Denis. In a later, undated letter [1939?], Folder 533, ibid., Guy tells St. Denis that she has a friend who is a college graduate, speaks several languages, can clean well, and would work for fifty cents per hour. Guy encloses her key to St. Denis's apartment with the letter, perhaps suggesting that her friend is a replacement for cleaning services Guy had been providing.

31. *Kykunkor* survives only in a few photographs, reviews, and programs. See photographs in DC/NYPL; program of the Little Theater performance, 18 June 1934, Asadata Dafora Papers, Manuscripts, Archives and Rare Books Division, Schomburg Center for Research in Black Culture, New York Public Library, Astor, Lenox and Tilden Foundations, New York, New York. Reviews include *New York Times*, 9 May 1934; *New Yorker*, 19 May 1934, 14–15; Joseph Arnold, "Dance Events Reviewed," *American Dancer* 7, no. 10 (July 1934): 12; and others noted below.

32. *Daily Mirror*, 19 May 1934.

33. *Esquire*, August 1934.

34. Souvenir Program, n.d. [1935?], Dafora Papers.

35. *New York Times*, 9 May 1934; *New York Post*, 19 May 1934; *New Yorker*, 19 May 1934; Souvenir Program, n.d. [1935?], Dafora Papers.

36. *New York Amsterdam News*, 7 July 1934. I have found no evidence that the film was ever made.

37. Souvenir Program, n.d. [1935?], Dafora Papers.

38. Torgovnick, *Gone Primitive*, 244–45.

39. Locke quoted in Lewis, *When Harlem Was in Vogue*, 303, 154. Zora Neale Hurston received support from Mason from 1927 to 1932, and Mason held all the technical rights to the folklore she collected during that time; see Dearborn, *Pocahontas's Daughters*, 64–65. Dearborn also claims that Mason and Locke demanded an attention to folk culture and African traditions that the African American artists supported by Mason did not always want to pursue (65). Lewis's account suggests that Locke felt more ambivalent about that focus as well.

40. *New York Amsterdam News*, 23 June 1934.

41. Ibid., 19 May 1934.

42. Ibid., 23 June 1934; Sherrod, "Dance Griots," 293.

43. William Grant Still to Katherine Dunham, n.d. [1936?], Box 1, Folder 7,

Katherine Dunham Collection, Special Collections, Morris Library, Southern Illinois University, Carbondale, Illinois.

44. *Dance Observer* 3, no. 6 (June–July 1936): 64.

45. Press release, Edna Guy Programs, DC/NYPL.

46. Accounts of Dunham's life include Dunham, *Touch of Innocence;* Beckford, *Katherine Dunham;* Aschenbrenner, *Katherine Dunham;* and a consolidated article on Dunham's influence, Joyce Aschenbrenner, "Katherine Dunham: Anthropologist, Artist, Humanist," in Harrison and Harrison, *African-American Pioneers,* 137–53.

47. Katherine Dunham, "Thesis Turned Broadway," *California Arts and Architecture,* August 1941, 19, reprinted in Clark and Wilkerson, *Kaiso!,* 55–57.

48. A full exposition of Mead's work on gender roles can be found in Mead, *Male and Female.*

49. On the history of anthropology in the 1920s and 1930s, see Marcus and Fischer, *Anthropology as Cultural Critique;* Clifford, *Predicament of Culture;* Stocking, *Race, Culture, and Evolution;* Gleason, "Americans All." A debate on the persistence of racism in the discipline of anthropology even as it changed from scientific racism to an enculturation model of cultural relativism began in the late 1960s. See William S. Willis Jr., "Skeletons in the Anthropological Closet," in Hymes, *Reinventing Anthropology,* 121–52; Remy, "Anthropology: For Whom and What?"; Hsu, "Prejudice and Its Intellectual Effect"; Harrison and Harrison, *African-American Pioneers.*

50. Melville Herskovits, "The Negro's Americanism," in Locke, *The New Negro,* 353–60. Ruth Benedict, in *Patterns of Culture,* also uses the example of African Americans in the United States to demonstrate the success of acculturation: "[M]ost Harlem traits keep still closer to the forms that are current in white groups" (13).

51. Stuckey, *Going through the Storm,* 199.

52. Herskovits, *Myth of the Negro Past,* 76.

53. Katherine Dunham to Melville Herskovits, 9 March 1932, Box 7, Folder 12, Papers of Melville Herskovits, Northwestern University Archives, Evanston, Illinois. See also Kate Ramsey, "Melville Herskovits, Katherine Dunham, and the Politics of African Diasporic Dance Anthropology," in Doolittle and Flynn, *Dancing Bodies,* 196–216.

54. Dunham did eventually publish her findings in 1946 in *Katherine Dunham's Journey to Accompong.* It was an unconventional anthropology book. Essentially a descriptive travelogue of her experiences, the book offered neither scholarly analysis nor statements of broader impact about anthropology or the West Indies. This book and another of Dunham's, *Island Possessed,* have received renewed interest recently

among some anthropologists because of their descriptive style. As the discipline of anthropology has struggled with questions about objectivity and the limitations of one's own cultural myopia, Dunham's subjective approach has received praise. See Joyce Aschenbrenner, "Anthropology as a Lifeway: Katherine Dunham," a 1978 lecture reprinted in Clark and Wilkerson, *Kaiso!*, 186–91; Harrison and Harrison, *African-American Pioneers*, 19–20. My thanks to Yvonne Daniel for originally calling my attention to this point.

A significant aspect of her journey, often overlooked, was her extensive use of a Kodak 16mm motion picture camera to visually record for the first time many of the scenes, rituals, and dances; see Roy Thomas, "Focal Rites: New Dance Dominions" (1978), reprinted in Clark and Wilkerson, *Kaiso!*, 112–16.

55. Melville Herskovits to Katherine Dunham, 8 May 1937, Box 7, Folder 12, Herskovits Papers. More recent research into the place of nonwhites in anthropology suggests that other factors may have contributed to Dunham's leaving academia. Hsu, "Prejudice and Its Intellectual Effect," argues that nonwhites have generally had the role of fact gatherers rather than theoreticians, stemming at least in part from the belief then that it was impossible to be objective about "your own" people.

56. Description of *L'Ag'Ya* from Program, 8 May 1950, Katherine Dunham file, Archives of the Museum of the City of New York; Clark, "Katherine Dunham's *Tropical Revue*." For a more analytical review of *L'Ag'Ya*, see VèVè Clark's "Performing the Memory of Difference in Afro-Caribbean Dance: Katherine Dunham's Choreography, 1938–1987," in Fabre and O'Meally, *History and Memory*, 188–204.

57. Clark, "Performing the Memory of Difference," 197.

58. Katherine Dunham to Melville Herskovits, 23 June 1935, 28 December 1935; Melville Herskovits to Katherine Dunham, 6 January 1936, Box 7, Folder 12, Herskovits Papers. In this last letter, Herskovits wrote: "I am not surprised that the natives are amazed at the way you pick up the dances, and that it induces them to believe that you probably have an inherited *loa* that makes this possible." Herskovits's view of field work differed from Dunham's, although he did not deride her in these letters. In his *Life in a Haitian Valley*, however, Herskovits describes his methodology, clearly arguing that it is not wise to "go native." "This may be feasible among some folk—in the South Seas, perhaps—but let it be stated emphatically that this is neither possible nor of benefit among West African Negroes and their New World Negro descendants" (322). In his opinion, respecting the "dignity" of set caste lines and, most of all, not opening yourself up to ridicule laid the foundation for good ethnography. Hsu, "Prejudice and Its Intellectual Effect," and Harrison and Harrison, *African-*

American Pioneers, suggest how this view might have contributed to the racism within the discipline of anthropology.

59. Marcus and Fischer, *Anthropology as Cultural Critique,* 130.

60. Hazel Carby argues that Hurston romanticized the rural folk of the American South, finding words and speech patterns around which to conceptualize an essentialist view of blackness; see "The Politics of Fiction, Anthropology, and the Folk: Zora Neale Hurston," in Awkward, *New Essays on Their Eyes Were Watching God,* 71–93, esp. 87. For a discussion of Hurston as a feminist, see Gwendolyn Mikell, "Feminism and Black Culture in the Ethnography of Zora Neale Hurston," in Harrison and Harrison, *African-American Pioneers,* 51–69.

61. Frederick L. Orme, "The Negro in the Dance: As Katherine Dunham Sees Him," *American Dancer* 11, no. 5 (March 1938): 46; Katherine Dunham, "The Future of the Negro in the Dance" (1938), reprinted in *Dance Herald: Black Dance Newsletter* 3, no. 4 (Winter 1978): 3.

62. Rose, *Jazz Cleopatra,* 167–70.

63. *New York Times,* 20 September 1943; unidentified magazine, 4 February 1941, Dunham Clippings, 1938–45, Barzel Collection.

64. See *Ebony* 6, no. 3 (January 1951): 56; *Christian Science Monitor,* 20 January 1947; Lloyd, *Borzoi Book of Modern Dance,* 266; John Martin, *John Martin's Book of the Dance,* 180–81; *Dance Observer* 13, no. 6 (June–July 1946): 76–77.

65. Martin quoted in Bogle, *Brown Sugar,* 98–101. The part of Georgia was given to Lena Horne in the MGM movie version. Bogle suggests that perhaps Dunham was "too brazen" for the movie.

66. *Boston Herald,* 20 and 23 January 1944. The city censor's move caused a wave of protest against him among Boston critics. In particular, they lamented that Boston would continue its reputation and "black name" in theatrical circles for being especially puritanical. Clark, "Katherine Dunham's *Tropical Revue*"; Martin Sobelman to Katherine Dunham, 5 April 1941, Box 2, Folder 2, Dunham Collection.

67. Robinson, *Last Impresario; Boston Herald,* 23 January 1944.

68. Copy of personal letter dated 27 February 1945 [name unclear], Pearl Primus Manuscripts, DC/NYPL; *Dance Observer* 10, no. 8 (October 1943): 88; Lloyd, *Borzoi Book of Modern Dance,* 266; *New York Times,* 18 March 1979.

69. Lillian Zwerdling, interview by the author, 23 July 1993.

70. *Dance Observer* 10, no. 8 (October 1943): 90; *Dance Magazine* 18, no. 11 (November 1944): 14.

71. *Afro-American* (Baltimore), 22 July 1944; John Martin, *John Martin's Book of the Dance,* 183.

72. *Dance Observer* 11, no. 9 (November 1944): 110–11, and no. 10 (December 1944): 122–24. Also illuminating are comments of two other white critics addressing different audience reactions to a dance concert in North Carolina that included a white and black troupe: see *Dance Observer* 11, no. 7 (August–September 1944): 80–81.

73. Franziska Boas, "The Negro and the Dance as an Art," *Phylon* 10, no. 1 (1949): 38–42. A more contemporary and theoretical look at the distinction between dancing for a white or black audience can be found in Hazzard-Gordon, "Afro-American Core Culture."

74. Audience composition remains a barely tangible issue. My judgment that the audience was predominantly — if not exclusively — white is drawn from the assumptions I see the critics making; I believe they are commenting on a white audience as well as to a white readership. Critics probably would have noted if there were an unusually large number of African Americans in the audience. See sources mentioned in note 72. Also, the lack of black public support for concert dance by African Americans drew concern, especially in the 1960s and 1970s; see *Dance Magazine* 53, no. 10 (October 1979): 81.

75. *Chicago Defender,* 22 May 1937.

76. *Crisis* 47, no. 3 (March 1940).

77. *New York Amsterdam News,* 25 September 1943.

78. *Yank* 2, no. 42 (7 April 1944): 14.

79. *New York Amsterdam News,* 12 February 1944.

80. Ibid., 29 April 1944.

81. Ibid., 12 February 1944.

CHAPTER FOUR

1. Shawn, *American Ballet,* 20–22. See also Ted Shawn, "Ballroom Dancing of Present Day Described as Form of Imbecility," *Boston Herald,* 30 April 1936.

2. For prescriptive evidence from the time period about the association of homosexuality among men interested in the arts, see Terman and Miles, *Sex and Personality,* and sources cited in Minton, "Femininity in Men." For a novel of the period that links homosexuality and dance, see Levenson, *Butterfly Man.* On the history of homosexuality and gay men, *Gay New York* by Chauncey is indispensable. Also helpful are Weinberg, *Speaking for Vice;* Bérubé, *Coming Out;* D'Emilio, *Sexual Politics, Sexual Communities;* and Sedgwick, *Epistemology of the Closet.* For a new anthology that considers many issues in sexuality in dance, see Desmond, *Dancing Desires.*

3. Chauncey, *Gay New York,* chap. 11. For histories of masculinity of this period,

see Mosse, *Image of Man;* Bederman, *Manliness and Civilization;* Kimmel, *Manhood in America;* and Kimmel and Messner, *Men's Lives.* On nationalism and sexuality, see Mosse, *Nationalism and Sexuality,* and Parker, Russo, Sommer, and Yaeger, *Nationalisms and Sexualities.*

4. Poindexter, "Ted Shawn," 80, 84. See also the only published biography of Shawn, Terry, *Ted Shawn.*

5. Ted Shawn, "The Female of the Species," Folder 625, Denishawn Collection, DC/NYPL.

6. Terry, *Ted Shawn,* 15.

7. Carman, *Making of Personality,* 207–11; Bliss Carman to Ted Shawn, 13 November 1912, quoted in Poindexter, "Ted Shawn," 143.

8. Shelton, *Divine Dancer,* 119–20; Shawn with Poole, *One Thousand and One Night Stands,* 25.

9. Shelton, *Divine Dancer,* 123.

10. Ibid., 218–21. Beckman went on to marry a daughter of a wealthy investment banker (ibid., 227).

11. *Berner Tagblatt,* 4 May 1931, translation of article in Ted Shawn Scrapbook, TS.

12. Shawn's first proclamation of this mission was an article in *New York Dramatic Mirror,* 13 May 1916.

13. "Shawn's Art Form for Athletes," no publication name, n.d. [mid-1930s?], Folder 628, TS; Poindexter, "Ted Shawn," 238–41.

14. Poindexter, "Ted Shawn," 284; confirmed by the meticulous route lists Shawn kept, which have been preserved in TS.

15. Catalog, "Shawn School of Dance for Men," Ted Shawn Programs, DC/NYPL.

16. Chauncey, *Gay New York,* 284–85.

17. Terry, *Ted Shawn,* 107.

18. Carpenter, *Love's Coming of Age,* 120–40.

19. Sherman and Mumaw, *Barton Mumaw, Dancer,* 72–73.

20. Ibid., 124.

21. Letter from Ted Shawn to Ruth St. Denis quoted in Shelton, *Divine Dancer,* 267.

22. Ted Shawn, "The Dancers' Bible: An Appreciation of Havelock Ellis' *The Dance of Life,*" *Denishawn Magazine* 1, no. 1 [1924]: no pagination. Shawn also recommended Ellis in *American Ballet* and *Dance We Must.* Ellis at least accorded Shawn some attention; he wrote the introduction for Shawn's *American Ballet.*

23. Lucien Price to Ted Shawn, 10 July 1962, Folder 380, TS.

24. Lucien Price to Ted Shawn, 14 December 1935, Folder 52, ibid.

25. Lucien Price to Ted Shawn, 8 February 1934, Folder 39, ibid. Barton Mumaw claims that Price and Shawn "always talked in a heightened way about male sex"; see Barton Mumaw to Jane Sherman, 30 May 1979, Barton Mumaw Collection, Jacob's Pillow Dance Festival Archives, Becket, Massachusetts.

26. Lucien Price to Ted Shawn, 21 February 1935, Folder 47, TS. For another re-iteration of this view, see Lucien Price to Ted Shawn, 6 January 1935, Paige Box 9, Joseph Marks Collection, Harvard Theatre Collection, Houghton Library, Harvard University, Cambridge, Massachusetts (hereafter HTC).

27. Lucien Price to Ted Shawn, 1 September 1963, ibid. During the same month Shawn corresponded with Pillow photographer John Lindquist about this maga-zine and strategies on how to get such material through the U.S. mail. Ted Shawn to John Lindquist, 15 and 26 September 1963, Correspondence Box 3, Folder 3, John Lindquist Collection, HTC.

28. Lucien Price to Ted Shawn, 28 September 1960, Paige Box 9, Marks Collec-tion.

29. Ibid.; Lucien Price to Ted Shawn, 14 August 1961, Folder 380, TS; John Schu-bert to Lucien Price, 22 October 1938, Paige Box 9, Marks Collection.

30. Jonathan Weinberg, "Substitute and Consolation: The Ballet Photographs of George Platt Lynes," in Garafola with Foner, *Dance for a City,* 129–52. For how Lynes and Lindquist fit into a larger artistic tradition of male nude photography, see Ellenzweig, *Homoerotic Photograph.*

31. The Harvard Theatre Collection houses the John Lindquist Collection, which includes some correspondence and a massive amount of photographic material. For a general overview of the collection and biography of Lindquist, see Lucker, "John Lindquist Collection." About circulation of photographs, see letter to John Lindquist from unidentified man [Jon?], 11 February 1961, Correspondence Box 1, Folder 5, Lindquist Collection. Shawn and Lindquist had an understanding that Shawn would see *all* pictures taken by Lindquist before anyone else saw them. While Shawn was worried about particular pictures "falling into the wrong hands," he also built up quite a picture collection for his own use and enjoyment. Ted Shawn to John Lindquist, 17 July 1965, Correspondence Box 3, Folder 3, ibid.

32. Kirstein, *Mosaic,* 214. Also see the discomfort expressed by John Martin, *New York Times,* 11 February 1934.

33. Terry, *Ted Shawn,* 14. Shawn's eradication of feminine influence in dance may have come from a growing bitterness toward women fueled by his hurt over the early death of his mother and the philandering of St. Denis, which he believed prompted

him to turn to men for love and affection. Although Shawn admitted to Terry that he "'guessed' his homosexuality was always there 'deep down,'" he never stopped believing that if St. Denis had been faithful to him he would have been satisfied in marriage with her (130).

34. Ruth Murray, "The Dance in Physical Education," *Journal of Health and Physical Education,* January 1937, no pagination, reprinted in *JOHPER: Selected Articles on Dance* 1 (1930–57), DC/NYPL.

35. Walter Camryn, "Male Dancers," n.d., Box 1, Stone-Camryn Collection, Newberry Library, Chicago, Illinois.

36. Ted Shawn, "Men Must Dance," *Dance* (East Stroudsburg, Pa.) 1, no. 2 (November 1936): 10.

37. Shawn, *Dance We Must,* 119.

38. Ted Shawn, "Dancing Originally Occupation Limited to Men Alone," *Boston Herald,* 17 May 1936.

39. Chauncey, *Gay New York,* 52–55, 344.

40. *Dancing Times,* October 1934, 12; *Des Moines Register,* 2 April 1934.

41. Sam Bennett, "Horton Dance Group Startles Pasadenans in Modern Show," [January 1937?], Folder 4, Box 10, Lester Horton Collection, Library of Congress, Washington, D.C.; Weidman quoted in John Selby, "The Dance Takes Hold of Life," *San Francisco Chronicle,* 16 January 1938, Weidman clipping file, DC/NYPL.

42. Ted Shawn, "Dancing for Men," *Physical Culture,* July 1917, 16.

43. Shawn, "Dancing Originally."

44. Shawn, "Men Must Dance."

45. Shawn, "Dancing Originally."

46. Shawn quoted in "Found Dancing Wasn't for Sissies," no publication name [*Springfield Republican* or *Berkshire Eagle?*], n.d. [1934?], Ted Shawn clipping file, DC/NYPL.

47. Shawn quoted in *Columbia Missouri Christian College Microphone,* 20 March 1934.

48. Shawn, "Dancing Originally."

49. Margaret Lloyd, "The Dance as a Manly Art," *Christian Science Monitor,* n.d. [1938?], clipping file, Shawn and His Men Dancers, DC/NYPL.

50. *News and Leader,* 14 February 1932.

51. My analysis is based on a film of the piece dated 1934–40, DC/NYPL.

52. Shawn, "Dancing Is Unique among the Arts in That Human Body Is the Medium," *Boston Herald,* 5 May 1936.

53. Shawn, *American Ballet,* 65.

54. Ibid., 81.

55. Offstage, Shawn's own body preoccupied him too, and his weight bounced dramatically in response to intense periods of dieting and training followed by laxity. Shawn continued to send pictures of himself nude to a select audience throughout his life (found in Lindquist Collection). Including one in a letter to Barton Mumaw taken when Shawn was nearing his seventy-fourth birthday, he kidded about his "Narcissus complex." Sherman and Mumaw, *Barton Mumaw, Dancer,* 223.

56. *Chicago Daily News,* 9 April 1934.

57. *New York Times,* 11 February 1934.

58. Price quoted in Sherman and Mumaw, *Barton Mumaw, Dancer,* 129.

59. Ibid., 124–29.

60. Doris Humphrey to her parents, 19 December 1928 postmark, Folder C271.18; Doris Humphrey to Charles Woodford, Spring 1939, Folder C425.2, DH.

61. Drier, *Shawn the Dancer,* no pagination.

62. Harry Gribble to John Lindquist, 18 January 1940, Correspondence Box 1, Folder 1, Lindquist Collection. Emphasis in original.

63. Lucien Price to Ted Shawn, 28 December 1935, Folder 52, TS.

64. Melosh, *Engendering Culture,* 205–8.

65. For a detailed account of women in Soviet iconography, see Bonnell, "Peasant Woman in Stalinist Political Art." Shawn's display of the nearly nude male body fit into a "rediscovery of the human body" common in early-twentieth-century America and Europe. George Mosse argues that the search for a more genuine image of strength rose to counter the artificiality of modernism and then was easily folded into nationalist and fascist movements based on eugenic ideas in Germany and Italy. Mosse, *Image of Man,* 95, and *Nationalism and Sexuality,* chap. 3. The Greek model of male nudity dominated the imagery and had been resurrected by J. J. Winckelman, a German art historian with homosexual inclinations, in the late eighteenth century and revived again in the twentieth century. Mosse discusses Winckelman's influence in *Nationalism and Sexuality,* 11–14. For an analysis of the "natural" body in dance during this period, see Daly, *Done into Dance.* Also, "nature" required tuning. In Shawn's case, the practicalities of performing nearly nude required a weekly all-over shave in an attempt to achieve a "sexless impersonality"; see Sherman and Mumaw, *Barton Mumaw, Dancer,* 105.

66. "Mussolini Writes a Signed Article Expressly for Our Readers," *Physical Culture* 65, no. 6 (June 1931): 18–20, 80–81; Benito Mussolini, "Building a Nation's Health," *Physical Culture* 68, no. 1 (July 1932): 14–15, 64, 68. Shawn appeared on the cover of the July 1917 *Physical Culture* and was featured in the November 1924 issue.

Shawn and Macfadden had a personal friendship as well; Shawn and his company stayed at Macfadden's Florida home and spa in 1936 (Shawn Newsletter, January 1937, Barton Mumaw Collection, HTC). Macfadden's interest in dance was inspired by his first wife, Mary, who had studied "nature dancing"; see Ernst, *Weakness Is a Crime,* 83. See also Fabian, "Making a Commodity of Truth."

67. Burt, *Male Dancer,* 110.

68. Sherman and Mumaw, *Barton Mumaw, Dancer,* 144, and Burton Mumaw to Jane Sherman, 30 May 1979, Mumaw Collection, Jacob's Pillow Dance Festival Archives.

69. That same year Limón and Lawrence married, to much surprise. The marriage lasted until Limón's death, but it is unclear whether it was more of a creative partnership than a romantic one.

70. Gene Martel, "Men Must Dance," *New Theatre,* June 1935, 17–18. See also Ezra Friedman and Irving Lansky, "Men in the Modern Dance," *New Theatre,* June 1934, 21, and Walter Ware, "In Defense of the Male Dancer," *American Dancer* 11, no. 7 (May 1938): 15, 48.

71. *New York Times,* 16 March 1936.

72. Burt, *Male Dancer,* 109. The experience of African American gay male dancers deserves greater attention, although the evidence is hard to find. For initial interpretations, see Thomas DeFrantz, "Simmering Passivity: The Black Male Body in Concert Dance," in Morris, *Moving Words,* 107–20.

73. Limón also ended up viewing Graham's technique as distinctly feminine; see Garafola, *José Limón,* 53.

74. Program, June 1929, Folder 1, Box 12, Horton Collection. See also Lester Horton, "American Indian Dancing," *American Dancer* 2, no. 11 (June 1929): 9, 24, 32. For Shawn's views, see Sherman, "American Indian Imagery."

75. Ted Shawn, "Shawn Trains Dancers in Berkshire Refuge," *Berkshire Evening Eagle,* 27 June 1936.

76. "Ted Shawn: His Career as a Dancer," no author, n.d. [mid-1930s?], Folder 628, TS.

77. "Ted Shawn To-Day: Success of His Male Ballet," *Dancing Times,* October 1934, 10–11.

78. *Cornell Daily Sun,* 2 November 1934.

79. Shawn, "Shawn Trains Dancers."

80. *Dallas Times Herald,* 24 February 1937.

81. Walter Terry, "Leader of the Dance," *New York Herald Tribune,* 18 February 1940.

82. Russell Rhodes, "Shawn and His Men Dancers at Last Reach Broadway," *Dancing Times*, April 1938, 31–32.

83. *Theatre Journal* 1, no. 2 (April 1936), Folder 3, Box 10, Horton Collection.

84. Film in DC/NYPL. For a detailed narrative of *Kinetic Molpai*, see Sherman and Mumaw, *Barton Mumaw, Dancer*, 270–77.

85. Quoted in program for performance at Majestic Theater in New York, 27 February 1938, Ted Shawn Programs, DC/NYPL.

86. Ibid.; Ted Shawn, "Asceticism of Dark Ages Almost Buried in America, Shawn Says," *Boston Herald*, 4 June 1936.

87. Shawn targeted Terry to set the record straight: see Ted Shawn to Walter Terry, 30 January 1938 and 30 December 1938, Folder 517, TS. See also Shawn's interaction with Doris Humphrey, Charles Weidman, and Pauline Lawrence that he describes in a letter to Walter Terry, 7 April 1939, Folder 519, ibid. Terry eventually responded with two articles lauding Shawn in the *New York Herald-Tribune*, 18 February 1940 and 12 May 1940.

88. Sherman and Mumaw, *Barton Mumaw, Dancer*, 149–52, 177–81; audio interview with Peter Hamilton, 19 June 1967, DC/NYPL. Hamilton claims that Weidman was only interested in a "Pygmalion relationship" in which Weidman could guide the other person. Weidman took on that kind of relationship again with a young Japanese American sculptor in the late 1960s. Interviews by the author with Graham company member Dorothy Bird Villard, 12 May 1995, and Humphrey-Weidman member Lee Sherman, 16 December 1994, confirm that homosexuality provided connections, particularly in getting in Broadway shows in the 1940s and 1950s, although some kind of connection was probably always common, as when Tamiris hired her husband, Daniel Nagrin, as the lead dancer in *Annie Get Your Gun* (1946). But Sherman, who was in the Humphrey-Weidman Group for much of the 1930s, and Bob Kosinski (interviewed by the author, 14 December 1994), another male dancer who worked with Weidman in the 1960s, said they felt isolated by their heterosexuality. Not only did people outside the dance world assume they were gay, other male dancers did as well and attempted to pick them up. "There was an inside circle I was not a part of and didn't necessarily want to be because I knew that I was not [gay]," according to Sherman. Both claimed it did not really matter and that they had very positive experiences in dance.

89. Agnes de Mille boldly declared that gay men sought out the arts as a way to express their "neurosis." More surprisingly, the gay ballet dancer and choreographer Jerome Robbins wrote in a 1956 letter that he "somewhat agree[d]." De

Mille quoted in Easton, *No Intermissions,* 97–98; Jerome Robbins to Leland Heyward, [1956], Folder 1, Ballets: U.S.A., DC/NYPL. For de Mille's provocative views on dance and sex, see her autobiography, *Dance to the Piper,* especially chap. 8.

90. Newton, *Mother Camp.* For a survey of drag roles and the people who played them, see Roger Baker, *Drag.*

CHAPTER FIVE

1. Terry, *Ted Shawn,* 139.

2. Recent scholarly work has uncovered the ties to Communist activities and concerns in the 1930s that rooted the development of modern dance in overtly political debates. See Graff, *Stepping Left;* Prickett, "Marxism, Modernism, and Realism"; Garafola, "Of, by and for the People." Franko, *Dancing Modernism / Performing Politics,* offers a more theoretical treatment of the relationship between political and aesthetic ideas (see especially chap. 2 for an account of this dynamic in modern dance during the 1930s).

3. How politics affected art and culture in the 1930s remains one of the most vibrant questions among scholars. Denning, *Cultural Front,* offers the most substantial revision of Warren Susman's assessment of the era as conservative and predominantly marked by white middle-class concerns, a revision that the development of modern dance supports (see Susman, "Culture and Commitment," in *Culture as History,* 184–210). Other authors who critique Susman's assessment include Doss, *Benton, Pollock;* Stowe, *Swing Changes;* Erenberg, *Swingin' the Dream;* and Lary May, *Big Tomorrow.*

4. Biographical information on Chilkovsky and Geltman is scarce. An oral history of each in FTP-GMU provides some biographical information. Chilkovsky may have grown up in Philadelphia (she lived out her adult life there); Geltman was Jewish, but she did not identify her heritage beyond that.

5. Graff, *Stepping Left,* 42–43, claims that Dudley's advocacy of leftist ideals came from associations with other leftist artists.

6. Reminiscences of Edith Segal, 27 February 1981, Oral Histories of the American Left, Tamiment/Wagner Archives, New York University; Segal quoted in Stacey Prickett, "'The People': Issues of Identity within the Revolutionary Dance," in Garafola, "Of, by and for the People," 15. Also see reminiscences of Edith Segal, January, February 1991, DC/NYPL.

7. Mishler, *Raising Reds,* 92–94.

8. Graff, *Stepping Left*, chap. 2.

9. Betts, "Historical Study of the New Dance Group," 7; reminiscences of Nadia Chilkovsky, 25 May 1978, FTP-GMU.

10. This slogan appears on a 4 June 1933 program of the Workers Dance League, DC/NYPL. The program was for the first Workers Dance Spartakiade, a kind of competition among dance groups, held at the New School for Social Research in New York.

11. *Daily Worker,* 10 January 1934. See also David Allan Ross, "The Dance of Youth: Propaganda from the Left," *Forum and Century* 94 (August 1935): 115–19.

12. Nell Anyon, "The Tasks of the Revolutionary Dance," *New Theatre,* September 1933, 21.

13. Workers Dance League statement quoted in *New Dance,* January 1935; review of Workers Dance League, probably by Edna Ocko, *New Theatre,* September 1933, 20.

14. *Daily Worker,* 10 January 1934.

15. Workers Dance League Programs, January and April 1934, DC/NYPL.

16. Jane Dudley, "The Mass Dance," *New Theatre,* December 1934, 17–18. See also an earlier article on how to instruct children: Kay Rankin, "Workers' Children Dancing," *Workers Theater,* March 1932, 26.

17. *Daily Worker,* 14 June 1934; *New Theatre,* July–August 1934, 28. The debate was taken up again by Robert Forsythe in "Speaking of Dance," *New Masses* 12 (24 July 1934): 29–30; Forsythe supported Gold's position and called for more joy and hope about the revolution in dance and other art forms as well.

18. Harry Elion, "Perspectives of the Dance," *New Theatre,* September 1934, 19. See also preceding months (April, May, June 1934) for more debates about "bourgeois" technique.

19. Paul Douglas in *New Theatre,* November 1935, 27, and Horace Gregory in *New Masses* 14 (22 January 1935): 28.

20. *New Masses* 14 (5 March 1935): 27; (19 March 1935): 21.

21. For example, see the debate between Edna Ocko, dance critic of *New Theatre,* and Michael Gold of the *Daily Worker* over what constitutes good political art, in *Daily Worker,* 14 June 1934, and *New Theatre,* July/August 1934. This issue of *New Theatre* includes a longer exposition on the problem of content and style in modern dance by Emanuel Eisenberg entitled "Diagnosis of the Dance" (24–25).

22. Ocko quoted in Williams, *Stage Left,* 132.

23. Denning, *Cultural Front,* 58–64.

24. Helen Priest Rogers notebook (1934), Bennington College Archives, Bennington, Vermont.

25. *New York Times,* 25 December 1938.

26. De Mille, *Martha,* 168; *Dance,* June 1930, January 1931; *Theatre Arts Monthly* 15 (March 1931): 179.

27. Doris Humphrey used this ploy. Humphrey quoted in Siegel, *Days on Earth,* 111.

28. De Mille, *Martha,* 168.

29. *Theatre Arts Monthly* 16 (May 1932): 351–52.

30. Barbara Page Beiswanger, "National Section on Dance: Its First Ten Years," *Journal of Health, Physical Education and Recreation (JOHPER),* May–June 1960; Mildred C. Spiesman, "Dance Education Pioneers," *JOHPER,* January 1960; Hawkins, *Modern Dance in Higher Education;* Ross, *Moving Lessons.* The argument over where dance should be placed—in physical education or fine arts departments—was waged from the beginning and continues today. Overwhelmingly, surveys indicate that dance was placed in physical education departments. See the opposing arguments in *Educational Dance* 1, no. 3 (August–September 1938) and 2, no. 10 (April 1940).

31. Solomon, *In the Company of Educated Women,* 44, 63.

32. Leigh quoted in Brockway, *Bennington College,* 39–40. Brockway noted another significant factor in the history of the first women students at Bennington: 80 percent of their mothers had not gone to college, while 75 percent of their fathers had gone and expected their sons to attend their alma mater. Thus, if the same impulse applies for mothers, the majority of these mothers would have had less preference about where their daughters went to college (40).

33. Ibid., 56–58.

34. Ibid., 125–26, and chap. 16.

35. The first conception was a five-year plan, but the school's success prompted its continuation. In 1939 the Bennington Summer School of the Dance moved to Mills College in California in the hopes of attracting more attention to modern dance on the West Coast. There 170 people attended, 50 percent of whom were from the Far West; see Kriegsman, *Modern Dance in America,* 86. In 1940 Bennington instituted a larger Summer School of the Arts where dance was a part of other offerings in music, drama, and theater design, although dance continued to attract the most students. Notably, more men also attended the School of the Arts that year than in previous summers, but Kriegsman's statistics do not indicate if the number of male dance students increased (my assumption is that it did not, particularly in 1942 after American participation in World War II began). This school lasted through the summer of 1942, after which time the rationing of fuel for the war caused Bennington

to close for some of the winter and extend its classes into the summer. A summer dance program started again at Connecticut College in 1948 as the American Dance Festival and continues today at Duke University in Durham, North Carolina.

36. Kriegsman, in *Modern Dance in America,* draws on the program applications provided by Mary Jo Shelly and gives a description of each summer's program with statistics; for 1934, see p. 42; 1935, p. 49; 1936, p. 57; 1937, p. 69; 1938, p. 78; and, for geographical percentages, p. 15. For a description of the black woman who passed as white and later went on to teach dance at Spelman College, see the reminiscences of Faith Reyher Jackson, 21 April 1979, CUOHROC, 45.

37. Ford quoted in Kriegsman, *Modern Dance in America,* 273.

38. Ethel Butler quoted in ibid., 269.

39. Public relations catalog, n.d. [1935?], clipping file, Shawn and His Men Dancers, DC/NYPL.

40. Humphrey quoted in Humphrey and Cohen, *Doris Humphrey,* 154.

41. *Ballet Review* 9, no. 1 (Spring 1981) is devoted to interviews with participants from the Bennington summers, many of whom corroborate the view that collaborations did not occur. Other reminiscences about the Bennington school downplay the antagonisms between the leading dancers, remarking that the greater division was with ballet rather than between the physical education teachers and the professional students. For example, see William Bales and Jane Dudley, interview with Tobi Tobias, 7 March 1977, DC/NYPL, 52–59. Marian Van Tuyl Campbell remembers that people conversed under a Graham tree and a Humphrey tree after dinner; see Campbell's reminiscences, 10 May 1979, CUOHROC, 75.

42. Kazan quoted in Ciment, *Kazan on Kazan,* 17. Alex North, the lover of Anna Sokolow and brother of Joseph North, an editor of *New Masses,* also added Communist ideas to conversations on politics.

43. Reminiscences of Helen Alkire, 4 October 1979, CUOHROC, 34. Another summer student, Helen Knight, was asked to choreograph for the Chicago chapter of the New Dance League but refused, worried that she would endanger her public school job because of the league's association with leftist politics. Reminiscences of Helen Knight, 19 September 1979, ibid., 46. For talk of the politics permeating Bennington, see the reminiscences of Helen Alkire, Louise Allen, Helen Knight, Norman and Ruth Lloyd, and Faith Reyher Jackson, ibid.

44. Tamiris may have not been invited because the directors of the summer school did not want the influence of her politics and organizing abilities, or they may have thought she was not as talented as the others. Humphrey liked her per-

sonally but did not think she was a competent dancer; see Doris Humphrey to her parents, 12 December 1931 postmark, Folder C286.10, DH.

45. Klehr, *Heyday of American Communism,* chap. 11; Wald, *New York Intellectuals,* chap. 3; Naison, *Communists in Harlem,* chap. 7; Denning, *Cultural Front;* Graff, *Stepping Left,* chap. 5.

46. *New Theatre,* April 1935, 28.

47. Advertisement for New Dance League printed in the program of the National Dance Congress, [May 1936], clipping file, National Dance Congress, DC/NYPL.

48. *New Theatre,* April 1935, 28.

49. Kolodney, "History of the Educational Department." The conflict between an American or Jewish focus arose in the 1950s and again more recently; see ibid., chap. 12, on the 1950s, and, from the current director of dance at the Y, Finkelstein, "Doris Humphrey and the 92nd Street Y." For extended treatment of the importance of the 92nd Street Y, see Jackson, *Converging Movements.*

50. Deborah Dash Moore charts this general transition within the Jewish population in New York in *At Home in America.* See also Feingold, *Time for Searching.*

51. Clipping file and published *Proceedings of the National Dance Congress,* DC/NYPL.

52. New Dance League, Report of Annual Conference, May 1936, clipping file, New Dance League, DC/NYPL; *Dance Herald* 1, no. 6 (April 1938).

53. Constitution of National Dance Congress, clipping file, National Dance Congress, DC/NYPL.

54. *Christian Science Monitor,* 2 June 1936.

55. Ibid.

56. Leonard Dal Negro, "Return from Moscow: An Interview with Anna Sokolow," *New Theatre,* December 1934, 27. Franko, *Dancing Modernism/Performing Politics,* 27, notes that there was not as much fervor against ballet in the radical magazines because of its popularity in the Soviet Union. For a view of the sustained interaction between modern dance and ballet, see Sally Banes, "Sibling Rivalry: The New York City Ballet and Modern Dance," in Garafola with Foner, *Dance for a City,* 73–98.

57. *Daily Worker,* 29 March 1936. Daniel Aaron notes this turn from condemnation to praise in the case of writers and the Communist Party: "[A]fter 1935 the party preferred to concentrate on the popular literary figures whose sympathy, even if qualified, they could exploit for publicity purposes." Aaron, *Writers on the Left,* 309. Wald sees a similar appeal to liberals among writers; see *New York Intellectuals,* chap. 3.

58. *New Theatre,* September 1935, 27.

59. *New York Times,* 13 March 1936.

60. Nicholas Wirth, "Mary Wigman—Fascist," *New Theatre,* August 1935, 5; Manning, *Ecstasy and the Demon,* 272–73.

61. *Dance Herald* 1, no. 2 (December 1937). This action roused a debate within the organization because the full board of directors had not given guidance and approval of the telegram. The New York chapter was chastised for its "wrong . . . method of procedure."

62. *Dance Observer* 4, no. 4 (April 1937): 41.

63. Flanagan, *Arena,* 52. For information on the Dance Project and dance within the Theatre Project see Roet, "Dance Project"; Lally, "History of the Federal Dance Theatre"; Graff, *Stepping Left,* chap. 4.

64. *New Theatre,* January 1935, 29.

65. Miriam Raphael Cooper, interview by the author, New York City, 8 December 1994; Don Oscar Becque, audio interview, n.d., DC/NYPL; Flanagan, *Arena,* 68. Oral histories of workers in the Federal Theatre and Dance Projects attest to the zealotry of the dancers; see reminiscences of Philip Barber, 11 November 1975; Add Bates, 30 November 1976; Charles K. Freeman, 20 February 1976; Fanya Geltman Del Bourgo, 16 December 1977; George Kondolf, 21 February 1976; Sue Remos Nadel and Paula Bass Perwolin (interviewed together), 23 October 1977; and Robert Sour, 31 October 1977, all in FTP-GMU.

66. Correspondence folders, Papers of the Federal Theatre Project, Works Progress Administration, Record Group 69, National Archives, Washington, D.C.

67. George Kondolf, one of the directors of the New York City Federal Theatre Project, thought that the Workers' Alliance (of which the CPC was a part) "was a direct arm of the local Communist Party"; see reminiscences of George Kondolf, 21 February 1976, FTP-GMU. The CPC endorsed the Farmer-Labor Party in the 1936 presidential election, expressing dissatisfaction with Roosevelt's dictatorial style. A speaker from the Farmer-Labor Party attended a meeting of the Dancers Local of the CPC on 10 June 1936; see *Federal Dance Theater Bulletin* 1, no. 3 [n.d., May 1936?], gift of Lea Wallace, ibid.

68. Reminiscences of Fanya Geltman Del Bourgo, 16 December 1977, ibid.

69. In an interview by the author, 8 December 1994, Miriam Raphael Cooper made this point explicit, and it is corroborated by the virulence of political activism on the project. Jane Dudley claims that the core of the WPA was mostly Communist Party members. Reminiscences of Jane Dudley, [1981], Oral Histories of the American Left, Tamiment/Wagner Archives, New York University.

70. Don Oscar Becque to Ted Shawn, n.d. [1940?], Folder 83, TS.

71. *Dance Herald* [newsletter of the American Dance Association] 1, no. 4 (February 1938).

72. Minutes of Audition Meetings (12/13 December 1938), Dance Coordinator Folder, Box 246, Papers of the Federal Theatre Project, Works Progress Administration, Record Group 69, National Archives.

73. Hallie Flanagan to John Martin, 10 January 1939, General Correspondence, Box 27, ibid. George Kondolf, the head of the New York City Theatre Project, claimed that the Workers Alliance may have "hurt the project" because of its radical politics; see Kondolf's reminiscences, 21 February 1976, FTP-GMU, 10–11.

74. *Dance Observer* 6, no. 5 (May 1939): 218–19.

75. Ibid., no. 8 (October 1939): 263. See related articles in ibid., 267–68, and ibid., no. 9 (November 1939): 279.

76. Ellfeldt, "Role of Modern Dance," claims that 76 percent of the ninety-seven colleges and universities that responded to the question said that they first offered modern dance after 1930 (117). Lucile Marsh, in "Terpsichore Goes to College," *Dance Magazine* 18, no. 7 (June 1943): 4–5, decries the dominance of the "New York Moderns." See also Sally Banes, "Institutionalizing Avant-Garde Performance: A Hidden History of University Patronage in the U.S.," in Harding, *Contours of the Theatrical Avant-Garde,* 217–38.

77. Isabel Kane, "A Survey of Modern Dance in Colleges and Universities in California," *Educational Dance* 2, no. 4 (October 1939): 9; results continued in the following issue. Another survey sponsored by the Whitney Foundation and conducted through the Bennington Summer School of the Dance by Mary Jo Shelly indicated that one-third of the universities that responded offered modern dance classes (short mention of the survey in Mary Jane Hungerford, "National Conference and Convention," *Educational Dance* 2, no. 1 [May 1939]: 3–5). This number does not correspond with the Kane survey nor with the Ellfeldt survey cited in note 76. See also Arslanian, "History of Tap Dance."

78. Ellfeldt, "Role of Modern Dance," 112. Numbers from Frances Davies, "Survey of Dance in Colleges," show a more startling dichotomy. Folk, square, and country dancing were taught in 100 percent of the seventy-four schools surveyed, modern dance in 99 percent, tap in 82 percent, social and ballroom in 69 percent, and ballet in a lowly 3 percent (16).

CHAPTER SIX

1. Reminiscences of Welland Lathrop, 22 September 1979, CUOHROC, 54.

2. Shawn, foreword to *American Ballet,* no pagination.

3. Whitman, "Democratic Vistas" (1871), in *Complete Poetry and Collected Prose,* 463. For a detailed discussion of the use of Whitman by the American left, see Garman, "'Heroic Spiritual Grandfather.'"

4. Graham quoted in "Graham Interprets Democracy," *Daily Worker,* 7 October 1938.

5. Lester Horton to Hollywood Bowl Association, 6 April 1937, Folder 13, Box 4, Lester Horton Collection, Library of Congress, Washington, D.C.

6. Humphrey quoted in Humphrey and Cohen, *Doris Humphrey,* 94.

7. Steinberg, *Other Criteria,* 299–300. Steinberg names Fry as a part of the school of formalist art criticism and spends a great deal of time dismantling its assumptions and arguing for reducing the importance of formal criteria in judging art, an indication of ongoing debates in art history over form and its meaning.

8. Susan Leigh Foster has described this mode of art as one of replication, following the trope synecdoche named in the literary criticism of Hayden White. See Foster, *Reading Dancing,* chap. 1. She lays out the comparison between choreographers Deborah Hay, George Balanchine, Martha Graham, and Merce Cunningham and the respective tropes they embody: metaphor, metonymy, synecdoche, and irony (ibid., 42–43). For a more in-depth exploration of emotion in modernism, see Franko, *Dancing Modernism/Performing Politics,* especially chaps. 1 and 2, and "Nation, Class, and Ethnicities."

9. Amy Koritz discusses this in a comparison of Eugene O'Neill and Martha Graham, "Re/moving Boundaries: From Dance History to Cultural Studies," in Morris, *Moving Words,* 88–106.

10. "Shaker Art," *Time,* 26 August 1940, Folder Z13.15, and other miscellaneous documents on the Shakers, DH; Siegel, "Four Works by Doris Humphrey," 29–30. More recent historical examination has shown that celibacy and pronouncements of equality of men and women amongst the Shakers did not necessarily carry over in daily life and the governing of the sect, particularly after the death of the founder, Ann Lee. See Brewer, "'Tho of the Weaker Sex.'" In the 1930s, however, Humphrey's belief in the gender equality of the sect was reasonable. The 1955 revival of *The Shakers* at Connecticut College brought one of the two remaining brothers of the sect to the performance, and Humphrey told him she attained her information about the Shakers from their literature and pictures, and from contemporaneous

comment about them. At the time she choreographed the dance, she had neither visited the community nor spoken to a member. *Dance Magazine* 29, no. 9 (September 1955): 4.

11. Doris Humphrey, "On Choreographing Bach," reprinted in Humphrey and Cohen, *Doris Humphrey*, 255.

12. My analysis of *The Shakers* is based on three different performances captured on film in 1955, 1959, and 1963, DC/NYPL. Reconstructions are probably truer to the original because the piece was recorded in Labanotation. The 1955 performance was probably revived with the help of Humphrey herself (she died in 1958).

13. Joseph M. Gornbein, "Shakers: A Group Dance by Doris Humphrey," a paper for a college philosophy course submitted 23 January 1940 (college unnamed), Folder M150.1, DH.

14. *The Shakers* had a small recital premiere at Hunter College, 12 November 1930. The Dance Repertory performance was its first formal showing. It was also included in a musical revue entitled *Americana* that played in Philadelphia in the fall of 1932, along with other works by Weidman and Humphrey, including Weidman's *Ringside—Madison Square Garden,* on boxing. The dance offerings made the show a success, according to the reviewer from Philadelphia's *Public Ledger.* See *Public Ledger,* 19 September 1932, and program of *Americana* in Folder C303.2, DH.

15. Shawn quoted in Sherman, "American Indian Imagery," 367.

16. My analysis is based on a film of the piece in "Primitive Rhythms," dated 1934–40, in DC/NYPL.

17. Lester Horton, "American Indian Dancing," *American Dancer,* June 1929, 9, 24, 31.

18. McBride, *Molly Spotted Elk,* 128, 224–25.

19. Naum Rosen, "The New Jewish Dance in America," *Dance Observer* 1, no. 5 (June–July 1934): 51, 55; Martha Graham, "The Dance in America," *Trend* 1, no. 1 (March 1932): 6.

20. McDonagh, "Conversation with Gertrude Shurr," 19.

21. Draft of a letter from Doris Humphrey to Ted Shawn and Ruth St. Denis, n.d. [early 1928?], Folder C272.1, DH. For an indication of Graham's view, see McDonagh, "Conversation with Gertrude Shurr," 19–20.

22. Doris Humphrey to her parents, 20 October 1927 postmark, Folder C268.8, DH.

23. For general work on the physical dimensions of anti-Semitism that persist throughout history see Gilman, *The Jew's Body;* essays in Howard Eilberg-Schwartz, *People of the Body;* Robert Singerman, "The Jew as Racial Alien: The Genetic Com-

ponent of American Anti-Semitism," in Gerber, *Anti-Semitism in American History,* 103–28. These physical stereotypes also held strength within the Jewish community, as seen in the efforts by the Zionist movement at the beginning of the twentieth century to sponsor sports and gym clubs to make the "New Jew" strong and manly; see Hyman, *Gender and Assimilation,* 142. Peter Levine, in *Ellis Island to Ebbets Field,* 16–25, argues that challenging these images in America through sport was part of an attempt by Jewish men to be seen as American. How these physical stereotypes affected Jewish women still needs further attention; see my "'Angels Rewolt!'"

24. Miriam Raphael Cooper, interview by the author, New York City, 8 December 1994.

25. For accounts of anti-Semitism in the 1930s in higher education, see Marcia Graham Synnott, "Anti-Semitism and American Universities: Did Quotas Follow the Jews?," in Gerber, *Anti-Semitism in American History,* 233–71.

26. Quote from Lee Sherman in interview by the author, 16 December 1994, New York City; point reiterated by Miriam Raphael Cooper in interview by the author, 8 December 1994, New York City. Cooper believed that the leaders of the modern dance movement were generally anti-Semitic. She was very quick to state that the anti-Semitism was no more or less than that which suffused the society at large and would not cite any specific incidents.

27. Helen Alkire commented that "you could pinpoint who studied with whom." Reminiscences of Helen Alkire, 4 October 1979, CUOHROC, 53. George Bockman claimed that the Humphrey-Weidman company allowed for individuality but that "some other companies made everybody a facsimile of everybody else." Reminiscences of George Bockman, 2 May 1979, ibid., 8. On Graham crackers, see reminiscences of Kathleen Slagle Partlon, 15 August 1979, ibid., 66.

28. My analysis of *How Long Brethren?* is based on extant photographs, programs, reviews, and production notes in DC/NYPL and in the Papers of the Federal Theatre Project, Works Progress Administration, Library of Congress, Washington, D.C. (hereafter FTP-LOC).

29. *How Long Brethren?,* Lighting Plot folder, Box 1019, Production Title File, Production Records, FTP-LOC.

30. Humphrey, *Art of Making Dances,* 57. See also Doris Humphrey, "Position [of modern dance] in social scene," lecture-demonstration notes, n.d. [1936?], Folder M58.1, DH.

31. *Daily Worker,* 21 May 1937.

32. Reminiscences of Fanya Geltman Del Bourgo, 16 December 1977, FTP-GMU.

33. See program notes of a 22 November 1955 performance at the Broadway Theater, Dunham Programs, DC/NYPL. For an account of *Southland,* see Hill, "Katherine Dunham's *Southland.*"

34. My analysis of *Barrelhouse Blues* is based on a re-creation featured in the American Dance Festival documentary *Free to Dance,* telecast 24 June 2001 on PBS as part of its *Great Performances* series.

35. Lenore Cox, "Scanning the Dance Highway," *Opportunity* 12, no. 8 (August 1934): 246–47.

36. *New York Herald Tribune,* 19 February 1940.

37. *Federal Theatre* 2, no. 4 (April–May 1937): 28.

38. Helen Tamiris, "Selections from the First Draft of an Uncompleted Autobiography," Helen Tamiris Collection, DC/NYPL, 48.

39. Manning argues this point for both *How Long Brethren?* and *American Document;* see "Black Voices, White Bodies" and "*American Document* and American Minstrelsy," in Morris, *Moving Words,* 183–202. For an account of this kind of representation in movies, see Clover, "Dancin' in the Rain," and Rogin, *Blackface, White Noise,* which delves into the role of Jews in this process.

40. Production Bulletin, "A Festival of American Dance," Production Title File, Box 1008, Production Records, FTP-LOC; quote from reminiscences of Myra Kinch, 21 February 1976, FTP-GMU.

41. Margaret Lloyd, "Horton Revives Dance Group," *Christian Science Monitor,* 11 January 1947, Folder 8, Box 10, Horton Collection.

42. Reminiscences of Bella Lewitzky, 3 February 1967, Folder 11, Box 1, ibid., 19; Program, 26 April 1937, Folder 2, Box 12, ibid.

43. Sam Bennett, "Horton Dance Group Startles Pasadenans in Modern Show," [January 1937?], Folder 4, Box 10, ibid. See also Herbert Matthews, "Lester Horton Dancers Recital Highly Lauded," in the same folder.

44. Libretto of *American Document* reprinted in *Theatre Arts Monthly* 26, no. 9 (September 1942): 565–74. Very small snippets of film survive; my analysis derives from the libretto, photographs, reviews, and oral histories of participants in the production. In "*American Document* and American Minstrelsy," Susan Manning has written a full account of the dance, tracing changes from its premiere at Bennington to its revival in 1944. She notes parts of the libretto that may have undergone change from 1938 to its publication in 1942. See also Costonis, "*American Document.*"

45. Libretto, *American Document,* 566.

46. *Daily Worker,* 7 October 1938.

47. Lincoln Kirstein, *Nation* 147, no. 10 (3 September 1938): 231.

48. Reminiscences of Alwin Nikolais, 7 November 1979, CUOHROC, 41.

49. Owen Burke, "An American Document," *New Masses* 29 (18 October 1938): 29. Burke remarks on changes from the Bennington version in August to the New York version in October and heralds the change from a final solo to this final company action. I am describing the company finale because I believe it is the ending most audiences saw, in New York and on the national tour afterward.

50. I invoke here the meaning of invention that Eric Hobsbawn outlines in his influential *Invention of Tradition.*

51. Melosh, *Engendering Culture;* Park and Markowitz, *Democratic Vistas.*

52. *New Masses* 29 (18 October 1938): 29.

53. Lincoln Kirstein, *Nation* 147, no. 10 (3 September 1938): 231.

54. *New Republic* 78 (9 May 1934): 365; *New York Times,* 26 April 1934; *Dance Observer* 5, no. 8 (October 1938): 116.

55. For Kirstein's view of ballet in America, see "Blast at Ballet" (1937) in Lincoln Kirstein, *Three Pamphlets Collected.* On the intertwining of ballet and modern dance, see Sally Banes, "Sibling Rivalry: The New York City Ballet and Modern Dance," in Garafola with Foner, *Dance for a City,* 73–98.

56. Philip, "Billy the Kid Turns 50." Eugene Loring discussed the concurrence of Americana themes in both ballet and modern dance during this time in his reminiscences, 18 September 1979, CUOHROC, 10–11.

57. For de Mille's account of *Rodeo,* see her autobiography, *Dance to the Piper,* 240–41, and chap. 25. For an analysis of the gender dynamics in *Rodeo,* see Banes, *Dancing Women,* 185–94.

58. Eugene Loring speaking in the *Omnibus* viewing of *Billy the Kid,* telecast 8 November 1953, DC/NYPL.

59. Lincoln Kirstein, "About 'Billy the Kid,'" *Dance Observer* 5, no. 8 (October 1938): 116.

60. Banes, "Sibling Rivalry," discusses many of the interactions between ballet and modern dancers and choreographers from the 1930s to the present day and admits ballet trumped modern dance in popularity and institutionalization. I believe that the social and political dynamics I am drawing out offer reasons as to why that occurred.

61. My analysis of *Appalachian Spring* is based on photographs of the work in the 1940s, later filmed versions, and current performances of the piece.

62. O'Donnell quoted in Copland and Perlis, *Copland,* 44–45.

63. Script quoted in Shirley, "For Martha," 71.

CHAPTER SEVEN

1. John Martin, "The Dance Completes a Cycle," *American Scholar* 12, no. 2 (Spring 1943): 205–15. Martin insisted that modern dance had infused American ballet with its new energy and ended the article with a plea for renewed attention to modern dance.

2. *New Masses* 57 (27 November 1945): 30–31.

3. See editorial in *Dance Observer* 7, no. 5 (May 1940): 63, decrying the denunciations of Walter Terry, and another editorial in ibid. 8, no. 2 (February 1941): 19, about Edwin Denby.

4. Doris Humphrey, "A Home for Humphrey-Weidman," ibid. 7, no. 9 (November 1940): 124–25.

5. George W. Beiswanger, "Lobby Thoughts and Jottings," ibid. 9, no. 9 (November 1942): 116.

6. Ibid. 9, no. 2 (February 1942): 19.

7. Ibid. 11, no. 3 (March 1944): 35.

8. "This Is the Civilian," n.d., Folder M142.1, DH; Doris Humphrey, "New Dance," [1936], in Humphrey and Cohen, *Doris Humphrey,* 238.

9. Magriel, *Art and the Soldier.*

10. Ted Shawn to Walter Terry, 28 May 1943, Folder 521, TS.

11. Bérubé, *Coming Out,* 20, on occupational choice exam, and chap. 3.

12. Ted Shawn to Walter Terry, 20 November 1942, Folder 520, TS.

13. Unspecified publication [*Stars and Stripes?*], December 1944, Folder 143, TS.

14. Walter Terry to Ted Shawn, 15 January 1944, Folder 143; Ted Shawn to Walter Terry, 20 November 1942, Folder 520, ibid.; Terry, *Invitation to Dance,* 77.

15. Walter Terry to Ted Shawn, 15 January 1944, Folder 143, TS.

16. Barton Mumaw talks of this from his own experience in the military. See Sherman and Mumaw, *Barton Mumaw, Dancer,* 161–62. See also Bérubé, *Coming Out.*

17. Terry quoted in Sherman and Mumaw, *Barton Mumaw, Dancer,* 172.

18. Barber, "Pearl Primus," 12–15, 114–15; John Martin, *John Martin's Book of the Dance,* 182–83; Lloyd, *Borzoi Book of Modern Dance,* 268; *Current Biography* (1944), 551. See also Perpener, *African-American Concert Dance,* chap. 7.

19. *Dance Observer* 11, no. 6 (June–July 1944): 67.

20. *Dance Magazine,* April 1946, 30–31, 55–56; Lloyd, *Borzoi Book of Modern Dance,* 274; *Ebony* 6, no. 3 (January 1951): 56.

21. *Theatre Arts* 34, no. 2 (December 1950): 40–43; *Ebony* 6, no. 3 (January 1951): 54.

22. Pearl Primus, "Out of Africa," in Sorell, *Dance Has Many Faces,* 155–58; *Dance Magazine* 24, no. 7 (July 1950): 21–23.

23. For an extended analysis of the song and its impact, see Margolick, *Strange Fruit.*

24. My analysis is based on a re-creation of the dance in the American Dance Festival documentary *Free to Dance,* telecast 24 June 2001 on PBS as part of its *Great Performances* series. See also Simmons, "Experiencing and Performing."

25. *Afro-American,* 22 July 1944.

26. Jane Kruger, "Pearl Primus Considers Her African Dance Correlation of Modern and Ancient Worlds," *Smith College Associated News,* 9 April 1948.

27. *New York Times,* 19 June 1988.

28. Denby, *Looking at the Dance,* 377–78. See also Stowe, "Politics of Café Society."

29. *Dance Observer* 11, no. 9 (November 1944): 110; *New York Post,* 27 March 1969; *New York Times,* 18 March 1979.

30. Pearl Primus Programs, Manuscripts, Archives and Rare Books Division, Schomburg Center for Research in Black Culture, New York Public Library, Astor, Lenox and Tilden Foundations, New York, New York.

31. Dunham's comment to the audience, 19 October 1944, reprinted in Clark and Wilkerson, *Kaiso!,* 88.

32. Alan Brinkley suggests that race and ethnicity rather than gender and class were the radical issues of the postwar world in "The New Political Paradigm: World War II and American Liberalism," in Erenberg and Hirsch, *War in American Culture,* 313–30.

33. Juana de Laban, "What Tomorrow?," *Dance Observer* 12, no. 5 (May 1945): 55–56.

34. Joseph Gifford, "Smoke Gets in Our Eyes," *Dance Observer* 12, no. 6 (June–July 1945): 65–66.

35. On the role of government-sponsored dance abroad, see Prevots, *Dance for Export.*

36. Richard Lippold, "On Saints in Buckets," *Dance Observer* 12, no. 10 (December 1945): 125–26.

37. Gertrude Lippincott, "Pilgrim's Way," *Dance Observer* 13, no. 7 (August–September 1946): 84–85. On the relationship between "good art and good politics," see the response to Lippincott by Mary Phelps, "Dancers or Donkeys?," *Dance Observer* 13, no. 9 (November 1946): 110–11, and also letters in the following issue.

38. Foster, *Reading Dancing,* 49.

39. John Cage, "Grace and Clarity," *Dance Observer* 11, no. 9 (November 1944): 108.

40. Doris Humphrey to her parents, 24 November 1930 postmark, Folder C279.6, DH. Linda Tomko addresses this difference in distinguishing modern dance from Progressive Era dance and ends her book by suggesting that humanist concerns may have continued into the 1930s. See Tomko, *Dancing Class,* 163–64, 219–20.

41. For an account of the specific setting out of which these events occurred, see Duberman, *Black Mountain College.*

42. Christine L. Williams, "The Glass Escalator: Hidden Advantages for Men in the 'Female' Professions," in Kimmel and Messner, *Men's Lives,* 193–204.

43. See Elaine Tyler May, *Homework Bound,* for a general account of this trend.

44. Helen Tamiris to Ted Shawn, [1942], including a flyer with names of supporters, none of whom were dancers, Folder 140, TS.

45. Reminiscences of Jane Dudley, [1981], Oral Histories of the American Left, Tamiment/Wagner Archives, New York University.

46. Helen Tamiris to Daniel Nagrin, n.d. [1965?], Helen Tamiris Collection, DC/NYPL. Tamiris wrote a scathing letter to the Ford Foundation in 1964 berating it for granting almost $8 million to support ballet while completely ignoring modern dance. Helen Tamiris to W. McNeil Lowry, 18 December 1964, ibid. She also devised a plan for a new repertory company to be called the American Modern Dance Theatre. Unlike the ill-fated Dance Repertory Theatre of the early 1930s, which depended on the cooperation of artists and their companies, Tamiris's plan proposed the formation of one company with leading stars and an ensemble to perform the works of the great modern choreographers—Graham, Humphrey, Holm, Weidman, and Tamiris herself. The plan was never realized. See "Proposed Plan for the Modern Dance," [1957?], Typescripts, ibid.

47. *Hearings of the House Committee on Un-American Activities,* 83d Cong., H1428-H-B, 5 May 1953, 1315–25. Victor Navasky, a historian of the anti-Communist purges in the entertainment industry, has suggested that the committee may have threatened to disclose Robbins's homosexuality if he did not testify and name names. Robbins denied this. Navasky suggests that Robbins may have let this rumor flourish because it provokes sympathy for his decision to testify. As Ring Lardner commented: "I don't know whether it's true or not, but if you were Jerry Robbins, wouldn't you like to have people believe that's the reason you did it?" Navasky, *Naming Names,* 75, 304. Robbins remained notoriously silent about this issue and about his personal life in general.

48. Connecticut College memo, 22 November 1954, and letter from Rosemary Park to Charles B. Fahs, 18 December 1954, Folder 2957, Box 320, Rockefeller Foundation/1.2/200R, Rockefeller Archive Center, North Tarrytown, New York.

49. Talk with John Martin, 5 February 1951, and interview with Anatole Chujoy, 3 March 1954, Folder 6, Box 1, Series 911, Rockefeller Foundation/3.1; Robert W. July's impressions of American Dance Festival, Connecticut College, 16–17 August 1956, Folder 2958, Box 320, Rockefeller Foundation/1.2/200R, ibid.

50. Kendall, "Ford Foundation Assistance."

51. Dvora Lapson, "The Jewish Dance," *Reconstructionist* 10 (26 May 1944): 13–17.

CODA

1. Ailey quoted in Emery, *Black Dance,* 274. See also Ailey with Bailey, *Revelations,* and Dunning, *Alvin Ailey.*

2. Ailey quoted in catalog to the exhibition "Black Visions '89: Movements of Ten Dance Masters," at the Tweed Gallery, New York City, DC/NYPL, 9.

3. For an overview of postmodern dance see Banes, *Democracy's Body* and *Terpsichore in Sneakers.*

bibliography

MANUSCRIPT COLLECTIONS

Becket, Massachusetts
   Jacob's Pillow Dance Festival Archives
      Barton Mumaw Collection
Bennington, Vermont
   Bennington College Archives
Cambridge, Massachusetts
   Harvard Theatre Collection, Houghton Library, Harvard University
      John Lindquist Collection
      Joseph Marks Collection
      Barton Mumaw Collection
Carbondale, Illinois
   Special Collections, Morris Library, Southern Illinois University
      Katherine Dunham Collection
      Mark Turbyfill Collection
Chicago, Illinois
   Newberry Library
      Ann Barzel Collection
      Stone-Camryn Collection
      Mark Turbyfill Collection
Evanston, Illinois
   Northwestern University Archives
      Papers of Melville Herskovits
Fairfax, Virginia
   Special Collection and Archives, George Mason University Libraries
      Federal Theatre Project Oral History Collection
New York, New York
   Dance Collection, Jerome Robbins Dance Division, The New York Public

Library for the Performing Arts, Astor, Lenox and Tilden Foundations
Denishawn Collection
Doris Humphrey Collection
Ruth St. Denis Collection
Ted Shawn Collection
Helen Tamiris Collection
Manuscripts, Archives and Rare Books Division, The Schomburg Center for
Research in Black Culture, The New York Public Library, Astor, Lenox and
Tilden Foundations
Asadata Dafora Papers
Oral History Research Office Collection, Columbia University
Tamiment/Wagner Archives, New York University
Oral Histories of the American Left
North Tarrytown, New York
Rockefeller Archive Center
Washington, D.C.
Library of Congress
Lester Horton Collection
Papers of the Federal Theatre Project, Works Progress Administration
National Archives
Papers of the Federal Theatre Project, Works Progress Administration
(Record Group 69)

PUBLISHED SOURCES

Aaron, Daniel. *Writers on the Left: Episodes in American Literary Communism*. New
York: Harcourt, Brace and World Press, 1961.
Adair, Christy. *Women and Dance: Sylphs and Sirens*. New York: New York University
Press, 1992.
Adamczyk, Alice. *Black Dance: An Annotated Bibliography*. New York: Garland
Publishing, 1989.
Ailey, Alvin, with A. Peter Bailey. *Revelations: The Autobiography of Alvin Ailey*. New
York: Carol Publishing Group, 1995.
Albright, Daniel. *Untwisting the Serpent: Modernism in Music, Literature and Other Arts*.
Chicago: University of Chicago Press, 1999.
Alexander, Charles. *Here the Country Lies: Nationalism and the Arts in Twentieth-
Century America*. Bloomington: Indiana University Press, 1980.

Allen, Robert C. *Horrible Prettiness: Burlesque and American Culture.* Chapel Hill: University of North Carolina Press, 1991.

Ammer, Christine. *Unsung: A History of Women in American Music.* Westport, Conn.: Greenwood Press, 1980.

Anderson, Benedict. *Imagined Communities: Reflections on the Origin and Spread of Nationalism.* New York: Verso Press, 1991.

Armitage, Merle. *Martha Graham: The Early Years.* New York: Da Capo Press, 1937.

Arslanian, Sharon Park. "The History of Tap Dance in Education: 1920–1950." Ed.D. diss., Temple University, 1997.

Aschenbrenner, Joyce. *Katherine Dunham: Reflections on the Social and Political Contexts of Afro-American Dance.* New York: Congress on Research in Dance, 1981.

Austin, Mary. *The American Rhythm: Studies and Reëxpressions of Amerindian Songs.* Boston: Houghton Mifflin, 1930.

Awkward, Michael, ed. *New Essays on Their Eyes Were Watching God.* New York: Cambridge University Press, 1990.

Baigell, Michael, and Julia Williams. *Artists against War and Fascism: Papers of the First American Artists' Congress.* New Brunswick, N.J.: Rutgers University Press, 1986.

Baker, Houston A., Jr. *Modernism and the Harlem Renaissance.* Chicago: University of Chicago Press, 1987.

Baker, Roger. *Drag: A History of Female Impersonation in the Performing Arts.* New York: New York University Press, 1994.

Baldwin, James. *Tell Me How Long the Train's Been Gone.* New York: Dell Publishing, 1968.

Banes, Sally. *Dancing Women: Female Bodies on Stage.* New York: Routledge, 1998.
———. *Democracy's Body: Judson Dance Theater, 1962–1964.* Ann Arbor: UMI Research Press, 1983.
———. *Terpsichore in Sneakers: Postmodern Dance.* Middletown, Conn.: Wesleyan University Press, 1987.

Banner, Lois W. *American Beauty.* Chicago: University of Chicago Press, 1983.

Banta, Martha. *Imaging American Women: Idea and Ideals in Cultural History.* New York: Columbia University Press, 1987.

Barber, Beverly Anne Hillsman. "Pearl Primus: In Search of Her Roots, 1943–1970." Ph.D. diss., Florida State University, 1984.

Barker, Barber. *Ballet or Ballyhoo: The American Careers of Maria Bonfanti, Rita Sangalli and Giuseppina Morlacchi.* New York: Dance Horizons, 1984.

Barzel, Ann. "The Lost 10 Years: The Untold Story of the Dunham/Turbyfill Alliance." *Dance Magazine* 57 (December 1983): 91–98.

Beckford, Ruth. *Katherine Dunham*. New York: Marcel Dekker, 1979.

Bederman, Gail. *Manliness and Civilization: A Cultural History of Gender and Race in the United States, 1880–1917*. Chicago: University of Chicago Press, 1995.

Begho, Felix O. "Black Dance Continuum: Reflections on the Heritage Connection between African Dance and Afro-American Jazz Dance." Ph.D. diss., New York University, 1984.

Beiswanger, Barbara Alice Page. "The Ideational Sources of the Modern Dance in America as Expressed in the Works of Two Leading Exponents, Isadora Duncan and Ruth St. Denis." Ph.D. diss., New York University, 1944.

Benedict, Ruth. *Patterns of Culture*. Boston: Houghton Mifflin, 1934.

Bérubé, Allan. *Coming Out under Fire: The History of Gay Men and Women in World War Two*. New York: Free Press, 1990.

Betts, Anne. "An Historical Study of the New Dance Group of New York City." M.A. thesis, New York University, 1945.

Bird, Dorothy, and Joyce Greenberg. *Bird's Eye View: Dancing with Martha Graham and on Broadway*. Pittsburgh: University of Pittsburgh Press, 1997.

Blair, Karen. *The Torchbearers: Women in Their Amateur Arts Associations in America, 1890–1930*. Bloomington: Indiana University Press, 1994.

Boas, Franz. *The Mind of Primitive Man*. New York: Macmillan, 1911.

Boas, Franziska. *The Function of Dance in Human Society*. New York: Dance Horizons, 1972.

Bogle, Donald. *Brown Sugar: Eighty Years of America's Black Female Superstars*. New York: Da Capo Press, 1980.

Bone, Richard. "Richard Wright and the Chicago Renaissance." *Callaloo* 9, no. 3 (1986): 446–68.

Bonnell, Victoria E. "The Peasant Woman in Stalinist Political Art of the 1930s." *American Historical Review* 98 (February 1993): 55–82.

Brandman, Russella. "The Evolution of Jazz Dance from Folk Origins to Concert Stage." Ph.D. diss., Florida State University, 1977.

Breslin, James. *Mark Rothko: A Biography*. Chicago: University of Chicago Press, 1985.

Brewer, Priscilla J. "'Tho of the Weaker Sex': A Reassessment of Gender Equality among the Shakers." *Signs* 17 (1992): 609–35.

Brockway, Thomas. *Bennington College: In the Beginning*. Bennington, Vt.: Bennington College Press, 1981.

Buhle, Mari Jo. *Women and American Socialism, 1870–1920.* Urbana: University of Illinois Press, 1981.

Burt, Ramsay. *Alien Bodies: Representations of Modernity, "Race," and Nation in Early Modern Dance.* New York: Routledge, 1998.

———. *The Male Dancer: Bodies, Spectacle, Sexualities.* New York: Routledge, 1995.

Butcher, Margaret Just. *The Negro in American Culture.* New York: Knopf, 1967.

Butler, Judith. *Gender Trouble: Feminism and the Subversion of Identity.* New York: Routledge, 1990.

Cahn, Susan. *Coming On Strong: Gender and Sexuality in Twentieth-Century Women's Sport.* Cambridge: Harvard University Press, 1994.

Carby, Hazel. *Reconstructing Womanhood: The Emergence of the Afro-American Woman Novelist.* New York: Oxford University Press, 1986.

Carman, Bliss. *The Making of Personality.* Boston: Page Company, 1929.

Carpenter, Edward. *Love's Coming of Age.* New York: Michell Kennerley, 1941.

Chauncey, George, Jr. *Gay New York: Gender, Urban Culture, and the Making of the Gay Male World, 1890–1940.* New York: Basic Books, 1994.

Cheney, Sheldon. *The Theatre: 3000 Years of Drama, Acting, and Stagecraft.* New York: Tudor Publishing Company, 1936.

Chernoff, John. *African Rhythm and African Sensibility: Aesthetics and Social Action in African Musical Idioms.* Chicago: University of Chicago Press, 1979.

Ciment, Michel. *Kazan on Kazan.* New York: Viking Press, 1974.

Clark, VèVè A. "Katherine Dunham's *Tropical Revue.*" *Black American Literature Forum* 16 (Winter 1982): 147–52.

Clark, VèVè A., and Margaret Wilkerson, eds. *Kaiso!: Katherine Dunham, An Anthology of Writings.* Berkeley: University of California Press, 1978.

Clifford, James. *The Predicament of Culture: Twentieth-Century Ethnography, Literature, and Art.* Cambridge: Harvard University Press, 1988.

Clover, Carol J. "Dancin' in the Rain." *Critical Inquiry* 21 (Summer 1995): 722–47.

Cohen, Barbara Naomi. "The Borrowed Art of Gertrude Hoffman." *Dance Data* 2 (1977): 2–11.

Cohen, Lizabeth. "Encountering Mass Culture at the Grassroots: The Experience of Chicago Workers in the 1920s." *American Quarterly* 41 (March 1989): 6–33.

Cohen-Stratyner, Barbara Naomi. "Ned Wayburn and the Dance Routine: From Vaudeville to the Ziegfeld Follies." *Studies in Dance History* 13 (1996).

Copeland, Roger, and Marshall Cohen, eds. *What Is Dance?: Readings in Theory and Criticism.* New York: Oxford University Press, 1983.

Copland, Aaron, and Vivian Perlis. *Copland: Since 1945*. New York: St. Martin's Press, 1989.

Corn, Wanda. *Grant Wood: The Regionalist Vision*. New Haven: Yale University Press, 1983.

Costonis, Maureen. "*American Document:* A Neglected Graham Work." In *Proceedings of 12th Annual Conference, Society of Dance History Scholars* (1989), 72–81.

Cott, Nancy F. *The Grounding of Modern Feminism*. New Haven: Yale University Press, 1987.

Creque-Harris, Leah. "The Representation of African Dance on the Concert Stage: From the Early Black Musical to Pearl Primus." Ph.D. diss., Emory University, 1991.

Crowley, Alice Lewisohn. *The Neighborhood Playhouse: Leaves from a Theatre Scrapbook*. New York: Vail-Ballou Press, 1959.

Crunden, Robert M. *Body and Soul: The Making of American Modernism*. New York: Basic Books, 2000.

Cunningham, Merce. *Chance Notes on Choreography*. New York: Something Else Press, 1968.

————. *The Dancer and the Dance: Merce Cunningham in Conversation with Jacqueline Lesechaera*. New York: M. Boyars, 1985.

Curry, Richard O., and Lawrence B. Goodheart, eds. *American Chameleon: Individualism in Trans-National Context*. Kent, Ohio: Kent State University Press, 1991.

Curtin, Kaier. "*We Can Always Call Them Bulgarians*": The Emergence of Lesbians and Gay Men on the American Stage. Boston: Alyson Publications, 1987.

Daly, Ann. *Done into Dance: Isadora Duncan in America*. Bloomington: Indiana University Press, 1995.

Daniel, Yvonne. *Rumba: Dance and Social Change in Contemporary Cuba*. Bloomington: Indiana University Press, 1995.

Davies, Frances. "A Survey of Dance in Colleges, Universities, and Teacher Training Institutions in the United States for the Year 1941–42." M.A. thesis, New York University, 1942.

Dearborn, Mary V. *Pocahontas's Daughters: Gender and Ethnicity in American Culture*. New York: Oxford University Press, 1986.

D'Emilio, John. *Sexual Politics, Sexual Communities: The Making of a Homosexual Minority in the United States, 1940–1970*. Chicago: University of Chicago Press, 1983.

D'Emilio, John, and Estelle Freedman. *Intimate Matters: A History of Sexuality in America*. New York: Harper and Row, 1988.

De Mille, Agnes. *Dance to the Piper*. Boston: Little Brown, 1958.

———. *Martha: The Life and Work of Martha Graham*. New York: Random House, 1991.

Denby, Edwin. *Looking at the Dance*. New York: Pellegrini and Cudahy, 1949.

Denning, Michael. *The Cultural Front: The Laboring of American Culture in the Twentieth Century*. New York: Verso, 1997.

Desmond, Jane. "Dancing Out the Difference: Cultural Imperialism and Ruth St. Denis' *Radha* of 1906." *Signs* 17 (Autumn 1991): 28–49.

———, ed. *Dancing Desires: Choreographing Sexualities On and Off the Stage*. Madison: University of Wisconsin Press, 2001.

———, ed. *Meaning in Motion: New Cultural Studies of Dance*. Durham, N.C.: Duke University Press, 1997.

Dewey, John. *Art as Experience*. New York: Minton, Balch and Company, 1934.

———. *Experience and Nature*. New York: Dover Publications, 1958.

Dixon-Gottschild, Brenda. *Digging the Africanist Presence in American Performance: Dance and Other Contexts*. Westport, Conn.: Greenwood Press, 1996.

Doolittle, Lisa, and Anne Flynn, eds. *Dancing Bodies, Living Histories: New Writings about Dance and Culture*. Banff, Canada: Banff Centre Press, 2000.

Doss, Erica. *Benton, Pollock, and the Politics of Modernism: From Regionalism to Abstract Expressionism*. Chicago: University of Chicago Press, 1991.

Douglas, Ann. *The Feminization of American Culture*. New York: Knopf, 1977.

———. *Terrible Honesty: Mongrel Manhattan in the 1920s*. New York: Farrar, Straus, and Giroux, 1995.

Drier, Katherine S. *Shawn the Dancer*. New York: A. S. Barnes, 1933.

Duberman, Martin. *Black Mountain College: An Exploration in Community*. New York: Anchor Books, 1973.

Duberman, Martin, Martha Vicinus, and George Chauncey Jr., eds. *Hidden from History: Reclaiming the Gay and Lesbian Past*. New York: Penguin Books, 1989.

Du Bois, W. E. B. *The Souls of Black Folk*. New York: Penguin Books, 1982.

Duncan, Isadora. *My Life*. New York: Liveright Publishing, 1927.

Dunham, Katherine. *Island Possessed*. New York: Doubleday, 1969.

———. *Katherine Dunham's Journey to Accompong*. New York: Henry Holt, 1946.

———. *A Touch of Innocence*. New York: Harcourt, Brace, 1959.

Dunning, Jennifer. *Alvin Ailey: A Life in Dance*. New York: Addison-Wesley, 1996.

Easton, Carol. *No Intermissions: The Life of Agnes de Mille*. Boston: Little, Brown, 1996.

Eilberg-Schwartz, Howard, ed. *People of the Body: Jews and Judaism from an Embodied Perspective*. Albany: State University of New York Press, 1992.

Ellenzweig, Allen. *The Homoerotic Photograph: Male Images from Durieu/Delacroix to Mapplethorpe*. New York: Columbia University Press, 1992.

Ellfeldt, Lois Elizabeth. "The Role of Modern Dance in Selected Women's and Coeducational Colleges and Universities." Ph.D. diss., University of Southern California, 1946.

Ellis, Havelock. *The Dance of Life*. 1923. Reprint, New York: Modern Library, 1929.

————. *Studies in the Psychology of Sex*. Philadelphia: F. A. Davis, [1900?]–1928.

Emery, Lynne Fauley. *Black Dance: From 1619 to Today*. Princeton, N.J.: Princeton Book Company, 1988.

Erenberg, Lewis. *Stepping Out: New York Nightlife and the Transformation of American Culture, 1890–1930*. Westport, Conn.: Greenwood Press, 1981.

————. *Swingin' the Dream: Big Band Jazz and the Rebirth of American Culture*. Chicago: University of Chicago Press, 1998.

Erenberg, Lewis, and Susan E. Hirsch, eds. *The War in American Culture: Society and Consciousness during World War II*. Chicago: University of Chicago Press, 1996.

Ernst, Robert. *Weakness Is a Crime: The Life of Bernarr Macfadden*. Syracuse: Syracuse University Press, 1991.

Etlin, Richard A., ed. *Nationalism in the Visual Arts*. Hanover, N.H.: University Press of New England, 1991.

Fabian, Ann. "Making a Commodity of Truth: Speculations on the Career of Bernarr Macfadden." *American Literary History* 5 (Spring 1993): 51–76.

Fabre, Geneviève, and Robert O'Meally, eds. *History and Memory in African-American Culture*. New York: Oxford University Press, 1994.

Fass, Paula S. *The Damned and the Beautiful: American Youth in the 1920s*. New York: Oxford University Press, 1977.

Fauset, Jessie. *There Is Confusion*. Boston: Northeastern Press, 1989.

Feingold, Henry L. *A Time for Searching: Entering the Mainstream, 1920–1945*. Baltimore: Johns Hopkins University Press, 1992.

Finkelstein, Joan. "Doris Humphrey and the 92nd Street Y: A Dance Center for the People." *Dance Research Journal* 28 (Fall 1996): 49–59.

Flanagan, Hallie. *Arena: The History of the Federal Theatre*. New York: Arno Press, 1980.

Fleischhauer, Carl, and Beverly W. Brannan, eds. *Documenting America, 1935–1943.* Berkeley: University of California Press, 1988.

Floyd, Samuel A., Jr. *The Power of Black Music.* New York: Oxford University Press, 1995.

Foster, Susan Leigh. *Reading Dancing: Bodies and Subjects in Contemporary American Dance.* Berkeley: University of California Press, 1986.

———, ed. *Choreographing History.* Bloomington: Indiana University Press, 1995.

———, ed. *Corporealities: Dancing, Knowledge, Culture, and Power.* New York: Routledge, 1996.

Foulkes, Julia L. "'Angels Rewolt!': Jewish Women in Modern Dance in the 1930s." *American Jewish History* 88 (June 2000): 233–52.

Fox-Genovese, Elizabeth. *Feminism without Illusions: A Critique of Individualism.* Chapel Hill: University of North Carolina Press, 1991.

Fraden, Rena. *Blueprints for a Black Federal Theatre, 1935–1939.* New York: Cambridge University Press, 1994.

Fraleigh, Sondra Horton. *Dance and the Lived Body: A Descriptive Aesthetics.* Pittsburgh: University of Pittsburgh Press, 1987.

Francis, Elizabeth. "From Event to Monument: Modernism, Feminism, and Isadora Duncan." *American Studies* 35 (Spring 1994): 25–45.

Franko, Mark. "Abstraction Has Many Faces: The Ballet/Modern Wars of Lincoln Kirstein and John Martin." *Performance Research* 3 (Summer 1998): 88–101.

———. *Dancing Modernism/Performing Politics.* Bloomington: Indiana University Press, 1995.

———. "Nation, Class, and Ethnicities in Modern Dance in the 1930s." *Theatre Journal* 49 (December 1997): 475–92.

Fraser, Steve, and Gary Gerstle, eds. *The Rise and Fall of the New Deal Order, 1930–1980.* Princeton, N.J.: Princeton University Press, 1989.

Friedman, Edna. "American Opinions on Dance and Dancing from 1840 to 1940." M.A. thesis, New York University, 1940.

Friedman, Kim C. "The Federal Dance Theatre in New York City: Legislative and Administrative Obstacles." M.A. thesis, American University, 1992.

Garafola, Lynn. *Diaghilev's Ballets Russes.* New York: Oxford University Press, 1989.

———, ed. *José Limón: An Unfinished Memoir.* Middletown, Conn.: Wesleyan University Press, 1998.

———, ed. "Of, by and for the People: Dancing on the Left in the 1930s." *Studies in Dance History* 5 (Spring 1994).

Garafola, Lynn, with Eric Foner, eds. *Dance for a City: Fifty Years of the New York City Ballet*. New York: Columbia University Press, 1999.

Garman, Brian K. "'Heroic Spiritual Grandfather': Whitman, Sexuality, and the American Left, 1890–1940." *American Quarterly* 52 (March 2000): 90–126.

Gates, Henry Louis, Jr. "The Trope of a New Negro and the Reconstruction of the Image of the Black." *Representations* 24 (Fall 1988): 129–55.

Gay, Geneva, and Willie Baber, eds. *Expressively Black: The Cultural Basis of Ethnic Identity*. New York: Praeger Publishers, 1987.

Gayle, Addison, ed. *The Black Aesthetic*. New York: Doubleday, 1971.

Gerber, David A., ed. *Anti-Semitism in American History*. Urbana: University of Illinois Press, 1986.

Giddings, Paula. *When and Where I Enter: The Impact of Black Women on Race and Sex in America*. New York: William Morrow, 1984.

Gilman, Sander. *The Jew's Body*. New York: Routledge, 1991.

Gilroy, Paul. *The Black Atlantic: Modernity and Double Consciousness*. Cambridge: Harvard University Press, 1993.

Glassberg, David. *American Historical Pageantry: The Uses of Tradition in the Early Twentieth Century*. Chapel Hill: University of North Carolina Press, 1990.

Gleason, Philip. "Americans All: World War II and the Shaping of American Identity." *The Review of Politics* 43 (October 1981): 483–518.

Gorn, Elliot J. *The Manly Art: Bare-Knuckle Prize Fighting in America*. Ithaca, N.Y.: Cornell University Press, 1981.

Gottschild, Brenda Dixon. *Digging the Africanist Presence in American Performance: Dance and Other Contexts*. Westport, Conn.: Greenwood Press, 1996.

Graff, Ellen. *Stepping Left: Dance and Politics in New York City, 1928–1942*. Durham, N.C.: Duke University Press, 1997.

Graham, Martha. *Blood Memory: An Autobiography*. New York: Doubleday, 1991.

———. *The Notebooks of Martha Graham*. New York: Harcourt Brace Jovanovich, 1973.

Haag, Pamela. "In Search of 'The Real Thing': Ideologies of Love, Modern Romance, and Women's Sexual Subjectivity in the United States, 1920–1940." *Journal of the History of Sexuality* 2, no. 4 (1992): 161–91.

Hanna, Judith Lynne. *Dance, Sex, and Gender: Signs of Identity, Dominance, Defiance, and Desire*. Chicago: University of Chicago Press, 1988.

Hansen, Miriam. *Babel and Babylon: Spectatorship in American Silent Film*. Cambridge: Harvard University Press, 1991.

Harding, James H., ed. *Contours of the Theatrical Avant-Garde: Performance and Textuality.* Ann Arbor: University of Michigan Press, 2000.

Harris, Neil. *Cultural Excursions/Marketing Appetites: Cultural Tastes in Modern America.* Chicago: University of Chicago Press, 1990.

Harrison, Ira E., and Faye V. Harrison. *African-American Pioneers in Anthropology.* Urbana: University of Illinois Press, 1999.

Hawkins, Alma H. *Modern Dance in Higher Education.* New York: Teachers College, 1954.

Hazzard-Gordon, Katrina. "Afro-American Core Culture Social Dance: An Examination of Four Aspects of Meaning." *Dance Research Journal* 15 (Spring 1983): 21–26.

———. *Jookin': The Rise of Social Dance Formations in African-American Culture.* Philadelphia: Temple University Press, 1990.

H'Doubler, Margaret. *The Dance.* London: Jonathan Cape, 1925.

Herskovits, Melville. *Life in a Haitian Valley.* New York: Knopf, 1937.

———. *The Myth of the Negro Past.* New York: Harper and Brothers, 1941.

Hill, Constance Valis. "Katherine Dunham's *Southland:* Protest in the Face of Repression." *Dance Research Journal* 26 (Fall 1996): 1–10.

Hobsbawn, Eric. *The Invention of Tradition.* New York: Cambridge University Press, 1983.

Horowitz, Dawn Lille. *Michel Fokine.* Boston: Twayne Publishers, 1985.

Hsu, Francis L. K. "Prejudice and Its Intellectual Effect in American Anthropology: An Ethnographic Report." *American Anthropologist* 75 (February 1973): 1–19.

Huggins, Nathan. *Harlem Renaissance.* New York: Oxford University Press, 1971.

Hughes, Langston, and Meltzer, Milton. *Black Magic: A Pictorial History of the Negro in American Entertainment.* Englewood Cliffs, N.J.: Prentice-Hall, 1967.

Hull, Gloria T. *Color, Sex and Poetry: Three Women Writers of the Harlem Renaissance.* Bloomington: Indiana University Press, 1987.

Humphrey, Doris. *The Art of Making Dances.* New York: Grove Press, 1959.

Humphrey, Doris, and Selma Jeanne Cohen, ed. *Doris Humphrey: An Artist First.* Middletown, Conn.: Wesleyan University Press, 1966.

Hutchinson, George. *The Harlem Renaissance in Black and White.* Cambridge: Harvard University Press, 1995.

Huyssen, Andreas. *After the Great Divide: Modernism, Mass Culture, Postmodernism.* Bloomington: Indiana University Press, 1986.

Hyman, Paula. *Gender and Assimilation in Modern Jewish History: The Roles and Representations of Women.* Seattle: University of Washington Press, 1995.

Hymes, Dell, ed. *Reinventing Anthropology.* New York: Pantheon Books, 1969.

Jackson, Naomi M. *Converging Movements: Modern Dance and Jewish Culture at the 92nd Street Y.* Hanover, N.H.: University Press of New England, 2000.

Jamison, Judith, with Howard Kaplan. *Dancing Spirit: An Autobiography.* New York: Doubleday, 1993.

Johnson, James Weldon. *Black Manhattan.* New York: Atheneum, 1977.

Jowitt, Deborah. *Time and the Dancing Image.* Berkeley: University of California Press, 1988.

Kazin, Alfred. *On Native Grounds: An Interpretation of Modern American Prose Literature.* New York: Reynal and Hitchcock, 1942.

Kendall, Elizabeth. "Ford Foundation Assistance to American Dance, 1959–1983." *Ford Foundation Report* (1983): 75–78.

———. *Where She Danced.* New York: Knopf, 1979.

Kern, Stephen. *The Culture of Time and Space, 1880–1918.* Cambridge: Harvard University Press, 1983.

Kessner, Thomas. *Fiorello H. LaGuardia and the Making of Modern New York.* New York: Penguin Books, 1989.

Kimmel, Michael. *Manhood in America.* New York: Free Press, 1996.

Kimmel, Michael S., and Michael A. Messner, eds. *Men's Lives.* Boston: Allyn and Bacon, 1995.

King, Eleanor. *Transformations: The Humphrey-Weidman Era: A Memoir.* Brooklyn: Dance Horizons, 1978.

Kirschke, Amy Helene. *Aaron Douglas: Art, Race, and the Harlem Renaissance.* Jackson: University Press of Mississippi, 1995.

Kirstein, Lincoln. *Mosaic: Memoirs.* New York: Farrar, Straus, and Giroux, 1994.

———. *Three Pamphlets Collected.* New York: Dance Horizons, 1967.

Klehr, Harvey. *The Heyday of American Communism: The Depression Decade.* New York: Basic Books, 1984.

Koestenbaum, Wayne. *The Queen's Throat: Opera, Homosexuality, and the Mystery of Desire.* New York: Poseidon Press, 1993.

Kolodney, William. "History of the Educational Department of the YM-YWHA." Ed.D. diss., Teachers College of Columbia University, 1950.

Kriegsman, Sali Ann. *Modern Dance in America: The Bennington Years.* Boston: G. K. Hall, 1981.

Kuzmack, Linda Gordon. *Woman's Cause: The Jewish Woman's Movement in England and the United States, 1891–1933.* Columbus: Ohio State University Press, 1990.

Lally, Kathleen Ann. "A History of the Federal Dance Theater of the WPA, 1935–1939." Ph.D. diss., Texas Woman's University, 1978.

LaMothe, Kimerer. "Passionate Madonna: The Christian Turn of American Dancer Ruth St. Denis." *Journal of the American Academy of Religion* 66, no. 4 (1998): 747–69.

Laufe, Abe. *The Wicked Stage: A History of Theater Censorship and Harassment in the United States.* New York: Frederick Ungar, 1978.

Lears, T. J. Jackson. *No Place of Grace: Antimodernism and the Transformation of American Culture, 1880–1920.* New York: Pantheon Books, 1981.

Levenson, Lew. *Butterfly Man.* New York: Castle Books, 1934.

Levine, Lawrence. *Black Culture and Black Consciousness: Afro-American Folk Thought from Slavery to Freedom.* New York: Oxford University Press, 1977.

———. *Highbrow/Lowbrow: The Emergence of Cultural Hierarchy in America.* Cambridge: Harvard University Press, 1988.

Levine, Peter. *Ellis Island to Ebbets Field: Sport and the American Jewish Experience.* New York: Oxford University Press, 1992.

Lewis, David Levering. *When Harlem Was in Vogue.* New York: Knopf, 1981.

Lipsitz, George. *Time Passages: Collective Memory and American Popular Culture.* Minneapolis: University of Minnesota Press, 1990.

Lloyd, Margaret. *The Borzoi Book of Modern Dance.* New York: Knopf, 1949.

Locke, Alain, ed. *The New Negro.* 1925. Reprint, with an introduction by Arnold Rampersad, New York: Atheneum, 1992.

Long, Richard A. *The Black Tradition in American Dance.* New York: Rizzoli, 1989.

Lucker, Amy. "The John Lindquist Collection at the Harvard Theatre Collection." *Performing Arts Resources* 20 (1996): 57–74.

McBride, Bunny. *Molly Spotted Elk: A Penobscot in Paris.* Norman: University of Oklahoma Press, 1995.

McCarthy, Kathleen. *Women's Culture: American Philanthropy and Art, 1830–1930.* Chicago: University of Chicago Press, 1991.

McClay, Wilfred M. *The Masterless: Self and Society in Modern America.* Chapel Hill: University of North Carolina Press, 1994.

McDonagh, Don. *The Complete Guide to Modern Dance.* New York: Doubleday, 1976.

———. "A Conversation with Gertrude Shurr." *Ballet Review* 4 (1973): 3–20.

———. *Martha Graham: A Biography.* New York: Praeger Publishers, 1973.

————. *The Rise and Fall of Modern Dance.* New York: Dutton, 1970.

Magriel, Paul. *Art and the Soldier.* Biloxi, Miss.: Special Service, Kessler Field, 1943.

Malone, Jacqui. *Steppin' on the Blues: The Visible Rhythms of African American Dance.* Urbana: University of Illinois Press, 1996.

Manning, Susan. "Black Voices, White Bodies: The Performance of Race and Gender in *How Long Brethren.*" *American Quarterly* 50 (March 1998): 24–46.

————. "Cultural Theft—or Love?" *Dance Theater Journal* 13 (Autumn 1997): 32–35.

————. *Ecstasy and the Demon: Feminism and Nationalism in the Dances of Mary Wigman.* Berkeley: University of California Press, 1993.

Marcus, George E., and Michael M. J. Fischer. *Anthropology as Cultural Critique: An Experimental Moment in the Human Sciences.* Chicago: University of Chicago Press, 1986.

Margolick, David. *Strange Fruit: Billie Holiday, Café Society, and an Early Cry for Civil Rights.* Philadelphia: Running Press, 2000.

Marquis, Alice Goldfarb. *Art Lessons: Learning from the Rise and Fall of Public Arts Funding.* New York: Basic Books, 1995.

Martin, Carol. *Dance Marathons: Performing American Culture in the 1920s and 1930s.* Jackson: University Press of Mississippi, 1994.

Martin, John. *America Dancing.* New York: Dodge Publishing Company, 1936.

————. *John Martin's Book of the Dance.* New York: Tudor Publishing Company, 1963.

————. *The Modern Dance.* New York: Dance Horizons, 1966.

May, Elaine Tyler. *Homework Bound: American Families in the Cold War Era.* New York: Basic Books, 1988.

May, Henry. *The End of American Innocence: A Study of the First Years of Our Own Time, 1912–1917.* New York: Knopf, 1959.

May, Lary. *The Big Tomorrow: Hollywood and the Politics of the American Way.* Chicago: University of Chicago Press, 2000.

————, ed. *Recasting America: Culture and Politics in the Age of Cold War.* Chicago: University of Chicago Press, 1989.

Mazo, Joseph. *The Alvin Ailey American Dance Theatre.* New York: William Morrow, 1978.

Mead, Margaret. *Male and Female: A Study of the Sexes in a Changing World.* New York: Morrow Quill Paperbacks, 1977.

Melosh, Barbara. *Engendering Culture: Manhood and Womanhood in New Deal Public Art and Theater.* Washington: Smithsonian Institution Press, 1991.

Miller, Tyrus. *Late Modernism: Politics, Fiction, and the Arts between the World Wars.* Berkeley: University of California Press, 1999.

Minton, Henry L. "Femininity in Men and Masculinity in Women: American Psychiatry and Psychology Portray Homosexuality in the 1930s." *Journal of Homosexuality* 13 (Fall 1986): 1–21.

Mishler, Paul C. *Raising Reds: Young Pioneers, Radical Summer Camps, and Communist Political Culture in the United States.* New York: Columbia University Press, 1999.

Moore, Deborah Dash. *At Home in America: Second Generation Jews.* New York: Columbia University Press, 1981.

Morgan, Barbara. *Martha Graham: Sixteen Dances in Photographs.* New York: Duell, Sloan and Pearce, 1941.

Morris, Gay, ed. *Moving Words: Re-Writing Dance.* New York: Routledge, 1996.

Mosse, George L. *The Image of Man: The Creation of Modern Masculinity.* New York: Oxford University Press, 1996.

———. *Nationalism and Sexuality: Respectability and Abnormal Sexuality in Modern Europe.* New York: Howard Fertig, 1985.

Mulvey, Laura. "Visual Pleasure and the Narrative Cinema." *Screen* 16 (Autumn 1975): 6–18.

Myers, Gerald, ed. *African American Genius in Modern Dance.* Durham, N.C.: American Dance Festival, 1994.

———, ed. *The Black Tradition in American Modern Dance.* Durham, N.C.: American Dance Festival, 1988.

Naison, Mark. *Communists in Harlem during the Depression.* New York: Grove Press, 1983.

Natason, Nicholas. *The Black Image in the New Deal: The Politics of FSA Photography.* Knoxville: University of Tennessee Press, 1992.

Navasky, Victor. *Naming Names.* New York: Viking Press, 1980.

Newton, Esther. *Mother Camp: Female Impersonators in America.* Englewood Cliffs, N.J.: Prentice-Hall, 1972.

Nochlin, Linda. *Women, Art, and Power.* New York: Harper and Row, 1988.

Park, Marlene, and Gerald Markowitz. *Democratic Vistas: Post Offices and Public Art in the New Deal.* Philadelphia: Temple University Press, 1984.

Parker, Andrew, Mary Russo, Doris Sommer, and Patricia Yaeger, eds. *Nationalisms and Sexualities.* New York: Routledge, 1992.

Peiss, Kathy. *Cheap Amusements: Working Women and Leisure in Turn-of-the-Century New York*. Philadelphia: Temple University Press, 1986.

Peiss, Kathy, and Christina Simmons, eds. *Passion and Power: Sexuality in History*. Philadelphia: Temple University Press, 1989.

Pells, Richard. *The Liberal Mind in a Conservative Age: American Intellectuals in the 1940s and 1950s*. New York: Harper and Row, 1985.

———. *Radical Visions and American Dreams*. New York: Harper and Row, 1973.

Perpener, John O., III. *African-American Concert Dance: The Harlem Renaissance and Beyond*. Urbana: University of Illinois Press, 2001.

Philip, Richard. "Billy the Kid Turns 50: An American Dance." *Dance Magazine* 62 (November 1988): 41–42.

Poindexter, Betty. "Ted Shawn: His Personal Life, His Professional Career, and His Contributions to the Development of Dance in the United States of America from 1891 to 1963." Ph.D. diss., Texas Women's University, 1963.

Polcari, Stephen. *Abstract Expressionism and the Modern Experience*. New York: Cambridge University Press, 1991.

Powys, John Cowper. *In Defence of Sensuality*. New York: Simon and Schuster, 1930.

Prevots, Naima. *Dance for Export: Cultural Diplomacy and the Cold War*. Middletown, Conn.: Wesleyan University Press, 1998.

Prickett, Stacey L. "Marxism, Modernism, and Realism: Politics and Aesthetics in the Rise of American Modern Dance." Ph.D. diss., Laban Centre for Movement and Dance, 1992.

Remy, Anselme. "Anthropology: For Whom and What?" *Black Scholar* 7 (April 1976): 12–16.

Riis, Thomas. *Just Before Jazz: Black Musical Theater in New York, 1890–1910*. Washington: Smithsonian Institution Press, 1989.

Robinson, Harlow. *The Last Impresario: The Life, Times, and Legacy of Sol Hurok*. New York: Penguin Books, 1994.

Rodgers, Audrey T. *The Universal Drum: Dance Imagery in the Poetry of Eliot, Crane, Roethke, and Williams*. University Park: Pennsylvania State University Press, 1979.

Roet, Marian. "Dance Project of the WPA Federal Theatre." M.A. thesis, New York University, 1949.

Rogers, Frederick Rand, ed. *Dance: A Basic Educational Technique*. New York: Macmillan, 1941.

Rogin, Michael. *Blackface, White Noise: Jewish Immigrants in the Hollywood Melting Pot*. Berkeley: University of California Press, 1996.

Rose, Phyllis. *Jazz Cleopatra: Josephine Baker in Her Time*. New York: Doubleday, 1989.

Rosenwaike, Ira. *Population History of New York City*. Syracuse, N.Y.: Syracuse University Press, 1972.

Ross, Janice. *Moving Lessons: Margaret H'Doubler and the Beginning of Dance in American Education*. Madison: University of Wisconsin Press, 2000.

Ruyter, Nancy Lee Chalfa. *Reformers and Visionaries: The Americanization of the Art of Dance*. New York: Dance Horizons, 1979.

Sachs, Curt. *World History of the Dance*. New York: W. W. Norton, 1937.

St. Denis, Ruth. *Ruth St. Denis, An Unfinished Life*. New York: Harper Publishers, 1939.

Sayler, Oliver M., ed. *Revolt in the Arts: A Survey of the Creation, Distribution and Appreciation of Art in America*. New York: Brentano's, 1930.

Schlundt, Christena L. *Tamiris: A Chronicle of Her Dance Career, 1927–1955*. New York: New York Public Library Astor, Lenox and Tilden Foundations, 1972.

Scott, William, and Peter Rutkoff. *New York Modern: the Arts and the City*. Baltimore: Johns Hopkins University Press, 1999.

Sedgwick, Eve. *Epistemology of the Closet*. Berkeley: University of California Press, 1990.

Selden, Elizabeth. *The Dancer's Quest*. Berkeley: University of California Press, 1935.

Shawn, Ted. *The American Ballet*. New York: Henry Holt, 1926.

———. *Dance We Must*. Pittsfield, Mass.: Eagle Printing and Binding Company, 1950.

———. *Every Little Movement: A Book about François Delsarte*. Pittsfield, Mass.: Eagle Printing and Binding Company, 1954.

———. *Gods Who Dance*. New York: E. P. Dutton, 1929.

———. *Thirty-three Years of American Dance, 1927–1959, and the American Ballet*. Pittsfield, Mass.: Eagle Printing and Binding Company, 1959.

Shawn, Ted, with Gray Poole. *One Thousand and One Night Stands*. New York: Da Capo Press, 1979.

Shelton, Suzanne. *Divine Dancer: A Biography of Ruth St. Denis*. Garden City, N.Y.: Doubleday, 1981.

Sherman, Jane. "The American Indian Imagery of Ted Shawn." *Dance Chronicle* 12 (1989): 366–82.

Sherman, Jane, and Barton Mumaw. *Barton Mumaw, Dancer: From Denishawn to Jacob's Pillow and Beyond*. New York: Dance Horizons, 1986.

Sherrod, Elgie Gaynell. "The Dance Griots: An Examination of the Dance Pedagogy of Katherine Dunham and Black Pioneering Dancers in Chicago and New York City, from 1931–1946." Ed.D. diss., Temple University, January 1998.

Shirley, Wayne D. "For Martha." *Ballet Review* 27 (Winter 1999): 64–95.

Shurr, Gertrude. *Modern Dance Techniques and Teachings*. New York: A. S. Barnes, 1949.

Siegel, Marcia B. *Days on Earth: The Dance of Doris Humphrey*. Durham, N.C.: Duke University Press, 1993.

———. "Four Works by Doris Humphrey." *Ballet Review* 7, no. 1 (1978–79): 16–36.

Simmons, Michelle. "Experiencing and Performing the Choreography of Mna, Pearl Primus—'Strange Fruit.'" *Talking Drums! The Journal of Black Dance* 5 (January 1995): 8–9.

Singal, Daniel Joseph. "Towards a Definition of American Modernism." *American Quarterly* 39 (Spring 1987): 7–26.

Soares, Janet Mansfield. *Louis Horst: Musician in a Dancer's World*. Durham, N.C.: Duke University Press, 1992.

Solomon, Barbara. *In the Company of Educated Women: A History of Women and Higher Education in America*. New Haven: Yale University Press, 1985.

Sommer, Sally. "Loïe Fuller: From the Theater of Popular Entertainment to the Parisian Avant-garde." Ph.D. diss., New York University, 1979.

Sorell, Walter. *Dance through the Ages*. New York: Grosset and Dunlap, 1967.

———. *Hanya Holm: The Biography of an Artist*. Middletown, Conn.: Wesleyan University Press, 1969.

———, ed. *The Dance Has Many Faces*. New York: World Publishing Company, 1951.

Stansell, Christine. *American Moderns: Bohemian New York and the Creation of a New Century*. New York: Metropolitan Books, 2000.

Stearns, Marshall, and Jean Stearns. *Jazz Dance*. New York: Schirmer Books, 1968.

Steinberg, Leo. *Other Criteria: Confrontations with Twentieth-Century Art*. New York: Oxford University Press, 1972.

Stocking, George. *Race, Culture, and Evolution: Essays in the History of Anthropology*. New York: Free Press, 1968.

Stodelle, Ernestine. *Deep Song: The Dance Story of Martha Graham*. New York: Schirmer Books, 1984.

Stott, William. *Documentary Expression and Thirties America*. New York: Oxford University Press, 1973.

Stowe, David W. "The Politics of Café Society." *Journal of American History* 84 (March 1998): 1384–1406.

———. *Swing Changes: Big Band Jazz and New Deal America.* Cambridge: Harvard University Press, 1994.

Stuckey, Sterling. *Going through the Storm: The Influence of African American Art in History.* New York: Oxford University Press, 1994.

———. *Slave Culture: Nationalist Theory and the Foundations of Black America.* New York: Oxford University Press, 1987.

Susman, Warren. *Culture as History: The Transformation of American Society in the Twentieth Century.* New York: Pantheon Books, 1984.

Tamiris, Helen. "Tamiris in Her Own Voice: Draft of an Autobiography." Translated, edited, and annotated by Daniel Nagrin. *Studies in Dance History* 1 (Fall/Winter 1989): 1–64.

Terman, Lewis M., and Catharine Cox Miles. *Sex and Personality: Studies in Masculinity and Femininity.* New York: Russell and Russell, 1968.

Terry, Walter. *Dance in America.* New York: Harper and Row, 1971.

———. *Frontiers of Dance: The Life of Martha Graham.* New York: Thomas Y. Crowell, 1975.

———. *Invitation to Dance.* New York: A. S. Barnes, 1942.

———. *Ted Shawn: Father of American Dance.* New York: Dial Press, 1976.

Thomas, Helen. *Dance, Modernity, and Culture: Explorations in the Sociology of Dance.* New York: Routledge, 1995.

Thompson, Richard Farris. *Flash of the Spirit: African and Afro-American Art and Philosophy.* New York: Vintage Books, 1983.

Thorpe, Edward. *Black Dance.* New York: Overlook Press, 1990.

Tischler, Barbara. *An American Music: The Search for an American Musical Identity.* New York: Oxford University Press, 1986.

Tobias, Tobi. "A Conversation with Martha Graham." *Dance Magazine* 58 (March 1984): 62–67.

Tomko, Linda J. *Dancing Class: Gender, Ethnicity, and Social Divides in American Dance, 1890–1920.* Bloomington: University of Indiana Press, 1999.

Torgovnick, Marianna. *Gone Primitive: Savage Intellects, Modern Lives.* Chicago: University of Chicago Press, 1990.

Van Vechten, Carl. *The Dance Writings of Carl Van Vechten.* New York: Dance Horizons, 1974.

———, ed. *Selected Writings of Gertrude Stein.* New York: Vintage Books, 1962.

Wald, Alan M. *The New York Intellectuals: The Rise and Decline of the Anti-Stalinist Left from the 1930s to the 1980s*. Chapel Hill: University of North Carolina Press, 1987.

Ware, Susan. *Holding Their Own: American Women in the 1930s*. Boston: Twayne Publishers, 1982.

Warren, Larry. *Lester Horton: Modern Dance Pioneer*. New York: M. Dekker, 1977.

Weber, Nicholas Fox. *Patron Saints: Five Rebels Who Opened America to a New Art, 1928–1943*. New York: Knopf, 1992.

Weinberg, Jonathan. *Speaking for Vice: Homosexuality in the Art of Charles Demuth, Marsden Hartley, and the First American Avant-Garde*. New Haven: Yale University Press, 1993.

Whitman, Walt. *Complete Poetry and Collected Prose*. New York: Literary Classics of the United States, 1982.

Williams, Jay. *Stage Left*. New York: Scribner, 1974.

Wisher, Peter. "Modern Dance for Men: A Manual for Male Teachers of Physical Education." Ed.D. diss., Pennsylvania State University, 1952.

Woll, Allen. *Black Musical Theatre: From Coontown to Dreamgirls*. Baton Rouge: Louisiana State University Press, 1989.

index

of, 117, 118, 119, 177. *See also* Arts; Modernism

Cunningham, Merce, 154, 170–71, 173, 177, 182

Cuyjet, Marion, 55

Dafora, Asadata, 52, 58–66, 77, 109, 143, 180, 183

Dagger Dance (Shawn), 136

Dance halls, 11–13, 23, 51, 145, 157, 165. *See also* Social dance

Dance Observer, 74, 87, 112, 128

Dance of Sports (Weidman), 96

Dance Repertory Theatre, 1–2, 6, 14, 36, 112, 135

Dance schools. *See* Training, dance

Dancers Union, 123–24

Dances of Women (Humphrey), 44–45, 46

Death of Adonis (Shawn), 92

Decade (Humphrey), 159

Deep Song (Graham), 122

de Lavallade, Carmen, 180

Del Bourgo, Fanya Geltman, 105, 125, 143

Delsarte, François, 9–10, 30, 82

de Mille, Agnes, 56, 112

Democracy, 2–3, 5, 34, 54, 122–23, 131–32, 142, 150–52, 157, 160, 168–69, 177

Denby, Edwin, 159

Denishawn, 11, 22, 24, 29, 58, 79, 82, 83, 136, 139; influence of, 30–33, 102; scorn for, 17, 20, 25

Depression. *See* Great Depression

Deren, Maya, 170

Dewey, John, 34, 114

Diaghilev, Serge, 8

Dies Committee. *See* House Committee on Un-American Activities

Dionysius. *See* Nietzsche, Friedrich

Dixie to Broadway, 23

Dodge, Roger Pryor, 96

Dodson, Owen, 168

Dollar, William, 96

Douglas, Aaron, 23

Drag, 102–3

Du Bois, W. E. B., 40, 52–54

Dudley, Jane, 3, 35, 106, 109–10, 117, 160, 173

Duncan, Isadora, 8–11, 15, 25, 35, 81, 82, 130, 133

Dunham, Katherine, 34, 36, 52, 160, 164, 165, 168, 178, 179, 180, 182, 183–84; and anthropology, 66–72; choreography of, 64, 68–70, 143–45; critics' views of, 72–78; early career of, 55–58

Dunn, Robert, 182

Dust Bowl Ballads (Maslow), 153–54

East Side Sketches (Blecher), 138

Eddy, Mary Baker, 30, 82

Education. *See* Training, dance; Universities

Effeminacy, 3, 61, 80, 83, 86, 88–90, 94–95, 102–3, 177. *See also* Masculinity

Egypta (St. Denis), 30

Ellington, Duke, 39

Ellis, Havelock, 21, 35, 47, 84, 85, 86, 92

Emerson, Ralph Waldo, 82

Emotion, 18–20, 30, 132–33, 139, 171